Brigadier General
John Adams, CSA

ALSO BY LESLIE R. TUCKER

*Major General Isaac Ridgeway Trimble:
Biography of a Baltimore Confederate* (McFarland, 2005)

Brigadier General John Adams, CSA
A Biography

LESLIE R. TUCKER

McFarland & Company, Inc., Publishers
Jefferson, North Carolina, and London

LIBRARY OF CONGRESS CATALOGUING-IN-PUBLICATION DATA

Tucker, Leslie R., 1948–
　　Brigadier General John Adams, CSA : a biography / LeslieR. Tucker.
　　　　p.　　cm.
　　Includes bibliographical references and index.

ISBN 978-0-7864-7484-4
softcover : acid free paper ∞

　　1. Adams, John, 1825–1864.　2. Generals—Confederate States of America—Biography.　3. Confederate States of America. Army—Biography.　4. United States—History—Civil War, 1861–1865—Biography.　5. Tennessee—History—Civil War, 1861–1865—Biography.　I. Title.
E467.1.A23T83 2013
355.0092—dc23
[B]

　　　　　　　　　　　　　　　　　　　　　　2013034594

BRITISH LIBRARY CATALOGUING DATA ARE AVAILABLE

© 2014 Leslie R. Tucker. All rights reserved

No part of this book may be reproduced or transmitted in any form or by any means, electronic or mechanical, including photocopying or recording, or by any information storage and retrieval system, without permission in writing from the publisher.

On the cover: Brigadier General John Adams, CSA

Manufactured in the United States of America

McFarland & Company, Inc., Publishers
　Box 611, Jefferson, North Carolina 28640
　　www.mcfarlandpub.com

To my wife, Phebe

Table of Contents

Preface 1
Introduction 5

One. The Beginnings 19
Two. The Mexican War 40
Three. New Mexico Territory 76
Four. Minnesota 101
Five. Return to New Mexico 113
Six. California 130
Seven. War Begins 149
Eight. The Final Stage 181
Nine. Conclusions 203

Chapter Notes 207
Bibliography 219
Index 229

Preface

Gen. John Adams was a kingly man without the royalty usually attached to that class. He was a true type of the American, or rather Southern, soldier — ever modest, conservative, brave, and patriotic. He seemed not to know fear. To do his duty at all times and under all circumstances was ever his desire. No truer or braver officer ever gave his life in defense of his beloved Southland. The last words I heard of his saying was in that terrible and ever-memorable charge on the Federal works at Franklin. Riding in front of his brigade, he turned his face to his men and said in a cool calm, deliberate tone: "Follow me, my men!" In almost less time than it takes me to write, his horse sank down with his front feet resting on the enemy's breastworks, and he was pierced with seven bullets. I have seen it stated, as coming from a Federal officer who was in command on that portion of the line, that they could have captured Gen. Adams, but had to kill him to check his brigade, or else his men would have captured the works. He said he was the bravest man he ever saw. His troops were always willing to follow him, having implicit confidence in his skill and generalship. History has never done him justice, and I hope Tennesseans will see to it that the page that records his deeds is one of the brightest that adorns Southern history, for she never gave the South a truer, better, or braver officer. I hope to meet the surviving members of his staff at Memphis. It is indeed a very great pleasure to meet loved comrades now after the lapse of nearly forty years and to talk over those days of hardship and sacrifices, not unmingled with much pleasure.[1]

This is a biography of fallen Confederate general John Adams. There is not much in the way of personal papers that would allow us to understand the feelings of the man himself. Although we do not have his own interpretation of the events of his life, we do have considerable record of what he did, at least during the time that he served in the military.

This book has two main objectives: The first is to record in print

Preface

the deeds of this colorful and interesting Confederate general, a task which has not been done before now. The second is to use his life as a case study in Southern history and American history. There will be times when Adams will not be present for several pages. Nonetheless, those times will not be aimless wanderings but rather focused on the events and places where Adams was present. The idea is to fill in the missing pieces of his life with a description of what was going on around him. The life of John Adams that we know is the career of a military man. Like most people today or in the past, he was the product of his times and personal experiences. This is an account of one man's life, but history is the accumulation of such accounts. We cannot reach a conclusion on his life alone; however, his biography is of value if we accept it as one piece in the puzzle of history. For many years amateur and professional historians alike have looked to the militaristic strengths of Southerners as proof that they clung to a way of life that was being replaced with modernization. In their minds the southern cavalier was a knight out of the pages of Sir Walter Scott, though Don Quixote might be a better analogy. Many of those who fought for the "lost cause" fostered this delusion and thus became targets for the more recent revisionist historians.

In the case of General Adams, the man serves as an example of a career military officer who is as much a part of modern America and the progress of modernization as the democratic politician or the capitalistic businessman. Militarization was a slow process and men such as Adams were part of that process. We do not have the words of the man to tell of his experiences and the part he played in the building of the United States Army; nonetheless, a study of his life can reveal the interface between one American military leader and the historical events which occurred in his lifetime.

Four topics of nineteenth century American history are discussed in this study. One I call centralism versus localism, which deals with why John Adams chose to join his native state of Tennessee on the road to secession rather than remain loyal to the United States. The second is Manifest Destiny, which sent professional soldiers such as Adams to the West. The third is the relationship between the United States and the Indians, those who stood in the path of Manifest Destiny. Fourth is the common thread, the rise of the modern military. It is not always a disadvantage to be forced to peripheral sources when studying an individual, for in

Preface

many instances where a writer records his thoughts the historian is left with the task of deciding whether that person told the truth to himself or the reader. It is still necessary to evaluate the man's actions if we want to understand history. Historians do this all the time, thus so much disagreement in the profession. The Civil War is the most written about topic in American history, and yet historians have no consensus on even the causes for the war. This is probably due to our great desire to reduce a complex set of events to the simplest explanation. The actions of one man cannot explain the actions of millions, whether told in his words or whether his life is pieced together by an historian. Although it has been more than a century and a half since the war started, the discussion of it is as controversial today as it was then. A recent historiography of the topic will be discussed in the chapter in which Adams joins the Confederate cause. It will be shown that just when historians seemed to be approaching a consensus, extensive debate returns.

I want to especially thank Lynn Shaw of Tennessee, past commander-in-chief of the Sons of Confederate Veterans. Lynn has been active in historical and genealogical organizations for most of his life. In one of our discussions of the Civil War, he talked about his collection of biographies of Confederate generals. At the time I was still working on Isaac Trimble of Maryland. In anticipation of my next project, I asked him which biography he would like to see in print which has not yet been done. He answered John Adams. I hope he enjoys this one.

Introduction

One of the most horrific moments in what would later become known by Southerners as "the lost cause" took place at the Carnton House in Franklin, Tennessee. The afternoon and evening of November 30, 1864, included five hours of slaughter that we now call the Battle of Franklin. The more famous Pickett's Charge at Gettysburg involved crossing a mile of open ground; at Franklin the Confederates crossed two miles of open ground without any of the artillery preparation which they had during that devastating Pennsylvania adventure. On the morning of December 1, hundreds of wounded and dying sons of the South packed the plantation house, and the remains of four of the six generals killed that day lay on the back porch. These included Patrick R. Cleburne, Hiram B. Granbury, Ortho F. Strahl, and John Adams. The blood-stained floors attract tourists today, the tales of the ghosts that haunt the site fascinate many, but the image of these four fallen warriors is the crowning distinction of this otherwise stereotypical Southern mansion. This image of his life's end has also become the most distinguishing feature in the life of Brigadier General John Adams of the Confederate States of America.

John Adams, like the rest of us, is one piece of the fabric of American history, a history of which he is both part of and by which he was shaped. Four topics of nineteenth century American history are most relevant to his biography. The most important is perhaps the conflict between localism and centralism, which the South referred to as states' rights when states began to secede in in 1861. Many historians dispute this as the true cause, preferring instead to say it was over slavery. Regardless of the role of slavery in this issue, it boils down to the fact that the central government imposed its will on the states. That is states' rights. Adams

Introduction

chose to resign his service to the United States government and sided with his home state. He chose to defend the rights of his state over his nation. The second topic is American imperialism, which many prefer to discuss under the heading of Manifest Destiny when speaking of the nineteenth century. Adams served the United States in its western expansion. Third, related to the second, is the one of most interest in this age of ethnic interpretation of history: the relationship between the United States and the land's first inhabitants, who have traditionally been called Indians rather than the preferred term of today, Native Americans. Though he studied European warfare at West Point, most of his chosen career involved fighting Indians. Fourth is the development of a professional military. The years that he served in the American Army marked a stage in our nation's evolution from a people who feared a standing army to a nation which had troops stationed around the globe.

Since the life of John Adams covered only one link in the chain of American history, it is necessary to set the stage with a brief outline of where each of these four issues stood in the year that he graduated from the military academy, 1846. This establishes the basic assumptions on these topics used in discussing the life of John Adams.

Centralism versus Localism

One of the definitive eras of American history lingers as a controversial defining topic since the time of its occurrence. In recent years academia has leaned toward interpretations of the causes of the war which center on the abolition of slavery. Professional historians are aware of the fact that Lincoln denied that he fought to end slavery. They have read the Emancipation Proclamation and know that it only freed the slaves he had no control over. They are aware of the fact that many of the Northern men enlisted in the army to preserve the Union and would not have done so to end slavery. They know about the resolution passed by Congress which stated that the war was only to preserve the Union. Nonetheless, they insist that the war was caused by slavery. Many, if not most, Southerners have always claimed that the main issue they fought for was states' rights.

Few deny that slavery played a major role in the division of the

Introduction

United States in 1861. However, a larger issue was at stake. Since the founding of the country in 1776, one of the greatest barriers to survival of the United States revolved around the question of how much power should be granted to the national government. Not only was this a major issue in American history, but it was part of the development of Western European civilization in general.

The mid nineteenth century saw the rise of a national government in Germany and Italy where none had existed before. The British led the way in creating a strong central government; however, the consensus of British historians is that it was not until the reign of Queen Victoria that they truly achieved the Great Britain that some visionaries had in mind with the Unification Act of a century before. In many ways the struggle between centralism and localism that took place in America is similar to that which was occurring in other Western nations such as Germany, Italy, and even in the British Isles.

Remember, in 1776 there were thirteen separate states which came together, and rather than name their new nation they called themselves the United States of America. They first worked under the Articles of Confederation, which many thought weakened the central government to the point that they questioned its very survival. A new and stronger government was created when the Constitution was ratified, but there were still many who voted against it and even some, such as Thomas Jefferson, feared that it would result in the loss of the Republic.

Between 1787 and 1846, the people, North and South, questioned the limits of the authority of the central government. Timothy Pickering attempted to encourage interest in the independence of New England. Later, some of those at the Hartford Convention in Connecticut threatened separation over their disagreement with the War of 1812. Under President Jackson, South Carolina claimed the right of nullification over the tariff question and some even spoke of secession at that time. This had nothing to do with slavery but had everything to do with states' rights.

Issues over slavery existed at the time the nation was being formed. Leaders brought it up in the beginning; however, the Three-fifths Compromise proves that those who objected to slavery were willing to overlook it for the sake of unification. This compromise over the representation of the slave population in the House of Representatives

Introduction

helped to give the slave owners greater power than they would have otherwise enjoyed, but it seemed likely at the time that without it the Southern states might prefer to be on their own. This of course is the very nature of the debate. Yes it has to do with slavery; however, it also has to do with the question of the power the central government would have over those states which had slavery.

John Adams and his family had only a minor interest in the slave question. Adams himself never owned a single slave and he chose the military for a career. His future would not be affected one way or the other by slavery. These are the facts. John Adams had a career with the United States Army which he abandoned to join the Confederacy. This is all that we know for certain. Unfortunately, we do not have an explanation in his own words about why he made this decision; all we can do is speculate. It is most likely he was not motivated by any driving desire to preserve the institution of slavery. It seems logical to assume he was more motivated by the broader issue of localism versus centralism, or states' rights. When his home state of Tennessee seceded from the Union he resigned his commission in the United States Army and went home. In so doing he established that his state was his country and that he valued his connection to his home state more than he valued being an American.

Manifest Destiny

Many Americans deny that our nation is imperialistic. Even though no nation on earth expanded more than the United States during the nineteenth century, Americans then, and many now, did not see that as imperialism. In 1845, at the time John Adams attended West Point, a journalist named John L. O'Sullivan wrote an article which rationalized American conquest and still perpetuates the delusion that even though we conquer, we are not an empire. He began with the basic assumption that in 1776, "our national birth was the beginning of a new history, the formation and progress of an untried political system, which separates us from the past and connects us with the future only." We are not like those Europeans or others. "The American people never suffered themselves to be led on by wicked ambition to depopulate the land, to spread

Introduction

desolation far and wide, that a human being might be placed on a seat of supremacy." Our soldiers were not the "dupes and victims of emperors, kings, nobles, demons in the human form called heroes." Rather they were patriots who defended "our homes, our liberties, but no aspirants to crowns or thrones." The only reason for that rapid expansion of territory was "in defense of humanity, of the oppressed of all nations, of the rights of conscience, the rights of personal enfranchisement."[1] Such thinking clouds the minds of Americans today as much as it did in the time of John Adams. The goal here is not to prove or disprove this view but rather to establish the assumptions used here in an attempt at an objective evaluation of our history.

Beginning with the first permanent English settlement at Jamestown and extending well beyond the life and times of John Adams, people have come to America for land. This great hunger has fed the growth of the colonies and the United States. We like to claim people sought religious or political freedom, but it is clear that the desire for land is the driving force of American history. This is not to say that religion played no role, but that land was more important. There has been a cycle where the availability of land has led to a rapid population growth, as much due to natural growth as immigration, and the expanding population has fueled territorial expansion. None of the other colonies in the New World had as rapid population growth and no other colony or nation rivaled the imperialistic expansion. It is pursuit of property, not freedom, that produced the philosophy of manifest destiny, and thus the continued attacks on the native population.

Religion may have been a reason for the Puritans to go to Massachusetts; however, their struggle was actually as English citizens and members of the Anglican Church over practices which some felt resembled those of the Catholic Church. The hanging of Quakers and other such practices which forced Roger Williams and his friends to leave and start a more tolerant colony suggest that these Puritans did not seek religious freedom. Williams founded the colony of Rhode Island on the Enlightenment idea of a separation of church and state, whereas the Massachusetts Puritans wanted to control both the church and the government of the colony. In fact, their struggle in England continued so that in the mid seventeenth century Puritans removed the king and ruled the English Parliament and thus the entire empire. The Catholics of

Introduction

England found an early refuge in Maryland; however, by the end of the century they could not even vote there, and it is clear that the Church of England had become as dominant in that colony as in the rest of the Empire.

Regardless of the reason, the fact is they came and did so in large numbers, although much of the population growth was due to procreation. In the year of the *Mayflower* the English colonies numbered 2,300. In the next twenty years the population increased more than tenfold to 26,600; the next twenty years it tripled to 75,100; the next twenty years it doubled again to 151,500; and, by the beginning of the eighteenth century, the English colonies had a population of 250,900. No doubt some would argue that they came for freedom; however, they were still part of the British Empire, subjects to the English king, and prior to the end of the French and Indian War in 1763 very few seriously discussed the possibility of becoming an independent nation. Freedom does not require territorial expansion, but the desire for land and fortune does. With the growing population the colonists pushed deeper and deeper into the land of the first inhabitants. By 1760 the English colonies had 1,593,600 inhabitants. It was their hunger for land which sparked the French and Indian War which spread to Europe, where it was called the Seven Years' War.

At the end of that war the British government forbade expansion beyond the Proclamation Line of 1763, which in turn angered many of the common people. The rich men with their silk stockings and powdered wigs who voted on the Declaration of Independence spoke of the rights of men, but it was those buckskinned frontiersmen who penetrated into the French territory in 1754 with their longing for land. By 1800, less than twenty years after the Treaty of Paris, the population had grown to 5,308,483, and the new country had already added three new states with more to follow soon after.

Prior to 1840 immigration into the United States had barely begun. It was mainly natural growth that brought the head count up to 17,069,453. About a half century after the British barrier of 1763 had been removed, the former colonies had doubled in size with the acquisition of the Louisiana Territory, and by the time that John Adams graduated from West Point, wagon trains loaded with Americans traveled to the shore of the Pacific Ocean. American history is the result of rapid population growth which in turn resulted in territorial expansion, whether you call it Manifest Destiny or imperialism. The military career of John Adams was to support this growing nation. The victims of this expansion are those we call Native Americans today, but which were known as Indians in Adams's time.

The Indians

The Eurocentric philosophy that has helped us deny our imperialist ambitions have been greatly assisted with the belief that our noble ancestors conquered a wilderness. They did not conquer a wilderness, they conquered the Indians. Some would say that when the United States doubled in size in 1803 that it was not conquest, we purchased the land from the French. Did anyone ask the Indians? Did those who had occupied the land for thousands of years receive any of the money or did they sign the treaty surrendering the land to the United States? What Jefferson really purchased from Napoleon was an agreement that the French would not stand in the way of Americans conquering the Indian lands.

Back in 1620 when the Pilgrims numbered in the hundreds, they depended on the kindness of the first inhabitants for their survival. Many of the first Americans did not see any problem with the arrival of the white men, in fact they too benefited from trade with them. In 1637 the Puritans allied with other tribes in their war with the Pequot, though the burning of Fort Mystic with hundreds of women and children inside was not the normal Indian war tactics. By 1676 the Indians of New England began to realize that the white man's hunger for land would lead to the demise of their own way of life and they followed the Indian warrior Metacom, whom the English called King Philip.

In the South the relationship with the Indians did not begin so favorably, and in fact the colonists in Virginia had the first major conflict in 1623. Others followed in the 1640s and 1670s. The problems they had in 1676 caused historians to question if it was an organized attack since that is the same time that the Puritans had problems in the North. Either way, by the late seventeenth century it became clear that as the white population grew so did the demand for land, and thus they infringed deeper and deeper into the continent, pushing what they called savages back one way or the other.

Introduction

With the advance of the white population, the main conflicts took place on the frontier, or in the West. In the colonial days the French also lived in the West. There is no reason to think of them as any less racist than the English; however, their economy generated a more symbiotic relationship. The main industry of New France was the fur trade. The French colonists did not need nor demand possession over the home of the existing population. The Indians benefited from trade with the French. For this reason more of them sided with the French during the war that took place in the mid eighteenth century.

The Spanish tried to exercise more control over the conquered natives; however, they did not have the rapid population growth of the English colonies and so they did not have the same driving desire to clear the Indians from their habitats. In those parts of the Spanish colonies which became consumed by the United States, the Indians continued to live pretty much as they wished. The threat they posed on the Spanish settlements in the northern regions of New Spain, which became Mexico in 1822, made it difficult for them to attract settlers. This is why the Mexicans encouraged the Americans to come to Texas and California.

By the early days of independence for the former English colonies, the first inhabitants were anything but independent of European influences, whether dealing with the English, French, or Spanish. They had become as much a part of the world market economy as the white men since they traded, mainly various animal skins, with the white men to the point that they did not even know how to live as their ancestors had before the arrival of the Europeans.

What disgusts most people when talking about the first Americans is the rapid decline in population which resulted in the complete extinction of most of those cultures or civilizations which thrived in the western hemisphere prior to 1492. The more radical among us like to use the word genocide. Others have shrugged the whole thing off as the result of progress. In their view, the Indians did not make efficient use of the land, so it should be no surprise that it was taken over by the more industrious Europeans. This is the main assumption of the Manifest Destiny philosophy. The different views among the white population have resulted in changing policies toward the Indians from the very beginning up to and through the time in which John Adams dealt with the issues.

Introduction

There have been three basic approaches. Some wanted to draw borders between the Indians and European civilization. They felt that the leaders of the various cities, tribes, or nations should have the same status as any other foreign head of state. The more Eurocentric saw the presence of the Indians as a barrier to the advancement of civilization and as such they needed to be removed. Some simply wanted them pushed off their ancestral lands while others believed that "the only good Indian was a dead Indian." A very significant part of the population had a more liberal approach; however, these people clearly reflected a confidence in the superiority of their own civilization. The Christian thing to do was give them the word of God and teach them to live off the land as civilized people do. This third approach is called assimilation.

Modern Military

The Modern Age began about the year 1500. It is important for us to understand that when we speak of these historical eras we are defining them in terms of the advancements of Western civilization. Prior to 1500 Europe was in what we call the Middle Ages, medieval, or feudal period. The main distinction between then and the Modern Age is the economy. During the earlier period most people lived off the land, whereas in modern times there would be a transition toward a market economy. There have been many overlaps during the transition. We must realize that trade existed in the Middle Ages, and that many dreamed of being farmers in the Modern Age. Up until the 1920s most people in America were farmers, and it was not until after that time that more lived in urban areas. As Americans the most important aspect of the changes is that modern trade progressed to a world market. That is why Columbus sailed in the first place, seeking trade routes. That is what generated the growth of nationalism. The merchants sought protection while they did trade around the planet. That is what generated the burning desire to have stronger central governments. The more powerful the nation, the better the protection for the merchants who came from that nation.

Whether the smaller feudal states of the earlier era or the larger nations and empires of the later, they had warfare. Like most other aspects of European civilization, military arts changed. The driving force

Introduction

which enabled the Europeans to sail around the world, the driving force which allowed them to produce more goods, the driving force which changed warfare, was technology. The technological improvements which followed the Scientific Revolution gave the white men of Europe the advantage they needed to take over Africa, Asia, Australia, and the Americas.

The most influential technological change related to the military is the improved capability to launch projectiles toward the enemy. The primitive guns and cannons which the Spanish used in their first encounters with the natives of the Americas were not so complicated as to necessitate a change in their basic military strategies. They had a warrior class which came from the various ranks of the aristocracy. The common foot soldier came from the lower classes. They had a militia system where the bulk of the armies would be raised at war time and then would return to their more mundane lives and families after the war was over.

Technology had a major influence on the military commanders. The medieval aristocrat had little need for scientific knowledge. Many of them did not even know how to read and write — that is what clerks were for. After the scientific revolution the technology which gave winning armies their advantage became too complicated for a man who did not have the requisite training. This is why the seventeenth century saw the rise of military schools across Europe. A military commander needed much more than an aristocratic pedigree and the ability to ride a horse while waving a sword in the air. To be a successful military leader, a man needed to go to one of the academies and learn the skills that could lead to victory. It got to the point this artillery was more important than either the infantry or cavalry. As artillery became more complex the students of these academies needed to focus more and more on engineering. The greatest warriors during the days of the Civil War did not come from the aristocracy, but rather from the military academies.

A social change followed the Scientific Revolution which we call the Enlightenment. Those successful in the merchant economy and those successful on the battlefield did not always come from the aristocracy. It is not surprising that more and more of the new leaders rejected the rights that came with one's noble birth. Enlightenment thinking rejected the idea of divine right and replaced it with the idea of government by contract. These are the ideas incorporated by the founders of the United

Introduction

States. We Americans like to think that the likes of Washington, Jefferson, and Franklin created these concepts; however, many Englishmen will tell you that they came from England. The reality is that the modern liberal social thinking of the eighteenth century arose across Europe during this stage of development in Western civilization.

A conflict developed between the political philosophy of the Enlightenment and the change in the military. With the growth of a professional military, the liberal Enlightenment thinkers who were well schooled in history, especially ancient history, thought about the demise of the Republic of Rome. The founders of the United States created a republic and many of them feared that a standing army would produce a Caesar who would replace their republic with an empire. This is in fact a major contradiction in America today.

America had a civilian population which demanded a powerful military, while at the same time feared its influence. The common people wanted land, which led them to conflict with the Indians. They would expect the army to protect them. The New England merchants wanted a powerful navy to protect them on the seas. The southern planter wanted the army to help expand their borders and get more plantation land. This has created a system full of inconsistencies. Through the generations most Americans would be willing to serve, but many would resent the arrogance of the regular army. They did not want to see military control over the civilian government; however, they would consistently elect successful generals to the presidency.

Thomas Jefferson was one of the most outspoken against a standing army. It was during the seventeenth century when England first went in that direction. Jefferson's view was as much of the Enlightenment as it was American. Many of those in England had the same concerns. Shortly after the establishment of the United States, the government established the United States Military Academy at West Point, similar to those in Europe. The War of 1812 convinced many of the hesitant ones that men were needed trained in warfare. After 1815 an increasing number of generals and commanders came from those who studied the subject as opposed to those who rose up from the people. Nonetheless, between 1815 and 1846 many looked at the school as more of an engineering school, as many of those who graduated in engineering were encouraged to resign their commissions and work in the building of canals, turnpikes, and railroads.

Introduction

Shortly after he graduated from West Point, John Adams took off for the Mexican War. He and his classmates were members of a professional military called the Regular Army. During his lifetime Adams served in an army which some Americans wanted, while some disliked it.

These Issues During the Life and Times of John Adams

Adams was a man who became famous as a general during the ultimate American conflict between centralism and localism which we call the Civil War. The time in which Adams served the United States Army is the same time period which historians look to in seeking the causes of the Civil War, that is 1846 to 1861. As a professional soldier he lived and served in various parts of the United States. Apparently deep down inside he was still a Tennessean. After his native state seceded he resigned his commission in the United States Army in California and returned to the state of his birth. Regardless of one's position on the role that slavery played in the war versus the traditional southern claim that they fought for states' rights, the fact is that John Adams and his family did not depend on slavery for their livelihood. In his case he fought for his state against the might of the central government.

He spent most of his adult life in an army which was the product of Manifest Destiny. No sooner had he graduated than he headed down to Mexico where he did his part for the conquest of the northern part of that nation. He then fought to protect the American settlers in New Mexico, Minnesota, and California. The life and times of John Adams were a major part of American expansion and conquest.

Though he and his classmates at West Point studied the classical war strategies anticipated in a European style war, most of Adams's career involved fighting Indians. Most of the professional soldiers did not agree with the policies of the government, nor with the attitudes of many of the frontiersmen; however, they did their duty and fought the wars. The life and times of John Adams included one of the most controversial periods in the history of the relationship between white Americans and those who had formerly ruled the land.

The period between 1815 and 1865 marked a critical stage in the

Introduction

development of a professional army. During the Mexican War the nation called on the militia system of citizen soldiers, but most of the generals and field officers were West Point graduates. There were major conflicts between the volunteers and the regular Army. This is also a time when the army faced the issues which would have to be resolved to get men to make a career out of serving their country in the military. They would expect decent pay, housing, benefits, and the question of how to serve their country while providing for a family. The life and times of John Adams saw many changes that helped lead to the development of a professional officer class in the United States Army.

The life and times of John Adams is the biography of one man. It can also serve as a case study in a changing America. Like all of us, the events in history affected the flow of his life, and at the same time he played a role in changing his country.

ONE

The Beginnings

Richard W. Johnson arrived at West Point in June of 1844. A seventeen-year-old orphan from Kentucky, he knew nothing about the military traditions that he was going to follow. He had heard rumors that Winfield Scott planned a visit to the academy. When the young and naive country boy ascended the hill from the landing he heard the band playing on the plain. Years later Johnson recalled, "The drum major, with his party-colored trousers, bearskin cap, and huge baton with a brass ball on the end, was the most conspicuous person I saw, and at once I supposed that my eyes rested upon the hero of Lundy's Lane."[1] The mistake would have been somewhat justified if the young man had known about Scott's passion for fancy dress uniforms which earned him the nick name of "old fuss and feathers."

This was the time when John Adams also attended West Point. It was a time of transition for the military academy. Winfield Scott and the other generals of the day rose through the ranks due to their military prowess displayed during the War of 1812. In the army of the future the generals as well as other officers would be manufactured at West Point. Many Americans objected to the school as a playground for the American aristocracy; however, the reality is that men like the country boy Johnson and the Irish immigrant Adams were becoming increasingly more common. Ironically it is Scott, who had come up the old fashioned way, that campaigned for the creation of a professional officer corps. Ever since the wealthy creators of the United States claimed that "all men are created equal," more and more of the "people" thought of themselves as equal to any man with money or title. They increasingly found the deference associated with an officer class as distasteful. The period between the end of Scott's war and the beginning of the great war which would claim the life of John Adams marked a period of tumultuous change for the United States Army.

Few historians have studied the profession of arms during their formative years. Living in an age when bumper stickers urge the support of our troops, it may be difficult for some to understand how the average citizen saw the army as a threat to the American way of life rather than a defender. The biggest barrier to the army which Scott envisioned was the civilian population. In 1957, Samuel P. Huntington saw the years after the Civil War as the beginnings of a true military profession; however, he did acknowledge the roots of change in the 1830s and 1840s in his book *The Soldier and the State: The Theory and Politics of Civil-military Relations*. Marcus Cunliffe objected to Huntington's thesis as putting too much emphasis on its southern roots. In his 1968 book *Soldiers and Civilians: The Martial Spirit in America, 1775–1865*, Cunliffe saw an enthusiasm for all things military as being a part of American society. In 1986 Edward M. Coffman published *The Old Army: A Portrait of the American Army in Peacetime, 1784–1898*, in which he went into great detail on the peacetime military community but agreed with Huntington on his view that a true professional army began in the last of the nineteenth century. In 1992 William B. Skelton came out with his book *An American Profession of Arms: The Army Officer Corps, 1784–1861*, and said that "the early national and antebellum eras were crucial to the rise of the American profession of arms." He saw the first period, 1784 to the end of the War of 1812, as a foundation in which the American people accepted the need for a small regular army. However, he saw that "the emergence of a stable profession of arms occurred between the War of 1812 and the Civil War."[2]

Since the mid seventeenth century the modern age generated forces of change which would affect the military as much as the other ways of life. The key lay in technology. Before 1492 most people lived off the land, merchants had minimal influence, and war consisted of hand to hand combat with swords, maces, spears or other such weapons which would be delivered in person to the enemy. Only the aristocracy rode in the cavalry, and catapults offered very limited artillery capabilities. Since the fifteenth century, cannons and extremely primitive firearms appeared; however, it would not be until the English Civil War that they would began to play an important role. By the end of that century the

One. The Beginnings

leading European powers turned to the technology of their age as something that could serve them well during warfare. As a result merely being the son of an aristocrat would no longer be sufficient. The intellectual skill of the engineer would excel over the military prowess of a knight. By the eighteenth century they founded military schools. In 1751 Louis XV established the École Militaire, whose founding decree stated, "It is necessary that the ancient prejudice which has instilled the belief that bravery alone makes the man of war would give place imperceptibly to a taste for the military studies which we have introduced." In 1741 George II of England founded the Royal Military Academy at Woolrich.[3]

It was in the seventeenth century that the British developed their garrison system of colonial administration. Though in a decline, it was revived during the French and Indian War. The incident in Boston which the radicals of the day labeled the Boston Massacre came about because of this form of colonial control. That is why it is hard to understand why the new government of the United States used the same basic strategy. In the case of the Americans the main military threat came from the Indians. The people of the new nation generated conflict as they grabbed Indian land, and thus the Army had to defend the citizens. The situation only worsened after the acquisition of the Louisiana Territory in 1803 when the amount of land to be taken from the Indians doubled.[4]

The career of John Adams took place during this period of military change. Americans have been and many still are obsessed with what historians call American exceptionalism. Frederick Jackson Turner's frontier thesis does not command the respect that it once did, but the fact remains that the rapid expansion of the white population into Indian-occupied America is what drove the career of Adams as well as many of the others who were part of the West Point classes that graduated between the War of 1812 and the Civil War. The obsession of most Americans was land. Land was for the taking at the expense of the Indians. This was the key to conflict between the whites and the Indians but also between the civilian population and the Army.

The professional military was very small in the early days and in fact would continue to be small up to the beginning of the Civil War. Those who became the most aggressive toward the Indians were not the professional soldiers but most often the civilian or militia soldiers. In 1787 Lieutenant Colonel Harmar arrested a citizen at Fort Pitt for the murder of a peaceful Indian. He felt that the white inhabitants would come to the rescue of the man they saw as a victim of military justice. Harmar told the secretary of war, "It is the prevailing opinion of the people in general upon the frontiers, that it is no harm to kill an Indian." When officers of the Army tried to punish those who aggressed against the Indians, the civilian population would complain of the abuse of military authority.[5]

In addition to the Army being viewed as restricting the people from taking the lands of the Indians, there was a very basic philosophical objection to a professional or standing army. The militia system had its roots in medieval warfare where the king would send the word down the line through the aristocracy to raise an army for combat. The power of the British Empire reached its peak during the Enlightenment. The philosophers of this age who dreamed of republics saw the militia system as a way to limit the powers of potential dictators and tyrants. Europeans as well as the Enlightenment gentlemen who founded the United States received classical educations so that they were all aware that it was military commanders who turned the Roman Republic into an empire. This is an excellent example of the types of contradictions and conflicts brought about by modernization.

Modernization included the technology which generated a demand for professional soldiers while at the same time producing the Enlightenment philosophy that worried men about the threats such a military could pose. The new professional British Army battled the Americans as they struggled for independence. The average American saw the professional army as a threat to their liberty as well as a force which had prevented them from crossing the Proclamation Line of 1763. In other words, it is the British Army which prevented them from grabbing the Indian lands that they longed for. How could they possibly accept the same from an American army?

The Federalists had a greater grasp of the advantages of modernization while the Jeffersonians defended localism and agrarianism, and favored the militia over a professional army. By 1795 Congress became convinced of the need for engineers and artillery to defend the new nation. On May 9 of that year they created the Corps of Artillerists and Engineers, the beginning of the military academy. The creation of West Point with its books and training demonstrated that at least the Feder-

One. The Beginnings

alists grasped the reality of modernization, but it would not be until after the War of 1812 that we see the birth of the new army which General Adams would be a part of.

At the beginning of that war most of the officers were older men, many veterans of the war for independence. More political than military leaders, they were not terribly effective. New men began to rise through the ranks, a process that gave them the military skills needed for victory as well as a respect and love of the martial life. Three new brigadier generals specifically contributed to this change. The first, Alexander Macomb, had commanded the forces at Lake Champlain and stopped the British advance from Canada. The second, Edmund P. Gains, displayed tenacity and aggressiveness at Fort Erie. The third, and the most famous of the three today, was Winfield Scott. Even before the end of the war Scott had drafted plans for army expansion which included 65,000 men led by six lieutenant generals, thirteen major generals, and thirty-six brigadiers. He ended up with an army of 10,000 and the politicians would reduce that even more before the transition to a truly professional army would be completed.[6]

The War of 1812 gave birth to the infant army which the politicians not only hesitated to nurture but some even attempted to kill. The Jacksonian democratic reforms gave the civilian authorities that much more power as they tried to protect the interests of the Indian killing, land grabbing frontier population. Meanwhile, with the newly acquired power that the ballot box gave these buckskin clad men, more and more of them looked at those from the East with their powdered wigs and silver buckles as the American equivalent to the aristocracy that their fathers had tried to rid them of in 1776. The *North American Review* of 1832 summed up the attitude of the Jacksonians when it stated, "A large standing army has no advocates among us, and is wholly adverse to the spirit of our government and to the public sentiment."[7]

Even the aggressive President James K. Polk wanted to reduce the army in size. Only conflicts with the Indians produced tolerance to a military presence, but even then the numbers would be reduced as soon as the fight was over. Various states issued complaints. In 1833 the Tennessee legislature claimed West Point to be inconsistent and dangerous to the principles of free government. The Ohio legislature in 1834 called the academy "partial in its operations and wholly inconsistent with the spirit of American institutions." Though the evidence is to the contrary, the view persisted that admission policies favored the sons of the rich. Nonetheless, between 1815 and 1860 the Army increased the recruitment of officers from West Point graduates, and perhaps more important, by the time the Civil War began most of the commanding generals on both sides came from the Academy.[8]

One change that occurred shortly before Adams' entry into West Point was the foundation of cavalry. Adams went straight into the dragoons and most of his career was spent with a horse; he even died on one. George Washington saw little value in mounted soldiers, and the taint of aristocracy contributed to the view that men on horseback thought themselves as better than those on foot. This goes back to medieval warfare when only the aristocracy were mounted. After the war ended in 1815 the economy had a lot to do with government shying away from the additional expense of horses for soldiers.

The Indian wars again impacted American military, as the troubles during the 1830s led to the establishment of dragoons and later cavalry. During the Black Hawk War of 1832 a battalion of 600 volunteers played an important role in chasing those Indians to the West. The following year the War Department established the First Dragoons, which went by the moniker Black Hawks, no doubt due to the connection with the 600 who battled the Sauk warrior named Black Hawk the year before. Colonel Henry Dodge, who had commanded those men, became the first commander of the regulars, and his lieutenant was Stephen Watts Kearney, whom Adams would serve under upon his completion of training. The following year they would be joined by the Second Dragoons, and except for a brief period during the Mexican War when a third regiment would exist, these two would be the entire United States mounted army until the creation of the first and second cavalry in the 1850s.[9]

The philosophy of education at West Point also changed dramatically between the end of the War of 1812 and the time that Adams entered the school. On April 12, 1812, Congress passed a bill reorganizing the Academy, and Sylvanus Thayer reshaped the school into not only what Adams found upon his arrival but the institution which remains to this day. It is Winfield Scott who prepared the official manual of infantry tactics and drill based upon the French system. It would be revised but basically served as the guide for all of those who attended prior to the

One. The Beginnings

Civil War. The military strategy promoted by Baron Antoine-Henri de Jomini, who based his theories on the battles of Napoleon, had such an impact on those who fought the Civil War that it has been said that they went into battle with a sword in one hand and Jomini's *Summary of the Art of War* in the other.

What Napoleon did so well is grasp the main objective of destroying the army of the enemy. Though many military historians look to the world wars of the twentieth century as the beginnings of total war, others have argued that it began in the United States when the North and South battled each other. Napoleon at least laid the foundation for this strategy as he sought the complete destruction of his foe's army. The increasing importance of technology made it a necessity to attack the civilian population. If the armies of the enemy depended on the modern weapons of war, then total victory would require the elimination of the source of the new weapons, which would mean the destruction of that country's industrial capabilities. The civilian population would become at least collateral damage, but the civilian population which constituted the means of production became military targets themselves.[10]

Regionalism would increase between the end of the Mexican War and the secession of South Carolina in 1860, but it had begun by the time Adams arrived at West Point. The origins of Southern identity is one of the main topics in Southern history today, and the trend has been to regard it as a rather recent thing that has been called "the lost cause myth." Grady McWhinney considered the South to be predominantly a Celtic culture which has been in conflict with the Anglo-Saxon northern culture since before either one arrived in America. Regardless of which side one takes in this debate the fact is that the division between the two regions increased considerably in that time period we now call Antebellum. The myth at the time which persists today is that the school was dominated by aristocratic Southerners. There must have been some of those men there at the time Adams attended or else one of his classmates, George B. McClellan, would not have written home to his sister, "Some how or other I take to the Southerners. I am sorry to say the manners, feelings, and opinions of the Southerners are far, far preferable to those of the majority of the Northerners at this place. I may be mistaken, but I like them better."

Statistically the image of the militaristic Southerners, something argued by McWhinney, does not hold up. Between 1802 and 1861 graduates from the North outnumbered those from the South 1,122 to 627. Part of the explanation for the greater number from the North is the larger population; however, some is due to the greater success rate for the northern students. It is generally accepted that the people from the North assigned greater importance to education so that those from that region performed better academically. When we look at the breakdown based on population we do see a slight advantage for Southerners who served as officers in the Army. In 1797 the South accounted for 30.9 percent of the free population but provided 37.8 percent of the officer corps. This advantage increased some by 1860 when the South still had about the same percentage of the population with 30.6, but the number of officers increased to 43.2 percent. The stereotype of the Southern cavalry does hold up, with the South providing 60 percent of those appointed to mounted units. One does not need to be a historian to be aware of the fact that to this day there are more people in the South who love and raise and ride horses. It is only logical to accept that the region produced more men to serve in mounted regiments whether they be called dragoons or cavalry.[11]

The biggest shadow hanging over the early Army career of John Adams was the appropriations bill of 1845. The legislation, which was passed while Adams was a student, reflects not only the attitude that most Americans had toward West Point but also their view that the regular Army was aristocratic in general. The success of the Mexican War would temper these feelings slightly, but this would still be the boogie man which hung over those like Adams, who wished to make a career out of the military. Prior to the Civil War the North had a tradition of protesting the most to imperial aggressiveness, while those of the South supported the expansionist policies of Andrew Jackson and James K. Polk. Few in the South and West objected to the extermination or removal of Indians or Mexicans for access to more land. In other ways they did not differ with the common farmer of New England or the middle states who gave rise to Jacksonian democracy. Most of the average Americans viewed those in uniform as servants to the civilian authorities.

A vote on West Point appropriations for the year 1845 sparked the aggression of the civilian commanders in Congress. Congressman Hale of New Hampshire urged a revision which would abolish the institution after June 13, 1844. Congressmen Dana of New York supported the move. Dana called West Point "an aristocratic institution." He went on to say that "out of a population of eighteen or twenty million about one hundred individuals are annually selected as the exclusive recipients of the national bounty." He did not seem to be aware of the statistics which showed that a number of the sons of commoners were admitted, but he did have a point. In 1830 2.8 percent of those admitted were the sons of senators and congressmen.

He went on to denounce the "monopoly of military commissions" held by West Point graduates. Again, this could explain an attitude which prevails to this day where regular army officers, especially those from the Point, consider themselves the most knowledgeable when it comes to issues relating to the military. It could be argued that they do have the greatest technical knowledge; however, Dana claimed that this monopoly produced "positive evils" in the Army. He mirrored the philosophy of Jefferson as well as the Enlightenment philosophers of that day when he went on to say, "The main reliance of this country is and ever must be the militia." When we cover the relationship that existed between the volunteers and regular Army during the Mexican War we can see some validity in his exaggerated claim that "if war should occur and the Army and militia be brought in contact, the most disastrous consequences might ensue from their dissension." Dana called on his fellow congressmen to abolish "an expensive, extravagant and antidemocratic institution of little use, the occasion of many controversies between the officers and of discontent and degradation to the soldiers."

Despite the attempt to block the funding of West Point, the bill passed by a single vote. Obviously the military academy survived, since it is still with us, but we can see that many shared the view of Dana and Hale. This theme would continue throughout the military career of John Adams.[12]

In the Beginning

John Adams was certainly not of the aristocratic background that offended so many Jacksonians. Nathan Adams, John's grandfather, was born in Strabane, County Tyrone, Ireland, about 1765. The surname is English and the fact that he traveled back and forth between Ireland and the United States suggests that he was at least a little better off than even the average Scotsman who inhabited the Protestant counties of Northern Ireland. He left a portrait in which he appears to be prosperously dressed, which indicates he may have been well off even when compared to other Englishmen. Nonetheless, he was an immigrant and not from the old American gentry of either the North or the South. He married Martha Patton in 1784 and shortly after that they went to America. Martha was born at Strabane on April 24, 1768. They stayed in Philadelphia about three years and returned to Ireland. They went back to Philadelphia to stay in 1811, where Nathan died in 1816. Martha went west to be with her children and died in Nashville on January 15, 1854. They had three sons and eight daughters.[13]

Thomas Patton Adams, the son of Nathan and Martha, was born in Strabane on March 1, 1796. He went to America with his parents in time to begin his adult life in a new country. By 1815 Thomas and some of his brothers had moved to Nashville. The present state capital, established in 1779, is the oldest white settlement in middle Tennessee. The Adams men were far from the founding fathers; however, the city maintained some of the frontier spirit. The city was not called the state capital until 1827 and would not achieve permanent status as such until after the Adams family relocated to Pulaski. Thomas met Ann Tennant shortly after his arrival. Ann was born on March 1, 1799, at Dumfries, Scotland, the daughter of Christopher Tennant and his wife, Isabell Stothart. She met Thomas when she visited an uncle in Nashville in 1815. The two were married on November 18, 1819, by the Reverend William Hume, a Presbyterian minister.[14]

Thomas worked as a banker at a time when banking was still an adventure. Not subject to the regulations we have today, it did not take a great deal of capital to open doors in a building that could be no more than a log cabin. Though Thomas and his wife were both recent immigrants to the United States with no ties to any of the founding families, it does seem that they came from at least a middle class background. The fact that he cultivated capital rather than crops supports this supposition. He owned three lots of land on Sumner Street and Spruce Street in Nashville. Sometime between 1837 and 1839 he moved his wife and

One. The Beginnings

eight surviving children south to Pulaski, Tennessee. Pulaski served as the seat of Giles County, which was organized in 1809. It was hardly a frontier when Thomas arrived and worked as a cashier for the Planter's Bank. Chartered in 1833, this is one of the banks Andrew Jackson chose to deposit federal funds in during his war with Biddle over the Bank of the United States. When he died in 1841, he left land worth $3,000 and three slaves. This was a comfortable estate, but not that of a wealthy man.[15]

Another indication that Thomas did not come from one of the poor Irish immigrant families which flooded the United States during the antebellum years is the fact that he and his wife attached more importance to education than not only the potato famine refugees but the older Southern Jacksonians who dominated in Tennessee during this time period. His son John, the subject of this biography, was born in Nashville on July 1, 1825. John was accepted into the Wurtemberg Academy in Pulaski in 1838. Founded in 1812, the school provided the young John Adams with a traditional education in Latin, Greek, algebra, and French. In his application letters to West Point, the director of the school, Benjamin Mitchell, claimed that the boy acquired arithmetic and algebra "with much more ease than most of the scholars which I have instructed." His French teacher, Henry Mason, said that he "reads, translates, and understands readily all that is placed in his hands written in that language." The fact that John was accepted in West Point and that his brother Nathan went to law school shows that this family not only valued education but had ambition beyond farming.[16]

Although we cannot know to what degree, it seems safe to assume that the congressmen who recommended John for West Point had a personal acquaintance with the boy and his family. Aaron Venable lived in Nashville at the same time as the Adams family and later moved to Giles County. After serving in the state legislature, he became the Democratic congressman from 1839 to 1845, and then he became governor of the state. He wrote to the then-governor and the adjutant general's office and said that John came from a large and respectable family, and that the young man was of "more than ordinary capacity of good acquirements for his age and opportunities." John was accepted to the Point in March of 1841. Thomas died in Pulaski on April 10, 1841, before his son arrived at the military institute. Apparently he left his family with enough resources that John was able to continue with his education.[17]

At the Point

John apparently arrived by the expected date in June of 1841, one of several members of the famous class of 1846 to begin a year earlier than most of the class. This is such a distinguished class that a book has been written about them. One thing that helped to make them so famous is that they got an immediate chance to apply their newly acquired skills: the Mexican War began the year of their graduation. Fifty-three of the fifty-nine graduates fought in Mexico, four died there. Two more were killed fighting Indians in the 1850s. What has given them the most celebrity is the fact that during the Civil War ten of the survivors became Confederate generals, including John, and twelve became Union generals. This does include two of them, one Union and one Confederate, who graduated with the class of 1847. Among the many to achieve the rank of general were names of notoriety—Ambrose P. Hill, Thomas J. Jackson, George B. McClellan, Dabney H. Maury, Samuel B. Maxey, George E. Pickett, and Cadmus Wilcox.[18]

Despite the claims of the Jacksonians, or perhaps in response to their complaints, by the time Adams arrived candidates came from various walks of American life, including the lowliest of stations. As such they arrived at their new home by many modes of transportation. Those who did come from the American elite no doubt traveled in the style they had grown accustomed to. Perhaps a comfortable cabin on a river boat followed by a coach ride to the gates. Others rode horses or even walked, spending their nights on the road in front of a campfire. Regardless of how they arrived, once inside the confines of the academy they found themselves equals. They were measured purely by their personal accomplishments. No doubt those from privileged backgrounds had more in common with those who had shared the same life experiences. Likewise those who had worked with their fathers in the fields or a small merchant enterprise would hang with the birds of their same feather. Even the numerous journals and letters we have preserved for us today will not always reveal to what degree class jealousies may have entered

One. The Beginnings

the competition. No matter the background, almost all of those who would survive to graduation would share a bond of brotherhood once they completed their studies and put on the uniform of the United States Army. These bonds were not even completely broken when they chose opposing sides during the War Between the States.

When they arrived, that first June was spent going through the final stages of the entrance process, including physical and mental examinations. Adams was one of the dozen or so who had begun a year earlier. He would not have been among the 122 who went through the selection process in 1842, the largest entry class up to that time. Sixty would be the number to graduate, a survival rate which approximated 50 percent. It is difficult to be precise, as a few who started in 1842 ended up in the class of 1847, while some others, such as Adams, began earlier. For all, the process was much the same. The medical exam was a basic eval-

West Point, from Phillipstown (1831). This engraving by W. J. Bennett shows the original buildings of the United States Military Academy (Library of Congress).

uation where the candidates were weighed and measured to be sure they met the five foot minimum height. The board of three doctors would make sure their limbs showed no signs of ringbone and spavin, thump their chests for soundness of wind, look at their feet to see if they had bunions and look them over for any physical deformities or irregularities from childhood injuries. The eye exam involved holding a dime up at the other end of the room to make sure that the potential student could tell the difference between heads and tails; even a blind man would have a 50 percent chance. Some went home after the physical while the majority went on to the academic trials. Leaving behind the three doctors, candidates faced a board of thirteen Army officers. Thayer had placed high regard on the ability to speak French, but by far math would be the most important for what had become primarily an engineering school. A chalk board was where prospective students demonstrated their a mastery of the basic arithmetic skills of reduction, proportion, and fractions. Ninety-two of the 122 who went through this process in 1842 went on to begin classes. After the announcement of those who had passed, they received their knapsacks, packed up their clothes and marched into camp. Perhaps the biggest trials came from facing the upperclassmen who saw the plebes as "things," "animals," "reptiles," and "beasts." Before a good introduction to their rooms or educational facilities, they had to face what is still a ritual in the United States Army, the elimination of any individualism expressed by hairstyles. Men in those days often wore their hair long, some even with curls or perhaps held in place by bear grease or Macassar oil. All such displays of individual style disappeared.[19]

    The physical site and facilities inspired various emotions. The forty acre plain on which the academy was built was near the river and surrounded by crags and cliffs which at times must have seemed like the walls of a castle or a prison. Some saw the land as beautiful whether in the full green foliage of the summer time, the multicolored fall, or even in the lacy wintertime after a new fallen snow. The campus had only recently strived for impressive architecture. In 1836 builders erected the first chapel with a Roman basilica style. After fire destroyed the first academic building a couple of years earlier, the replacement was a new building in a more classical style. There was no such thing as a paved walkway connecting buildings and the only lighting came from whale-oil lamps. The roads varied from dusty to muddy to icy, and the travelers would have to face an Arctic wind in the wintertime. The only communication with the outside world was by boat, which meant they were completely isolated when the river froze.[20]

The cadet did not go to his room for comfort or rest, he went there to study or sleep, that is if he could in the heat of the warm months or the cold of the winters. Each room had an order posted:

> Bedstead—against door—Trunks—under iron bedsteads—Lamps—clean on mantel—Dress caps—Neatly arranged behind door—Looking Glass—between washstand & door—Books—neatly arranged on shelf farthest from door—Broom—Hanging behind door—Drawing books—under shelf fartherest from the door—Muskets—in gun rack and locks sprung—Bayonets in scabbards—Accoutrements—Hanging over muskets—Sabers—Cutlasses & swords—hanging over muskets—Candle Box—for scrubbing utensils—Against wall under shelf nearest door, & fire place—clothes—neatly hung on pegs over—bedsteads—Mattress & Blankets neatly folded—Orderly Board—over mantel—chairs—when not used under tables—Orderlies of rooms are held responsible for the observance of the above mentioned arrangement. By order of Lieut. E. J. Steptoe—1st Lieut. 1st Art. & Commd't compy.[21]

The uniform worn in the days of Adams predated Thayer and went back to a design which had not significantly changed since the days of Partridge. The color was "cadet gray." The shoes were heavy and clumsy and rose above the ankle to be fitted below the pantaloons. Socks were silk. The pantaloons were a gray cloth in winter and a white jean in the summer. The vest was single-breasted. The coat had three rows of eight yellow brass buttons. This was topped off with a bell-crowned black leather cap, seven inches tall, a polished leather visor, and an eight-inch black plume, which John Pope opined to "weigh about 5 Pounds and hurt my head extremely." The class of 1846 did benefit from the bold confrontation by Cadet Pope, who came in from furlough sporting pants that buttoned down the front. Faculty wives were shocked at the clear recognition of the male anatomy. One even denied entry to her house of any cadet dressed in such a way. They were ordered into their winter uniforms in early October and often suffered when the cold north wind struck as early as September. McClellan complained to his sister, "The weather has been quite cold today, at least it feels so to us, with our white pants, and no fires."[22]

The food did not offer much of a reprieve from the monotony and fatigue of study and drill. When they arrived at the tables the command was given "take seats," as explained by William Dutton, "& then such a scrambling you never saw." He added, "For breakfast we have the remains of the meat of the former days dinner, cut up with potato with considerable gravy & not more than two thirds of them get a bit. — bread cut in chunks, butter and coffee." They barely had enough to eat before the command "Squad rise" was given. For dinner they had some meat, such as roast beef or boiled fish, "& boiled potato & bread — no butter." For tea, the last meal of the day, they had tea, bread and butter. George McClellan claimed "Dr. Wheaton won't let any bread be brought on table younger than 20 hours." In a letter to his sister, he said, "Sunday dinner consists of 'Bull beef' & potatoes, I believe I'll cut it today, as I often do.[23]

"All is done to the strictest of regimentation," said William Dutton. He left us a good description: "A gun is fired in the place of an alarm clock at 4:30 A.M." A half hour later they are given the order "fall in there" to the beat of the drums. Roll is called and then they return to their rooms and have fifteen minutes to roll up their blankets, put them up, wash, and clean the room. "They have no mattresses and the five room mates cover the floor of the small ten by twelve room. The drums signal time for breakfast, which is followed by a march to the mess hall." The student paid for failure to follow the rules. "They are reported for speaking, raising a hand, or looking to the right or left." They had drill twice a day "& a good many faint away, but I like the whole of it." After tea they remained in their rooms, mainly for study, until 9:30. They were expected to spend ten hours a day on study. Lights had to be out after the 10:00 taps, and "after that the inspector happens in all times of night." McClellan claimed "the Sunday morning inspection occupied a good deal of time." Even on Sundays the regimentation of meal time and bedtime remained in force.[24]

All discipline was subject to the dreaded demerits. They lived by a code "more rigorous than those of Deuteronomy." The don'ts under Article XII, titled "DISCIPLINE," covered six pages, with an additional four pages under "MORE DISCIPLINE." The most frequent violations came from fighting, but the use of tobacco or consumption of alcohol certainly entrapped their share of victims. John Adams racked up an average num-

One. The Beginnings

ber for hair too long, arriving late for inspection, smiling in ranks, and once for throwing food at a waiter during mess. His most serious charge came when he deserted his post while on sentinel duty on the night of December 29, 1845.[25]

The course instruction in the age of Jackson fell into three main categories: military instruction, scientific instruction, and moral and religious instruction. Military instruction included infantry tactics, artillery tactics, engineering as related to military problems, horsemanship, and fencing. French was considered part of the military training, obviously reflecting the importance placed on the theories of Jomini.

Scientific instruction involved primarily mathematics, physics, electricity, and chemistry. No one could expect to be at the head of his class without the mastery of mathematics. Richard S. Ewell complained that this put those students from the South or the West at a disadvantage to the "down-east Yankees." This subject was also responsible for most of the failures in the academy. Moral and religious instruction included ethics and seemed to follow a distant third to the other two fields. Most who had studied at other colleges or universities were amazed at what the Point expected from them. John Adams finished twenty-fifth in his class of fifty-nine.[26]

Their mastery of the academic requirements was revealed every January and June at exam time. Questions could be general or specific and covered the entire course. They might be required to discuss the subject of friction, give its laws, and find a value for the coefficient of fraction by means of the inclined plane; prove the logarithms of the same numbers in different systems; draw a cross section of the human eye and to explain its construction and the optical principles upon which its efficiency depended; or to "show the method of constructing a Crown work for the defense of a bridge head and to show the dispositions which would be made to secure the passage of the river to a large army in the face of an Enemy."

The end of exams signaled a sigh of relief and cause for celebration. In 1842 they had a display of fireworks. "In the PM horses were attached to all the cannon on both sides of the plain & the way the cannon balls & bombs flew about was like hail. It seemed as if the earth would open, & the echoing from hill to hill produced an effect. Astonishing." William Dutton added, "In the evening they sent up rockets from every quarter

& the air was full of them, while every now and then large fire bombs were fired from the mortars shaking the earth, & lighting the vale as far up as Newburg & when several hundred feet from the ground would burst & those fragments would again burst with a noise." The celebrations concluded when "they placed candles around a hollow square and danced."[27]

They spent their first summer at West Point in an encampment on the plain, an annual summertime event. Beginning in early July they would spend the next two months living three or four to a tent. They were the first class to have board floors in the tents to protect them from the dampness of the ground. For furniture they had "1 pail, 1 wash bowl, 1 broom, 1 candle box, and candle stick, 1 looking glass, for each occupant, 1 Chair, 2 blankets, 1 Canvass bed cover, 4 Shirts, 2 pair shoes, 4 pair socks, 1 bandbox." Each man had a two foot square box to keep their belongings. This was not a restful summer retreat. The morning gun had them up at 4:00; they would be on the drill field by 5:00, in the mess hall by 6:30, parade at 8:00, and doing infantry or artillery drills for the rest of the morning. Many cadets were burned by the sun after hours of firing the cannons, which made a racket as they had never heard before. They had a midday meal at 1:00 followed by more military drills, parade at 6:00, stag dances, without girls, on the common until 9:00. For the better than nothing dances, candles were lit in two rows and the music came from fife, violin, and a drum. Bedtime was by 10:00, that is unless it was one's turn for guard. That first summer the plebes had the additional discomfort of being harassed by their elders, who felt obligated to do unto others as had been done unto them. Unfortunately they had to spend their nights at future encampments seeking their revenge. As stated by George Derby, "We shall do it next year to the next class of plebes, if we are so lucky as to be here."[28]

There were occasions for rest and amusement, though very limited. Sundays were not entirely a day of rest. As described by William Dutton, "I could not help contrasting in my mind the difference between a Sunday morning at home and here. There all is peace and quiet. Here accoutrements must be in their best order, & ¾ of an hour spent in evolutions." He went on, "But then from Inspection till the Church Drum, one can call home his thoughts or let them rove on home if he chooses without interruption, as there's no visiting on the sabbath." For

One. The Beginnings

church they were "obliged to sit for two hours on a bench without a back, squeezed up among a parcel of Cadets, and squeezed up more with ... belts," as they were obliged to wear their side arms to church.

They did have some free time on Sunday afternoons, but the cadets felt that the authorities did their best to see to it there was nothing to do. The only organized activity tolerated was a debating society which some turned to for amusement. The library did not subscribe to magazines of any sort, and each man was limited to one personal subscription. The only thing they offered for light reading was some history and a few novels. One was not allowed off the post, which did not matter for most as they had very little money to spend. They could only draw their $28.00 pay at the commissaries which carried clothes, mirrors, razors, and other essentials. Even those from wealthy families could not receive money from home, thus some found themselves even further restricted when they could not pay their tab. "Thayer and his successors forbade the cadets to drink, play cards or chess, gamble, use or possess tobacco, keep any cooking utensils in their rooms, participate in any games, read novels, romances, or plays, go off the post, bathe in the river, or play a musical instrument."[29]

One refuge that many found worth the cost in either currency or punishments was Benny Haven's. Getting caught there could result in dismissal. It was said three things made the institution worth the risk. First, the drinks, a favorite called the "hot flip." Second was the food, particularly the buckwheat flapjacks. One way to fund the food or drink was to smuggle out Mackintosh blankets since Benny knew how to turn such items into cash. The third was Benny himself. The proprietor came from the Hudson Valley and had served as a lieutenant in the War of 1812. After the war he turned to cutting "hoop poles," which were the young saplings used to make barrel hoops. On the side he turned his cottage into a tavern and found a use for the barrels he made. One of his most regular customers from the class of 1846 was George Pickett, a roommate of John Adams.[30]

The one thing that probably did most to lift the spirits of a depressed or fatigued cadet was the anticipation of the furlough which came after the third year. This feeling was best summed up by a man who was there at the same time as Adams. "Every moment is nearer than the preceding to that happy time known as furlough time, it is a period ever welcome to a cadet, its joys constitute his dreams by night, his thoughts by day." He went on to say, "It is the climax of his wishes and the boundary of his imagination, it is a period calculated to awaken the strongest idea of human happiness, it is liberty sweetened by confinement, and ease enhanced by previous labors."[31]

The day everybody worked for even more than furlough was graduation itself. This was what it was all about. To be a gentleman and officer in the United States Army, and though still faced with the regimentation of military life, it was expected to be easier than what they had already been through. Many even complained that the training did not prepare them for the life of a normal soldier. As one graduate claimed, "I think the sudden transition from the highest state of mental tension to one of perfect inactivity, which occurs in most cases on the graduation of a cadet, is exceedingly injurious." In the case of the class of 1846, they had something to fill the void: a good war.[32]

After graduation it came time to choose a corps, or be put into a particular corps depending on class ranking. The greatest status went to the engineers. The top four of this class, considered "species of gods," included Charles S. Stewart, George B. McClellan, Charles E. Blunt, and John G. Foster, in order of ranking. The next four were topographical engineers, called "topgods" or "demigods." Those remaining between the number nine rank through number twenty-seven, which included John Adams at number twenty-five, theoretically had their choice of artillery, infantry, mounted rifles, or dragoons, there was still no cavalry in the United States Army in 1846. Those who came after number twenty-eight would be in either mounted rifles, infantry, or dragoons. Adams ended up in the dragoons, which was said to be the bottom of the hierarchy where "a good, square seat in the saddle was deemed of more importance than brains." Adams had been selected for the artillery but petitioned to be in the lower status dragoons.[33]

They soon got their chance to prove what they learned, and all eagerly awaited their assignment in the war with Mexico. Manifest Destiny led the United States to take advantage of the volatile situation with Texas to seize and liberate other lands that today comprise the southwest quarter of the main forty-eight states. On news of the war McClellan wrote home to his sister, "Hip! Hip! Hurrah! Ain't it glorious! 15,000 regulars and 50,000 volunteers! Well, it appears that our wishes have at last been gratified and we shall soon have the intense satisfaction of fighting the crowd — musquitoes [*sic*] & Mexicans, &c." Apparently even the number two man of the class considered giving up a clinched position in the corps of engineers to ride with the dragoons. "I am in a very unpleasant state of uncertainty as to my part; I must wait the progress of events for a while, and then decide whether to try it in the Engineers, or the Dragoons. One thing is certain, I am determined to go to Mexico if it is possible to work it so."

John Adams passed his medical examination and met his future father-in-law, the surgeon Charles Mower McDougall of the medical staff, who had been on his board of examiners. He received his commission while at home in Pulaski, Tennessee. He was ordered on July 8 to proceed immediately to Fort Leavenworth in Kansas and report to Brigadier General S. W. Kearney. If the general and his command should be parted by time Adams reached them, then he was ordered to proceed with the reinforcement of volunteers from Missouri expected to follow. Adams did not reach Leavenworth until August 8, thus missing Kearney. Nonetheless, he was on his way with most of the men he graduated with and would soon find himself in Mexico.[34]

Two

The Mexican War

> I do not think I have previously spoken of the immense number of dogs in Mexico, — it seems to me beyond calculation; and being almost all a cross of the prairie wolf, have an exceedingly mean appearance. I did not see a gentlemanly dog in all Mexico. The pet dogs are called "Comanche;" but why I know not. They are without any hair, and of a dark slate color; and to me, the nastiest animals I know of to look at or to feel. And as to the dogs in general, I should advise a traveler never to stir out without a revolving pistol. The dogs have as strong a dislike to it as their masters, and the possession alone will be a sufficient safeguard from either cur or owner.[1]

The anxiety Frank Edwards expressed over cur or owner is typical of that felt by most of the Americans who traveled south for the war. The dogs, the land, and the people were such as few of the American soldiers had ever seen. It took little to justify exterminating dog or man alike if need be to bring forth the civilization they carried to the land. John Adams and his fellow West Point graduates took part in a chapter of American history, the Mexican War, and as such played a role in the evolution of American culture. We have almost nothing that reveals to us what Adams' thoughts were on the bigger issues of American history. It probably does not matter much, for as a professional soldier and officer he would have followed orders and done his job.

Manifest Destiny may have been coined by O'Sullivan in the 1840s, but whether you want to call it expansionism or imperialism, the people who founded the British colonies in North America have been grabbing land since their arrival. They escalated in the process after creating the United States. The justifications for the Mexican War were debated at the time that it happened. If not the best, it is at least a good example of the rationalization that has been a major part of the growth of the United

Two. The Mexican War

States from the original thirteen states to the fifty of today. O'Sullivan asserts the early exploits were not for the sake of expansion alone but part of America's destiny to spread the improved ways settlers had of doing things. The inhabitants may have been inferior to the invaders; however, in time they would learn to be like them. Some of those spreading the American way of life at times crossed the border that separates expansion from the cruelty of predecessor empires, but we like to think they are few and that the good that follows justifies such indiscretions.

There were many examples of such excesses in the Mexican War. So much so, there is no way they could have remained hidden from the future Confederate general John Adams. Adams took part in this war, so we can say that he did not find it morally reprehensible, at least not enough to keep him out of it. We have no reason to believe that he had any less enthusiasm to put his newly acquired martial skills to work as the rest of the West Point class of 1846 that he graduated with. All that we can do is speculate on his feeling, but we do know that he was a professional soldier and as such did the job he was sent to do.

With this war we see some of the issues which came with the growth and development of a professional army. We can see in this chapter of American history that the class of 1846, as well as the other West Point graduates, went far in justifying the creation, growth, and maintenance of at least a professional officer corps if not a professional army. They had a number of conflicts with the majority volunteers, and their glorious deeds were not always recognized by the citizen soldiers; however, they did prove themselves to those in the right places so that not only did the military academy survive the attacks of the Jacksonian Democrats, but became more and more of an American institution. John Adams and his fellow graduates were professional officers and went far to prove their value.

The Mexican War also serves as a reminder that there were people involved other than just the Mexicans and the Gringos. Those who deny American imperialism like to think that our ancestors conquered a wilderness. They did not. They conquered the land from people who had lived on it for thousands of years before the arrival of Europeans. We have traditionally referred to the "discovery" of America as the time when the first white people arrived. The existence of slavery has always tainted our founders' claims that all men were created equal; however, the relationship between the white settlers and the native inhabitants has also left a stain on the rationalizations of manifest destiny. We have traditionally called this war the Mexican War, but since the 1960s revisionism many textbooks prefer the name Mexican-American War. This does not change the fact that there were other nations involved — several other nations. We will never achieve a good understanding of this war, not to mention the years that followed in the newly conquered lands, without accepting the fact that there were others involved beside the Mexicans and the Americans. This would be those we call Indians or Native Americans.

This war serves as a major step in the evolution of policy of the United States toward the native inhabitants. We will see that at times some of these native people may have sided with the conquerors, some with the conquered, but in fact most struggled to preserve their own interests since they considered both the Mexicans and Gringos as invaders. Long after the treaty was signed, the new American claimants to Indian lands, with the help of John Adams, continued their war against these other nations.

Manifest Destiny

In the first half of the nineteenth century most Americans accepted the idea of territorial expansion; however, many opposed it. Prior to the Civil War most Americans were farmers and farmers need land. The wealthy ones, especially the southern planters, had developed wasteful habits of growing the same profitable crops despite the resulting depletion of their plantations; thus they needed new lands. The middle class farmers were always looking for an opportunity to get more or better land than what they already had. The lower classes, most of whom owned no land, came to America for the opportunity to become land owners. The immigrant population increased in the 1830s and 1840s, especially following the potato famine in Ireland. All of these forces contributed to the demand for more land.

Nonetheless, there were some who did not agree with the territorial aggressiveness which promised new lands. The largest segment of American society who would have objected to reckless expansion would have been the businessmen who did not directly profit from the ownership of farm land. They were the ones who paid the taxes to support the expense of a military. They were more interested in activity which would improve the competitive advantages for the United States in the world markets, such as banks, transportation or manufacturing.

These opposing views generated a regional and partisan split among the American population. The South chose the agricultural path to financial success. The growing importance of cotton left little motivation for the southern people to find a better way to make a living. Cotton was in big demand and thus very profitable. Southerners had the skill, land, and cheap slave labor supply to keep on this highly profitable path. Those in the North turned more toward the growing industrial revolution as a way to accumulate greater wealth. Thus the South favored territorial expansion, especially into lands that were warm enough to grow cotton, while more of those in the North resisted expansion. The West was becoming a distinctive region of its own. Most of those who went west did so to acquire land, and thus it is logical to believe that most Westerners favored continued territorial expansion. The agricultural southerners may have been the most motivated to move west, but there were plenty of northern farmers or immigrants who also wanted an opportunity to grab some of this land that could be easily taken away from its previous owners. Therefore it was the West and South which favored expansion while the North resisted it.

The Whig party attracted the more business oriented, and thus generally speaking, many of the wealthiest of the American people. The Democratic Party appealed more to the common man. This party was created by and for Andrew Jackson. The partisan divide was not purely class driven, as some of the successful planters were Democrats; however, more of the rich supported the Whig Party. The difference between the northern Whigs and the southern Whigs was primarily over the issues of slavery and of territorial expansion. This divide would become more and more critical after the end of the Mexican War.

Daniel Webster of Massachusetts expressed the objections that those in New England had to Manifest Destiny. "What do we want with this vast, worthless area? This region of savages and wild beasts, of deserts, of shifting sands and whirlwinds of dust, of cactus and prairie-dogs?" This included not only Texas, whose annexation he opposed, but also

California and Oregon. "What can we ever hope to do with the western coast, a coast of three thousand miles, rock-bound, cheerless, uninviting, and not a harbor on it?" It should be no surprise that Webster opposed the Mexican War.[2]

The regular army, West Point graduates, and professional officers such as John Adams naturally supported the war for the most part. This is one of the reasons that the lovers of liberty feared a professional army. War is the job of the soldier. The controversial issues of the 1840s, such as the annexation of Texas, the acquisition of Oregon, or the Mexican War may have caused some to feel anxious about war, but for the soldier it meant an opportunity to apply his chosen professional skills. Colonel Stephen W. Kearney actually regretted the easing of relations with Britain that resulted in a peaceful settlement of the Oregon question. Winfield Scott referred to peace societies, nullification, anti-masonry, Mormons, and abolitionists as "cankers of long peace & a calm world." He said "a good hot foreign war only could save the Union & our free institutions, by effectively curing the people of those moral distempers." Again, we do not know for certain what the attitude of John Adams was, but it seems safe to assume he was not much different from those he served with.[3]

Those who invaded Mexico for the United States, whether regular or volunteer, had the same attitude of racial superiority which our forebears possessed but which we do not like to think about today. According to an 1842 census of Mexico, the population consisted of four million Indians, a little more than two million mestizos, about one million whites and only six thousand blacks. The small black population reflects the lack of dependence on slave labor. Most Americans perceived the Mexicans in the same way they did blacks or Indians. They used descriptions such as "miserable ignorant, filthy race." One South Carolinian observed, "Not a white man among them, but some as black as Negroes as I ever saw." These views cannot be dismissed as only southern racism, as a Massachusetts man said, "how strong the contrast with the people of New England." Another man claimed they were the most "ignorant and degraded" people he had ever seen. Such attitudes may seem contradictory to what we think the United States stands for today; however, this is part of the rationalization of Manifest Destiny. No matter how wretched these people may have been, most Americans believed that in

Two. The Mexican War

time they would be able to improve their lives and give them opportunities they would never have under the government of Mexico.[4]

The principles which have been part of Manifest Destiny as well as those we use to justify American aggression today speak of such noble causes as the spread of democracy and capitalism. Many would argue that capitalism is necessary to support freedom and democracy. Critics of the American past as well as the present dismiss these ideas as rationalizations for greed. When we look at the involvement of Americans in New Mexico—where John Adams served—prior to 1846, there does seem to be a great deal of support for the latter interpretation. The governments of Spain, and later Mexico, have seen territorial expansion as a way to spread Christianity and improve the welfare of the state as a whole. American capitalism emphasizes the greater opportunities for the individual to profit. Capitalism is more individualistic than most other systems, including Spanish and Mexican Christianity.

The intent of first contact between Americans and that land that we call New Mexico today is not clear. There had been rumors of filibustering expeditions against Spanish possessions, including the famous General James Wilkinson and Aaron Burr plot. Regardless of Zebulon Pike's intent, his observations paved the way for the first commercial encounter, the mountain men. The Spanish successfully limited the influx of American fur trappers; however, in 1821 Mexico became independent. Shortly after that, the fad of beaver hats for the well to do gentlemen increased the number of Americans infringing upon Mexican lands. They established relations with Taos as the center for trade. It has been claimed that such men took as much as a $100,000 a year in beaver hides. By 1840 the little varmint became scarce and the trade began to die of natural causes.[5]

As the fur trade began to fade William Becknell of Franklin, Missouri, accidentally introduced the next phase of American interest in New Mexico. In 1822 he had found that the new Mexican rulers were receptive to the goods offered by the Gringo businessmen. Becknell did well and he returned home with a load of gold, silver, and furs. Soon others followed the Santa Fe Trail to the profits the land had to offer. It began with the small farmer investor but proved attractive to the larger merchant so that within a short period of time not only did the goods from the American frontier general store find their way to Santa Fe, but upscale New York merchandise began to appear. By the time the United States Army arrived in 1846 an assortment of American mountain men and merchants had already began to call New Mexico home. Some had taken Mexican wives but most would welcome a return to American citizenship and would lend a helping hand to the invading American forces.[6]

It appears that the intent of the first Americans in traveling to New Mexico was fuzzy in their own minds. The arrival of the Texans in 1841 is a perfect example. New Mexican writers depicted these men as opportunists who had every intention of taking their land and enslaving the Mexican people. The Texans later claimed that they were only interested in establishing trade relations. The specific interest in Santa Fe stemmed from their claim that the agreed upon border for the newly established Republic of Texas went to the Rio Grande. Santa Fe was the jewel of this river as well as the commercial center for the American businessmen. It is generally accepted that the Texans initially wanted to be annexed by the United States; however, since Whigs succeeded in delaying the annexation of a new southern slave state, some of the former Americans-turned-Texans began to have dreams of a new North American power which would spread from the Gulf of Mexico to the Pacific. The most common interpretation of the historical data is that this was simply a trading expedition sent by President Mirabeau B. Lamar; however, it seems reasonable to believe that these men were opportunists who could have been easily swayed toward the territorial expansion of the Republic of Texas.[7]

Regardless of their intent, the reception they received by the governor, General Manuel Armijo, laid the foundation for a revenge factor that would assist the Americans in their rationalization for the bad treatment of the Mexican population they found in their newly conquered lands. Some blamed the ruling class for the wretched conditions in which most of this population lived. It is in the interest of the ruling class in all nations at all times to keep the general population under their power. They also needed these people to fight their wars when necessary. The existing power structure of political and religious leaders in New Mexico persuaded the Pueblo Indians that the Texans intended to destroy their religion. Assisted by the 1,300 miles of dangerous lands that separated these men from their homes and supply lines, Armijo did what Santa

Anna could not do, he defeated the Texans. "The treatment accorded the Texans was among the most bestial ever meted out in the history of warfare. Many of the prisoners were shot down in cold blood, others were cruelly tortured, and most of them were forced into a death march southward." These are the memories which many Texans and Americans had of the Mexican government in New Mexico.[8]

Volunteers versus West Point

The divided America in the age of Jackson produced problems for the Army too. The Jeffersonian fears of professional military carried over to the age of Jacksonian Democracy so that the majority of the American population not only rejected the idea that the trained professional soldiers who came out of the United States Military Academy should be in command during the Mexican War, but saw them as a threat to the American way of life which was part of the philosophy of Manifest Destiny. Even though Jefferson spoke of all men being created equal, the reality is that he himself was a part of the tidewater aristocracy. These were the sorts of men who created the United States. Andrew Jackson, however, founder of the Democratic Party, was one of the common people. He was not only a general but was the victor in the Battle of New Orleans. By 1846 the common man had gone far in seizing control of the nation founded by aristocrats. The typical Jacksonian common man felt that he did not have to obey the commands of the sons of the elite who graduated from West Point.

As the volunteers filled the ranks of the invading army, they saw themselves as subservient to the Regular Army. Colonel William B. Campbell of the 1st Regiment of Tennessee Volunteers felt that there was a strong feeling of "jealousy & opposition to the volunteers, while the command & control of the army and all its departments is in the hands of the regular officers." He went on to say, "Volunteers have hard places, have fewer comforts or conveniences than regulars & when any thing is done all the praise is given to the regulars." One Ohio congressman who served during the war and swore to speak out against West Point specifically upon his return to the national legislature.[9]

The regulars not only felt entitled to special treatment, but they saw the politicians and frontiersmen who despised them as their inferiors. There is a difference between volunteers and militiamen. The latter were in the tradition of the militias raised at the time of the Revolution against the British. The volunteers were recruited for the sake of the Mexican War. Between 1832 and 1838 the regulars served with more than 43,000 volunteers and militiamen. "Nonetheless, regulars were virtually unanimous in their contempt for citizen-soldiers. The traditional adulation of such troops as the bulwark of American democracy appeared an affront to the officer corps, and a challenge to its claims to special expertise." We have been taught to admire the pioneers who built America; however, the regulars did not seem to share this view of their military contributions. During the Creek War, assistant surgeon Jacob Motte described them: "They presented a glorious display of dirks, pistols, and bowie-knives, with no scarcity of dirt." During the Mexican War, George B. McClellan, a member of the class of 1846, said they were "all hollowing, cursing, yelling like so many incarnate fiends— no attention or respect paid to the commands of their officers, whom they would curse as quickly as they would look at them." Lieutenant Thomas Williams said of the volunteers, "They are useless, useless, useless— expensive, wasteful — good for nothing."[10]

Thus we see a rivalry which divided the Regular Army from the volunteers; however, a partisan gap complicated the situation further. Few who opposed the war volunteered to fight and so they rarely participated in the conflicts which took place on the field of battle. Nonetheless, the Whig objectors motivated the favoritism President James K. Polk would show to his fellow Democrats. The president held a view of the Regular Army consistent with his frontiersmen constituency. He wanted to break the hold the West Point officers had on the Army, and he commissioned Democrats into the officer corps. In other words, because of the policies of Polk, many volunteers found acceptance in the attitude they had toward the professional soldiers. As a result of this attitude those in the Regular Army experienced a disrespectful attitude from the volunteers.[11]

The Indians

Mexicans and Americans alike thought of themselves as the rulers of the land both called New Mexico. They each believed that the original inhabitants were their subjects. Indians did not have the same view of the situation. John Adams, as did most of the Regular Army, spent most of his career dealing with Indian issues. Since the Indian Removal Act of 1830 the United States had a policy of removing the natives from their original habitat to make way for the land hungry white Americans. Some Americans had toyed with the idea of assimilation, and at the outbreak of the Mexican War there were still many who believed that this was the most Christian and humane way of helping the Indians. Of course what this philosophy did not take into account was the idea that maybe the Indians did not want to be helped. From the Black Hawk War in the Midwest to the removal of the Five Civilized Tribes in the South, it was clear that the government would make sure that the natives would not stand in the way of white American progress.

Generally speaking the volunteer and Regular Army differed considerably in their attitude toward the Indians. Since the volunteers usually came from pioneer stock, many had personal recollections of previous relations with the Indians. Quite often this meant that they could recall the death or even torture of a wife, or child, or a parent or other kin or neighbors at the hands of those they considered savages. The Regular Army, especially the West Point graduates, had been trained for traditional European style warfare. They did not study the guerrilla tactics used by the Indians. They considered such warfare as something that fit in their job description; however, it was not what they longed for. The war with Mexico, which offered a European trained adversary, is more what they had in mind when they marched southward. Conflicts with the Indians were merely a distraction. For the most part they would have chosen peace with the Indians. They knew what it would take to achieve this objective — leave them alone. It is the pioneer, the class that provided most of the volunteers, who usually sparked hostilities with their desire to seize the Indians' lands.

We have no more of a record on the personal feelings that John Adams held toward the Indians than we do for any of the other issues of his day; however, from his actions while he served in the Army, both during and after the Mexican War, suggest that he held a philosophy similar to that of most of his comrades. The scientifically rationalized racism which produced Social Darwinism did not really come until after the Civil War. Nonetheless, many of the professional officer corps believed in the superiority of the white man. They did not necessarily believe that it was due to their condition at birth. The Enlightenment philosophy which was the foundation for the Declaration of Independence and the United States Constitution was based on a basic assumption that the only difference between the successful man and the poor man was opportunity. Whether a beggar in the streets of London or New York or the Indian in the West, they were products of their environment. Thus many saw the Indian as someone who could be aided on the path of American progress, the underlying justification for Manifest Destiny. The early nineteenth century American soldier tended to be kinder than the later scientific racist who would climax with the Nazi final solution of exterminating inferior people. Though they in fact did exterminate many of the natives, it was an attempt to establish order on the frontier rather than to improve the stock of a master race.

While it was the Army that force-marched the Cherokee down the Trail of Tears, they saw these people as an example of those who could be helped by becoming "civilized." The Cherokee and the others labeled "The Five Civilized Tribes" were thus called because they developed their own written language, published newspapers, established schools, and some even dressed like white men, lived in the same kinds of houses, and owned slaves like the white men did. These were tribes believed to come from the higher order of Indians. Those in New Mexico, as well as most of the Plains Indians, were in the middle of the scale. The soldiers may have admired their martial skill; however, they "thought their character marred by treachery, thievery, cruelty, and other unpleasant traits." Those in California and the Rocky Mountains, whom Adams would deal with later in his career, fell into the third and last group in the white man's view of the native hierarchy. One captain described those Indians found at the mouth of the Eel River in California "as low on the scale of humanity as possible to conceive, of brutish habits, hideous repulsive features, and loathsome from disease."[12]

Charles Bent, who would later be made the American governor of New Mexico, not only understood the role played by the Indians but had a relatively enlightened attitude. Charles and his brother William were among those on the frontier who established private forts. Theirs, called Bent's Fort, became a center for trade on the Santa Fe Trail. They knew and understood the Indians. William's first two wives were

Two. The Mexican War

Cheyenne and his third was a Blackfoot half-breed. The original purpose for their fort was to conduct trade with the Indians in buffalo and deer skins, which later expanded to trading with the trappers who met the demand for beaver pelts. In the later days they traded with adventurers, explorers, wagon-trains, cowboys, as well as the trappers.

Their fort became a jumping off place for the United States troops invading New Mexico in 1846. It is no surprise that Charles was the first appointed American governor of the newly conquered land. Bent informed the secretary of state that there were more than Mexicans to deal with in his jurisdiction. In addition to the Pueblo Indians, he named eight other tribes which needed to be contained in order to have peace in the land. The largest of these, and therefore ones which will be covered here, included the Apaches with 6,000, the Navajos with 7,000, and the Comanches with 12,000. The others—which men like Adams would deal with for years after the treaty ending hostilities with the Mexicans— included the Southern Utes with 1,400, Hopis with 2,450, Kiowas with 2,000, Cheyennes with 1,500, and the Arapahos with 1,600.[13]

The Pueblos were those descended from the oldest inhabitants and builders of the famous and ancient cliff dwellings which can be found throughout the region in places such as Mesa Verde National Park. Not only did some of these people inhabit ancient pueblos at the time of the Mexican War, but they still live in them to this day. These are the people first encountered by the Spanish when they arrived in the area. Their lifestyle was not unlike similar civilizations found throughout the world whether it be Africa, Asia, or Europe. They had large nucleated villages surrounded by the fields they worked for their sustenance. Most of their days were spent in providing for or defending their families. They had established relations with the Spanish which came about after generations of conflict. At the time of the Mexican War many of the Mexicans and later the Americans lived among them.[14]

The first to seriously threaten the Pueblos, years before the arrival of the Spanish, were the Apache. They are considered different from Navajo, who will be discussed next, but both are part of the same culture and language group called Apachean. There was no political unity among the Apachean population, and even among those labeled Apache there were many sub groups such as the Chiricahua, Mescalero, and the ones most common in northern New Mexico, the Jicarilla. These tribes have become legendary from the earliest accounts of the Spanish through the more modern portrayals from Victorian western novels to Hollywood movies. They first arrived in the Southwest about 1000 A.D. Coronado offered the first European description of the people who followed the buffalo, which Coronado called cattle: "These natives are called Querechos. They do not cultivate the land, but eat raw meat and drink the blood of the cattle they kill." He went on to say, "They dress in the skins of the cattle, with which all the people in this land clothe themselves, and they have very well-constructed tents, made with tanned and greased cowhides, in which they live and which they take along as they follow the cattle." Under the leadership of Mangas Coloradas they initially signed a treaty with the Americans recognizing their rule over the former Mexican lands. John Adams and the United States Army would have to deal with them after the initial treaty due to the incursion into their lands resulting from the gold rush in the Santa Rita Mountains.[15]

The Navajo, the largest tribe in the United States today, migrated South with their tribal kin the Apache about 1000 A.D. Whereas the Apache maintained their nomadic Plains lifestyle the Navajo established a relationship with the Pueblo. The first Spanish records describe them as having large numbers of livestock and having large areas of their land in crops. Whereas the Apache at first accepted American rule, the Navajo did not recognize them as legitimate. In 1846 Charles Bent described them as an "industrious, intelligent, and warlike race of Indians, who cultivate the soil, and raise sufficient grain and fruits of various kinds for their own consumption." He added, "They are the owners of large herds, and flocks of cattle, sheep, horses, mules, and asses. It is estimated that the tribe possess thirty thousand head of horses, mules, and asses." The American soldiers would also have to deal with these people for many years after the peace with Mexico was settled.[16]

The people who struck fear into the hearts of Mexican, American, Pueblo, Apache, and anyone else they came into conflict with were the Comanche. Historically they appeared in the Southwest about 1700 when they broke off from the Shoshone people. Like the Apache they were never one unified tribal unit but rather basically independent smaller groups. Some have given them credit for being among the first of the American natives to master the use of horses. If not they at least have been among the greatest cavalrymen of all time. Warfare was a major

Two. The Mexican War

part of their culture and the horse was a big part of their military prowess. Many a John Wayne movie has been based on the decades of warfare between the Texans and the Comanche. The Republic of Texas failed to strike a peace settlement with their western challengers when the legislature failed to recognize an official boundary between Texas and Comancheria. This is a perfect example of the white man's inability to comprehend the Indian desire for their own sovereignty. The Comanche, like the Apache and Navajo, would continue to battle the Americans for many years after the treaty of Guadalupe Hidalgo, which ended hostility between the Americans and Mexicans.

The Invasion Begins

James K. Polk and the Democrats campaigned on the issue of territorial expansion. Northern Whigs had been successful for almost a decade in keeping the United States from annexing Texas on the theory that such a move would provoke a war with Mexico. Polk's appeal with the American people inspired Congress to take in the new state before the election, thus leaving Polk with nothing but his "54° 40' or fight" slogan. The plans for such a war had long been in existence. One army would enter Mexico from Vera Cruz, another was to hold Texas as far as the Rio Grande, from which they would move southward to Monterrey and Chihuahua, while New Mexico would be attacked by an army from Missouri. The final plan changed. One army would invade New Mexico, a third would help the Americans in California to establish American control on the Pacific, while a third would invade Mexico proper.

John Adams received orders to report to Fort Leavenworth, where he would join Stephen Watts Kearney in his invasion of New Mexico. Adams had been assigned to Company C which left Kansas with Kearney on June 29, 1846. Adams did not arrive at Leavenworth until August. He had alternate orders to join his company; however, he was then stricken with an attack of fever and was thus advised by an Army surgeon to not continue his travels. Adams would not reach New Mexico until October.[17]

Adams had been assigned to the First Dragoons and would remain part of the regiment until he left for the Confederate States of America.

It had been determined that mounted troops would be best for the mission given to Colonel Kearney. Mounted troops were referred to as "horse." Like the rest of the Army the mounted troops had regiments and companies; however, they had the additional organizational unit of squadron, which was composed of two companies. Dragoons usually had fifty men in a company instead of the hundred found in the artillery or infantry; however, on May 13, 1846, Congress raised their count to a hundred also. A government publication entitled *Cavalry Tactics* served as the basis for instruction for men like Adams.[18]

Mounted troops could not be expected to use the long barreled muskets issued to the infantry since it would be too difficult to wield such weapons from the back of a horse. The War Department developed a Model 1833 Hall carbine. Later in the war the Model 1847 cavalry musketoon was issued to those on horse. They also carried pistols. The Model 1842 and Model 1843 pistols were the same .54-caliber as the flintlock predecessors but utilized the more efficient percussion caps. These weapons were carried in leather holsters mounted on either side of the pommel of the saddle. It would not be until after the war when they would be carried on the soldier's belt. Though Samuel Colt had created a six shooter which had been issued on a trial basis to the dragoons as early as 1838, they stuck with the single shot variety throughout the Mexican War. Swords served as weapons for cavalry; however, the officers also liked to use them to display rank. The Model 1840, based on a French cavalry sword, were "edged weapons" designed to wound or kill. In 1840 the War Department authorized a M1840 foot officer's sword for those interested in a show of rank. Officers usually purchased their own swords. Accoutrements included leather belts, boxes, and slings as well as saddles, bridles and harnesses. The main dragoon accoutrement was a two inch wide white leather saber belt. On this belt was attached the sword, a cartridge box, pistol cartridge box, and a cap box.[19]

Stephen W. Kearney commanded the First Dragoons and seemed the best choice for commanding the invasion of New Mexico. He had served in the War of 1812 and thirty years on the frontiers of America. He had even ventured into the far West long before the war began. Before leaving Fort Leavenworth and during the lengthy stay at Bent's Fort, rumors circulated among the officers and men of the expedition. Some claimed that there would not be much of a fight while others insisted that the Mexicans fortified Santa Fe and Taos and were prepared for an epic struggle. They were determined to stick to the well traveled Santa Fe Trail and avoid the Cimarron cutoff. As they crossed the border into Mexico it was clear that Polk saw this as an exercise in Manifest Destiny. The objective was annexation of Mexican territory and not simply retaliation for any claimed infringements which had been used to justify the war. Whigs at the time, especially northern Whigs, as well as some historians today have seen the actions which started the war as nothing but a feeble excuse to grab the land which Americans wanted and Mexicans occupied.[20]

Bent's Fort had thrived for years since it was a jumping off point for any trapper, merchant or simply adventurer who wanted to cross the border into Mexican territory. Though part of Mexico, this placed called New Mexico had been separated by many miles from the rest of New Spain, which combined with its own unique Indian cultures developed a culture of its own. The Spanish settlements in this land centered on the main river that flowed out of the mountains and eventually found its way to the Gulf of Mexico. The Indians inhabited this waterway too. The Rio Grande watered their crops and their livestock and gave the European settlers what they needed for survival in such a wild land.

The mystical mountains and canyons limited the path one could travel from one place to another, but the further one ventured from the lifegiving waters of the Rio Grande the more hostile it seemed, not only the Indians but the land itself. As Lt. Adolphus Engelman noted, "All plants here have thorns, all the animals, sting or horns, and all men carry weapons and all deceive each other and themselves." Private Benjamin Franklin Scribner agreed, "The expression so common with us, 'All bushes have thorns, All insects have horns,' is almost true without exception. Even the frogs and grass hoppers are in possession of the last mentioned appendages."[21]

Santa Fe was the main target. The capital of New Mexico was described by some of the men as the "prairie dog capital." Like all towns in New Mexico it was constructed of adobe, having a plaza or public square in the center. Certainly not as grand as the still understated capital of the invading army, it was called "a collection of brick kilns, a dryland gathering of Mississippi flatboats." Though predating the arrival of the *Mayflower*, the Palace of the Governors was a "single-story four-hundred foot straggle of mud along the north side of the plaza." The streets

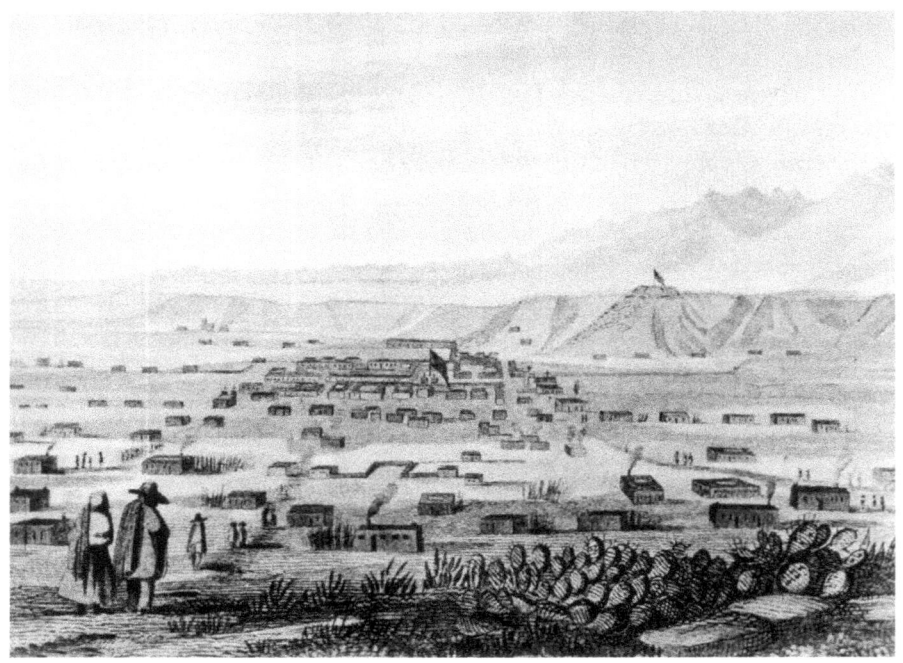

La Ciudad de Santa Fe from an engraving in the "Report of Lt. J. W. Abert of His Examination of New Mexico in the Years 1846–1847." This is the way things would have looked when John Adams first arrived (National Archives).

were full of donkeys and oxen, Indians, peons, trappers, and teamsters. Taos, the home of the Pueblo as well as a secondary cultural center for the Europeans, was not any better. "The main amusements seemed to be drinking, fornicating, and gambling.[22]

The governor of New Mexico and leader of the military resistance to the invasion was Manuel Armijo. It has been claimed that prior to the war he had the ambition of achieving independence for New Mexico. He came from a poor family but by starting out as a sheep thief he became a prosperous businessman. He owned caravans which traveled down the Santa Fe Trail capturing some of the profits to be made with the Missouri trade. He had a reputation as a cruel and greedy man, especially among Americans familiar with what happened with the Texans in 1841. As commander when the Texans arrived that year, Armijo had elevated his position with the people of his homeland, but to the Americans he was an object for

Two. The Mexican War

revenge as well as the man to defeat in this war. John Adams would later be exposed to other members of the governor's family who had accumulated most of the lands around Albuquerque, the base Adams was assigned to.[23]

The statement issued by Kearney to Armijo clearly reveals not only the justification for the war, but a plea to the governor for what Kearney sees as something which would be beneficial to the people of New Mexico:

> By the annexation of Texas to the United States, the Rio Grande from its mouth to its source forms at this time the Boundary between her & Mexico, & I come by orders of the Govt. To take possession of the Country, over a part of which you are now presiding as Governor — I come as a friend & with the disposition & intention to consider all Mexicans & others as friends who will remain quietly & peaceably at their homes & attend to their own affairs — such persons shall not be disturbed by anyone under my command either in their Persons, their Property or their Religion — I pledge myself for fulfillment of this promise — I come to this part of the United States with a strong Military force & a stronger one is following us as a reinforcement of us. We have many more troops than sufficient to put down any opposition that you can possibly bring against us, & I therefore for the sake of humanity call upon you to submit to fate, & to meet me with the same feeling of Peace & friendship which I now entertain for & offer to you & to all those over whom you are Governor.

We see here the two main tools of Manifest Destiny. "We are here to help you if you accept us, but if not we are prepared to conquer you."[24]

As Kearney's army headed toward Santa Fe it passed through several other settlements which both fascinated and repulsed the Americans. In some ways they started to look similar, and in fact the Spanish did have a habit of using the same plans for their churches and settlements in the New World. Las Vegas had dwellings "being low square blocks, sides and tops of sun-dried yellow bricks or adobe; the streets, and a large square, being the same color." Beyond Las Vegas lay Tecolote. "Very like Las Vegas—[it] was in the bottom of the valley; the scene must have been peaceful." San Miguel was "built of dull red adobes, in a dull red surrounding country." Nearby to San Miguel was the ancient walled town of Pecos. Apparently a settlement before the arrival of the Spanish, Cooke said, "Some contend that the Roman Catholic religion was only grafted on the Aztec; that the two were harmoniously blended; this is surely affirmed of the present religion of the Pueblos here." On August 12 they came in sight of Santa Fe.[25]

Brigadier General John Adams, CSA

As is usually the case in the spirit of Manifest Destiny, the Americans looked at themselves as liberators not conquerors. As such, Kearney needed to make sure that the people welcomed them as rescuers from those who had abused them in the past. Cooke described the governor as a greedy man who had taken advantage of his people and thus questioned their loyalty. Kearney stood before the mayor and people of Santa Fe:

> Mr. Alcalde and people of New Mexico [saluted the general]:
>
> I have come amongst you by orders of My Government, to take possession of your country, and extend over it the laws of the United States. We consider it, and have done so for some time, a part of the territory of the United states. We come amongst you as friends—not as enemies; as protectors—not as conquerors. We come among you for your benefit—not for your injury.
>
> Henceforth I absolve you from all allegiance to the Mexican Government, and from all obedience to General Armijo. He is no longer your Governor; [great sensation]. I am your Governor. I shall not expect you to take up arms and follow me to fight your own people who may oppose me; but I will now tell you, that those who remain peaceably at home, attending to their crops and their herds, shall be protected by me in their property, their persons, and their religion; and not a pepper, nor an onion, shall be disturbed.

Kearney promised them protection of their property and guaranteed them the freedom of their religion. Though this war would consist of numerous examples of the long history of American anti–Catholicism, Kearney believed in the religious freedom we claimed to stand for.[26]

Though Kearney implemented what he understood to be what America stood for and thus consistent with what O'Sullivan called Manifest Destiny, he did not act upon orders, and a few months later the president would object to his actions. Four months passed before the statements made by Kearney came to Polk's attention. The president frowned on the appearance that the military command established a permanent territorial government. Polk's words reveal the zeal with which Americans conquered this land: "The departure has been the offspring of a patriotic desire to give to the inhabitants the privileges and immunities so cherished by the people of our own country, and which they believed calculated to improve their condition and promote their prosperity." The president did not take any disciplinary action

Two. The Mexican War

against Kearney. "Any such excess has resulted in practically no injury, but can and will be early corrected in a manner to alienate as little as possible the good feelings of the inhabitants of the conquered territory,"[27] he said.

Kearney sought further military glory in California and thus did not stay long in the newly vanquished land. He almost immediately relinquished his governorship and appointed Charles Bent as the first real American governor. Bent was born in Charleston, Virginia, in 1797 of English and French parents. He was educated at West Point. He resigned from the Army and became a merchant. In 1829 he went down the Santa Fe Trail, and along with his brother founded the fort which bore their name on the Arkansas River, then the southern border of the United States. In 1832 he and his brothers, William and George, established a general merchandising business. He later established a business partnership with Colonel Ceran St. Vrain.

He and his brothers were not what many have called "ugly Americans" in that they respected the people and culture in this foreign land. It has already been pointed out that William had taken Indian wives. Charles married Maria Ignacia Jaramillo, a daughter of Don Francisco and Apolinia (Vigil) Jaramillo. Maria's sister, Josefa Jaramillo, married Kit Carson. Bent did maintain a sense of racial superiority over the natives of New Mexico, be they Spanish or Indian. He understood the people and apparently had enough respect for them to marry and live among them, but he recognized the difficulties in trying to govern them. He said, "There is no Stability to these people, they have no opinion of their one [own]."

Like other Americans, he believed himself a liberator of people who simply followed the lead of corrupt and bad leaders. "They are entirely governed by the powers that be, they are without exception the most Servile people that can be imagined." He went on, "They are Completely at the will of those in power let those be so Ignorant as may be ... they dare not express an opinion to that of their rules." He stated, "They are not fit to be free [people] they should be ruled by others than themselves.... Where that is no Morality, Honesty or Patriotism of character that people are not fit for self Government." There is no better word than racism to describe his claim that "the Mexican Character is made up of Stupidity, Obstinacy, Ignorance — duplicity and vanity."[28]

John Adams Arrives

We know that Adams made it into New Mexico by October 10, and we know he had orders to go with the Missouri volunteers who would follow Kearney. There is no record confirming it, but it does seem safe to assume that he traveled the Santa Fe Trail with Sterling Price and his men from Missouri. On September 25 General Kearney left for California, leaving Colonel Doniphan as the temporary military commander. Price arrived three days later to assume the command evacuated by Kearney. Adams had been delayed in his departure due to sickness and Price arrived in Santa Fe very ill. It is not known if this was the same illness that Adams had suffered from. The men had been fifty-three days on the trail, and two men and sixty horses had died from illness. It is no wonder that the men became ill since on their trip they had been forced to drink water that the horses refused. On the trail in the summer heat mosquitoes and buffalo gnats abounded, rattlesnakes were killed in camp, and blowflies infested the blankets. Some of the men became overcome by apathy while a blind fury had seized others.

Sterling Price was not an experienced commander as Kearney had been. He had been a congressmen from the state of Missouri and resigned in August of 1846 to become a colonel of a regiment of volunteers from his home state. His only military experience had been an occasional militia muster. Of course, this was not unusual in the days of Jackson and Polk. Price had been described as "in the prime of his young manhood, possessing a tall, straight, majestic figure of perfect proportions. His face fair and full, with regular, dignified feature, every appearance of manliness and gentility."[29]

By the time Adams arrived in New Mexico the Americans had made some progress in getting to know the land and the people. Naturally most of the soldiers were young men and even those who had someone waiting for them at home were a long way from female companions. Like so much about this land, the women both disgusted and pleased the invaders. One man described their "existence as listless in the extreme, as they have no intellectual resources, not even the accomplishment of music." Their dark eyes fascinated, especially when the women danced the fandango. These dances with their violins, guitars, and mandolins attracted the men who danced for hours with the senoritas. Even walking down the streets or in the plaza they would "carry themselves as if each one had been trained in a perfect walking school." Not so the Indian women, who "never walk well." When "you visit, the pretty daughter always sits in a corner with the mamma, who is not pretty, (mammas never being pretty,) close along side of her, for fear that you might sit too close to the lovely hope of maternal tenderness!"[30]

For some, food was probably first on their mind, but even the ladies' man eventually got hungry. Good food was scarce during the weeks on the trail, ill prepared army sustenance washed down with tainted water. Now in human settlement they experienced new culinary delights. The soil in the area of the Rio Grande produced well, though one thing the Americans offered their vanquished host was improved production techniques. The peppers and onions generated the most comments, and many of the men actually learned to love the green or red chilies. They would be brought to town strung together, and some even seemed to use them to decorate their homes. They had plenty of peas and beans, but none of the potatoes which so much of the world had grown to depend on. They lacked an assortment of vegetables. Fruits and nuts were more scarce than vegetables, though they did have a pine nut, or "pinones."[31]

Victorian standards of cleanliness had not penetrated into the formerly Mexican lands. However, one visitor noted, "In truth, the most wretchedly dirty and filthy men I have ever seen are among some of the Missouri 'free and independent' volunteers. Their quarters are but little better in condition than pig-sties, and their officers pay no attention to them." The observer added, "But the Mexicans— as I was going to say— are, generally, a very dirty people." A senorita who may have been adorned and appealing at the ball the night before could be found the next day in "her frock loosely thrown on, without ever hooking it in the back," and the garments would "awaken recollections, perhaps, of muslin having once been white."[32]

Some of the men, especially the officers and gentlemen, would try to create an environment they were accustomed to by seeking the same kind of amusements they knew at home. An occasional theatrical production would make it up from New Orleans, and if not, the soldiers sometimes arranged their own productions. There was limited reading material, even in Spanish. Some found diversion through fraternal organizations. Some grew anxious at the thought of soldiers conspiring with the Masons. So many Americans at this time feared this secret society that an Anti-Mason political party attracted many voters. The reform movement failed to curtail drinking among soldiers a long way from home. "American commanders issued orders forbidding the sale of liquor in camp, but regulars and volunteers had no trouble locating whiskey, brandy, and wine to slake their thirst." One officer took the bottle from a Mexican vendor, poured it over his head and then hit him with the empty bottle, but the soldiers banded together to get what they wanted from the locals, who understood the risk involved in such profit taking. The Temperance Movement did find some willing to sign a pledge of abstinence. Gambling vied with drinking to steal the money from the American soldiers. Faro, poker, seven up, whist, euchre, vingt-et-un, and chuck-a-luck were at times administered by professional gamblers who followed the army wherever it went.[33]

Officers such as John Adams were given money to hire servants to help make their life easier. The number of servants depended on one's rank. By law they were forbidden from having a private work for them. They had to turn to the native population for cooks, maids, laundresses, grooms, or whatever they needed. Those who owned slaves, which did not include Adams, were allowed to bring their slaves with them.[34]

Adams did not spend long in Santa Fe, as he had been assigned to Company G in Albuquerque under the command of Captain Henry John K. Burgwin. Albuquerque was a pretty large town, but the houses were widely scattered. There were a large number of farms in the middle part of the Rio Grande Valley. "On both banks of the river, the towns, villages, and ranchos or farm houses cluster so thickly together that it presents the appearance of one continued village from Algonones to San Tome, a distance of nearly sixty miles." The city of Albuquerque itself "stretched some 7 or 8 miles up and down the river." One soldier complained that to get to the plaza "I rode for miles as through a straggling village." The town had been founded in 1706 and the first structure built was the church named for its patron saint, San Felipe de Neri. In the early nineteenth century Albuquerque had become a nest for the Armijos, the family of the defeated governor. The First Dragoons, Companies B, I and G, had been assigned there to protect the locals from the Navajo. Kearney had promised the people of his domain freedom from the Indian raids.

Adams remained in the city until the end of the year, generally incapacitated due to his continued health problems.[35]

The Insurgency

Kearney wrongfully concluded that New Mexico had been conquered and that he was free to seek further adventure in California. There are a number of reasons that Kearney was wrong. Such is typical of the thinking of deluded conquerors. In many ways things have not changed all that much in the last hundred and sixty years; American soldiers today still honestly believe they are not conquering but rather liberating the people. Despite their complaints about the laziness, filth, or strange behavior of the natives, this is actually part of what justifies why they are there. There is hope for salvation. For the Americans, characteristics such as thievery, sneakiness, or rudeness are only the products of living under their evil and incompetent leaders. While promising the people that they were free to continue their religion, it is the Catholic clergy who were accused of reducing the people to such circumstance. This is part of the traditional American anti–Catholicism. One of the major objections to the Catholic Church since the beginning of the Reformation is the hierarchy. It is not surprising that the Protestant Americans would blame the Catholic clergy for what they saw as the dismal conditions that the natives lived in.

Though we might call this prejudicial thinking today, it does make sense that the leaders, religious or political, are responsible for the conditions in any nation. The common or poor of a land do all that they can just to survive. They generally do not see much difference in a change of leadership. Regardless of the time and place, the well to do and the leaders lose the most when they are replaced by conquerors. It is only natural to expect the most resistance would come from those who had previously been in charge. A common technique used by all rulers is to convince their subjects that by losing them they will be worse off. It does appear that the Americans were correct in blaming the clergy and wealthy for the events that transpired in New Mexico in 1847.

Kearney was long gone, so it was Sterling Price who first heard of a conspiracy to rebel in December of 1846. American soldiers busy liberating lands and spreading the good word of the American way of life often lose sight of the fact that people usually do not like someone else telling them what to do, especially foreigners who are not aware of their customs. Just as it is natural to believe that the former leaders would be most likely to lead a rebellion, it is likewise natural to expect some fear of the unknown among the conquered. By definition, when one is spreading a better way of life, that means they believe the old ways to be inferior.

Also, as time passed and boredom replaced the excitement of warfare, the men, many of whom were prone to drinking to begin with, probably did behave poorly. Such behavior gave credence to the claims of the fallen leaders that they must resist American occupation. The definitive leaders were Tomas Ortiz and Diego Archuleta. There were some members of the clergy supposedly involved in the conspiracy, such as Padre Antonio Jose Martinez. Many considered Martinez the chief architect of the rebellion; however, the Americans were never able to prove anything. He was one of the most brilliant men in New Mexico and supposedly realized that the coming of the Americans was a death blow to his power and prestige in the country. The rebels wanted to assassinate both General Price and Governor Bent. They wanted to rid their land of all Americans of distinction as well as those Mexicans who had supported their rule.

The first chosen date of December 19 was later changed to Christmas Eve, when the Americans would be less armed and partially incapacitated by celebration. At the sound of the church bell they were to enter the plaza, seize the artillery, and point it into the streets. No women were to be trusted with the plans; however, it has been claimed that it was a woman who passed them on to Price. On December 26, Bent wrote to the secretary of state: "So far as I am informed, this conspiracy is confined to the four northern counties of the Territory, and the men considered as leaders in the affair cannot be said to be men of much standing."[36]

The dissatisfaction with occupation had not been eliminated and more was to come. The bloodiest scenes took place in Taos on January 19, 1847. A few men had been made prisoner the night before and a mob gathered to force the alcalde to release them. It soon became clear to the lighter skinned residents of the town that they needed to take caution.

Two. The Mexican War

Charles Bent slowly accepted the fact that he was wrong to think that all were his friends and that they would not turn against him.

The mob approached the Bent home in Taos and hearing the crowd yelling outside, Bent's wife, her sister Josefa, the wife of Kit Carson, a woman named Mrs. Boggs, and an Indian slave woman began to dig a hole into the adjoining house using nothing but a fire place poker. Once this was completed, they followed the children whom they had pushed through the hole and urged Charles to join them. By that time he had been scalped by the invading Indians, though still alive. His daughter Teresina, only age five at the time, recalled many years later: "Some of the men came after him through the hole and others came over the roof of the house and down into the yard. They broke down the doors and rushed upon my father." She added, "He was shot many times and fell dead at our feet. The pleading and tears of my mother and the sobbing of us children had no power to soften the hearts of the enraged Indians and Mexicans."[37]

Others in the town suffered a similar fate. The circuit attorney, T. W. Leal, was scalped alive and dragged through the streets. Only after pleading did a kind Mexican end his suffering by shooting him. Stephen Lee, brother of the general, was killed on his own housetop. Narcissi Beaubien, son of the presiding judge of the district, hid in an outhouse with his Indian slave. Just when it seemed they would survive as the mob prepared to depart, a woman servant called out, "kill the young ones, and they will never be men to trouble us." The men returned and killed and scalped both. The crowd then headed toward Arroyo Hondo and Turley's Mill. The Pueblos on their way to Turley's killed two trappers named Harwood and Markhead. Like Bent, Turley failed to believe that he was in any danger until it was too late. Turley himself escaped into the mountains on the night following the second day of fighting; however, eight of his comrades had been killed and the mill sacked and gutted. No American was safe who happened to be in the path of murder and destruction. Following the destruction of the mill, they proceeded to the town of Mora where they killed eight more Americans.[38]

Colonel Price received word of the Taos massacre the next day. He also heard that the rebels were moving south toward Santa Fe and picking up new recruits along the way. He did not want to leave the capital unprotected, so he sent for a battalion from Albuquerque. We know that

John Adams was among the men from Albuquerque and thus participated in the defense launched by Price; however, we do not have details on the role he played. We know that his commanding officer, Captain Burgwin, was also among those on the expedition, but Adams was under the direct command of Captain William N. Grier. Price set out on January 23 accompanied by five companies of his second Missouri, Angney's infantry battalion, and a company of New Mexico volunteers and headed out toward Taos with a total of 353 men armed with mountain howitzers. Captain Burgwin and his men from the First Dragoons did not leave until January 27.[39]

The first encounter took place one day out of Santa Fe at a town called La Canada, or Santa Cruz. The rebels numbered fifteen hundred men, including some San Juan Pueblo Indians, under the command of Generals Tafoya and Chavez. Price forced the enemy from outside of their entrenchments in strong adobe houses and killed thirty-six of them, including General Tafoya, who bravely remained in the field after most had abandoned it. Price had two men killed and seven wounded. It was after that, on the 28th, that the men from the First Dragoons arrived along with another company of Missouri volunteers to put Price's headcount at 479. This is apparently when Adams joined the action. It is likely but not certain that Adams was involved in the fighting with his commanding officer, Captain Burgwin; however, we do not know if all of the men in the First Dragoons were together the whole time.[40]

From La Canada they traveled through a narrow pass known as Embudo, where the forest was dense and the road impracticable for wagons and cannons. The enemy occupied both sides of the canyon. Burgwin was sent with three companies to dislodge them. The sharpshooting skills of these men soon cleared the path for the rest of the American forces to pass into the town of Embudo. The men suffered most from the weather, as the snow thickly covered the mountains and several of the men were frost-bitten.[41]

On February 2 they arrived in Taos, where they found that the enemy had entrenched themselves in the famous Pueblo of Taos a few miles outside of the town. This ancient structure consisted of two large pyramidal apartment houses, each about 125 yards long and seven stories high. Each could hold about five hundred or six hundred men. The clear waters of Taos Creek ran between the two buildings. Nearby was the

Two. The Mexican War

Taos Pueblo as it appeared in a photograph dated 1941. At about 1,000 years it is the oldest continually inhabited dwelling in the United States. It probably did not look much different at the time of the revolt of 1680 or in the 1847 uprising against United States occupation (National Archives).

adobe mission church which faced north, with a corral to the south. It is the church which held the greatest number of the enemy. Price spent the whole day of the 3rd pounding the walls with his artillery. The next day they had managed to put a hole in the western wall of the church, and he then had his six-pounder brought around to that spot. He inched the cannon to within ten yards of the hole, where it became very threatening to those inside. Soon the church filled with smoke and the rebels evacuated, leaving little opposition to the storming First Dragoons. It was at this time that Captain Burgwin was hit and killed. Many of the enemy took refuge in the large houses on the east, and others headed into the mountains. Mounted men under Captains Slack and St. Vrain chased them, killing fifty-one of them with only a handful escaping. The remaining enemy finally surrendered and agreed to turn over the main leaders of the rebellion, Romero and Montoyo. Romero was killed by a bereaved relative, leaving only Montoyo to face trial.[42]

The trials took place shortly after the surrender. Montoyo was executed before the army on February 7. Fourteen others were tried for participating in the murder of Bent and the others on that bloody night. The jury was composed of those whose relatives had been killed on the nineteenth of January. A total of fifteen were hung. Of those, eight were Mexican and seven were Pueblo Indians. Several more were sentenced but they escaped the noose when the president pardoned them. Polk did not see how a Mexican could be accused of treason before the treaty officially made the land United States territory. They would have been soldiers fighting a war. Some of Price's officers, West Point graduates, said that the revolt would have never occurred if he had exercised the proper military discipline when he first arrived in New Mexico.[43]

1847

John Adams returned to Albuquerque after the insurgency had been put down. For the remainder of the year in New Mexico the only actions which involved Adams were with the Indian population and not those of Spanish descent. Before proceeding with details about Adams, a word should be said about the march made by Colonel Doniphan, even though it did not involve Adams in any way.

The Doniphan expedition is a good example of the harsh conditions facing those who occupied the newly conquered territory of northern Mexico. Alexander Doniphan was a volunteer officer leading a band of Missouri volunteers. On one hand he and his men were perfect examples of why some do not see the Americans as such noble crusaders. Likewise, they serve as a perfect example of why the West Point graduates such as Adams might look down on the volunteers with contempt. On the other hand, Doniphan and his men serve as a good example of why the American military has been successful most of the time. These volunteers were rude, crude, and in many ways downright repulsive, but they could endure much, and they could fight and win.

The colonel himself was quite an impressive individual. He was a good six and a half feet tall and weighed over 240 pounds. He had sandy red hair that stuck up like porcupine quills. His men said that he was "not afraid of the Devil or the God that made him." Nonetheless, he did have some humor and wore a habitual smile. He was popular with his men, who had unanimously elected him their colonel. He made them feel that they were part of the decision-making process. He was typical of the new Jacksonian American and definitely not of the West Point elite.[44]

When Kearney left, Doniphan had been preparing for a campaign south toward Chihuahua. Before leaving he received word from Kearney to settle the troubles with the Navajo before proceeding on his original mission. The Indians had a difficult time understanding how they could be the enemy of the new claimants to their land when they had been fighting a common enemy. Their chief, Sarcilla Largo, said, "Americans! You have a strange case of war against the Navajos. We have waged war against the New Mexicans for many years. We have plundered their villages, killed many of their people and have taken many prisoners. Our case was just." He then pointed out that the Americans waged war against the same people. "You now turn upon us for attempting to do what you have done yourselves. We cannot see why you have cause to quarrel with us for fighting the New Mexicans on the West, while you do the same thing on the East." Doniphan explained that now New Mexico was part of the United States and when the Navajo waged war against the people there they attacked citizens of the United States.[45]

The men who traveled with Doniphan endured incredible hardships. In the mountains of winter they lay on the ground "wrapped in blankets and skins, on the rugged earth or the frozen snow, and rose in the morning from beneath a newly-fallen coverlet of snow, with limbs benumbed, and icicles pendent in clusters from beard and hair." Farther south as they marched toward Chihuahua they crossed two deserts, one sixty miles wide. "Water was scarce, and so was game, but the area was rich in rattlesnakes, copperheads, tarantulas, and Mexican spies." They were outnumbered but they won battles at Brazito at Christmas in 1846, and again in Sacramento on February 28, 1847.[46]

They spent much of their time in the large settlement of El Paso. While there one Englishman reported on their lack of military discipline. Their camp was "strewn with the bones and offal of the cattle slaughtered for its supply, and not the slightest attention was paid to keeping it clear from other accumulations of filth." The men were "unwashed and unshaven, ragged and dirty." The Englishman claimed that "the most total want of discipline was apparent in everything." If anything it was worse after they took possession of Chihuahua on March 1. One woman recorded in her diary that the Missouri volunteers "who though good to fight are not careful at all how much they soil the property of a friend much less an enemy." She went on lamenting the loss of the people. "Their loved homes would be turned into quarters for common soldiers, their fine houses turned into stables, their public drinking fountain used as a bathing trough."[47]

Later Doniphan and his men turned their attention toward Indians again. They had begun a march toward Saltillo. On May 11 they reached Parras, where they skirmished with a band of Lapin Indians, who had robbed a local ranch and carried off women, children and livestock. Later they reached Monterrey, and after a brief stay there they went home by way of New Orleans to Missouri since the time they had volunteered for had expired. Senator Thomas Hart Benton made a special trip home from Washington to welcome the men of his state home.[48]

Most of 1847 was mundane for Adams compared to the heroic march of Doniphan. He had been attached to Company I as a second lieutenant under Captain William N. Grier. Most of his time was spent in Albuquerque. Men of his rank were permitted to sit in on councils of administration. He was also at times acting quartermaster and acting commissary of subsistence. From June 2 to July 5 of that year he was on a special detail to escort prisoners to Las Vegas. Near the end of the year he left Albuquerque with Grier in pursuit of a guerrilla chief called Cortes. On December 26 they marched south past San Miguel and did not return until the end of January. Then Adams was placed in temporary command of Company B. He joined up with the men in Albuquerque just in time to began Price's newly planned invasion of Mexico.[49]

On to Chihuahua

Perhaps because the war appeared to be concluding and Sterling Price did not want to miss out on all of the action, he made plans to move south; however, evidence suggests that the general honestly believed that he should invade Mexico. As early as August 14 and again on September 18, 1847, Price had requested permission to occupy Chihuahua and other provinces to the south. On November 20, adjutant-general Jones wrote to Price that expeditions to those places could be better conducted from Monterrey or Saltillo. Jones did add, "Should you; however, learn that a force is organized at Chihuahua with the design of marching on New Mexico ... you should make reasonable demonstrations and use your own discretion as to when it should be encountered." On January 21, 1848, Price wrote to Jones and claimed that measures were being taken under Governor Don Angel Trias to resist invasion from the United States. On February 4, Price received information from Lieutenant Colonel Lane, commander of the Missouri volunteers in El Paso, that he had documents which revealed that General Urrea was marching toward El Paso with three thousand men and that he expected more to arrive from Chihuahua. Price began accumulating an invasion force in El Paso.[50]

By February 23, Price had Companies B, G and I of the First Dragoons, under command of Major Benjamin Beall; six companies of Missouri Horse under command of Colonel John Ralls; five companies of Missouri Infantry under the command of Lieutenant Colonel Alton R. Easton; and a battalion of Santa Fe Volunteers, which consisted of three companies of horse and one of light artillery, under Major Robert Walker. Adams had been relieved of his temporary command of Company B and was made acting adjutant to the dragoon squadron serving directly under Major Beall. On March 1 the command under Price departed El Paso. They traveled with tents and carried eight days' provisions on pack mules. They needed to cross 300 miles of mountains and deserts.[51]

On March 6 the dragoons accompanied by Adams were ordered to advance on the town of San Geromino in order to take prisoner the Mexican General Manuel Armijo. From there they were to proceed to Durango and await further orders. After wandering the desert due to the confusion of their guide, the dragoons met a Mexican shepherd who reported that the Mexican General Don Angel Trias had abandoned Chihuahua and retreated to Santa Cruz de Rosales. Meanwhile, Price and his command had received the same information, as well as being informed that the treaty ending hostilities had been signed. Price did not allow this news to interfere with his plans. On March 7 the Americans occupied Chihuahua. They entered the city at eleven o'clock at night. Philip Gooch Ferguson described the scene, "As we marched through the silent and deserted streets, between long rows of stately buildings, the sound of the bugle gave rise to thrilling emotions and feelings impossible to describe." They camped at the edge of town.[52]

On March 8, Price led his 250 men, consisting of portions of Ralls', Beall's, and Walker's commands, the sixty miles to Santa Cruz de Rosales in pursuit of General Trias. The Mexicans, with a force estimated by Price at about 900, were well fortified within the city. They also had a greater supply of cannon and munitions. Ralls' and Walker's commands were dismounted to act as infantry, while Beall's dragoons with one company of Ralls' men were to act as a reserve to intercept the enemy in case of flight. Beall used his men as skirmishers. Company I was on the right between the Rio Conchos and the road to San Pablo; Company G was in the center guarding the road leading from the plaza of Santa Cruz de Rosales to the nearby ranches, and Company A was placed on the left guarding the main road leading to Durango. Price sent Ralls to the west side of the town and Walker to the southeast. Before hostilities began, Price did make a request for unconditional surrender. After this failed he lay siege to the city between March 9 and March 15 as he awaited the arrival of the artillery and other reinforcements. Those Mexicans in the church shouted out "Viva Mexico!" and "Benditos Gringos!" and "Santiago!" They then sent a white flag inquiring if they were in a state of hostilities, and pointing out that an armistice had been agreed upon.[53]

On the night of the 15th the awaited cannon and troops arrived, and on the 16th the first shot was fired and the battle began. Captain Love commanded the artillery, whose job it was to keep the housetops clear of Mexican infantry. The main strongholds were the church and a two story house. Philip Gooch Ferguson recorded, "It was a splendid sight to see the engines of death belching forth fire and smoke, to hear the loud roar of the contending batteries, to see the walls crumble as the balls struck them, the bombs exploding, and the balls whizzing in the air over our heads."

The house went first so that the main pocket of resistance was the church. A second shell from a 24-pound howitzer scattered these holdouts. By 8:00 P.M. the battle was over. Ferguson spent the night in the damaged church. "The next morning the sight that met the eye was shocking to behold. Piles of dead Mexicans were seen in various quarters, many of them most horribly mangled." It was not until after the battle that Price confirmed the rumors of an armistice.[54]

The Impact

The war changed more than just the borders between the United States and Mexico. Historians today look at the Mexican War as the starting point for the question of the expansion of slavery in the territories which climaxed with the secession of the Southern states. Many of the northern Whigs used the war as a political tool to weaken the Democratic Party by painting it as the party of the Southern planter class which had caused the war to begin with. In addition to the bigger picture, there were some more specific issues that followed the end of hostilities. One such issue for the Army was the awarding of what it called a "brevet." This was a temporary promotion without an increase in pay or allowances. Many of the men, especially West Point graduates, received brevet promotions, which seemed to cause more problems than these were worth.

The vagueness of the borders was another major concern. Following the American success Texas pushed for the expansion of its borders to the Rio Grande, a claim they had made since the days of independence. This in turn made it clear that no one knew what the exact borders of the new territories were.

It seems clear now that the Mexican War signaled the beginning of growing regional tensions that would not be resolved until the end of the Civil War. It began with the Northern Whigs, working with more radical abolitionists, claiming that the war came about due to the desire of the planters who wanted the Mexican land to expand their slave driven economic empires. The northern Whigs and abolitionists were intent on preventing the spread of slavery into the newly acquired territories. Many, if not most, Northerners supported this position, not so much out of concern for the slave as for the protection of their own economic interests. They believed that if the planter moved into the territories with their slaves there would be no way they could compete with their free labor. This Republican strategy of catering to the interests of the then successful abolitionists continued even after the war, causing U. S. Grant to say that the Mexican War was "one of the most unholy ever waged by a stronger against a weaker nation."[55]

John Adams was one of those given a brevet promotion for his "heroic" actions during the Battle of Santa Cruz de Rosales, which in turn helped to fuel a controversy in the Army. Adams had been brevetted a first lieutenant, having been commended by all of his superior officers for the accomplishments of his section and its "great execution upon the enemy's batteries and town." Congress had the authority to bestow this honorary rank upon an officer who performed a good service or heroic act during battle, a tradition which had been around since the War of 1812 but which became more contentious because of the great number handed out during the Mexican War. The promotion did not produce a pay increase; however, it caused problems when an officer of a brevet rank challenged another officer who held a true but lower rank. This situation generated so much controversy that President Polk, as commander-in-chief, declared the brevet rank inferior to actual rank. This had reversed a position previously taken by Major General Winfield Scott, who had been commanding general of the army at the time. From those at the top as well as through the ranks, many men became disturbed over the subject of brevet promotion.[56]

There were numerous issues over the political and legal status of the territory of New Mexico which Adams had found himself in at war's end, as well as a place where he would spend several of his future years. Texas had always claimed the Rio Grande as its western border, thus taking a big chunk of that land we call New Mexico today. In addition it was unclear what the southern boundary would be between the United States and Mexico. This became more important with the signing of the Treaty of Guadalupe Hidalgo. The Texans did surrender their claim to some of their northern lands when it was pointed out that Texas being north of 36° 30' would mean they could not have slavery under the terms of the Missouri Compromise.[57]

As these controversies heated up, John Adams continued his post war military service in New Mexico. Company I, the company of Lieutenant Adams, remained in Chihuahua until April 6, when it left for Buena Vista as a bearer of dispatches. Adams assumed command of the company for a brief period between the departure of Captain Grier until his replacement, First Lieutenant Joseph Whittlesey, arrived in Monterey. The company then went to Camargo and remained a week before returning to Chihuahua. Adams had been assigned to the duty of acting adjutant to the dragoon command until July 16, when Companies G and I left. Adams was then made acting adjutant to this squadron.[58]

Three

New Mexico Territory

Health continued to be a problem for the American soldiers as well as the rest of the population of New Mexico in the autumn of 1847. Assistant Surgeon Horace R. Wirtz reported that the hospital was full and that deaths averaged four per week, including soldiers and teamsters. Typhoid, a common visitor to those who lived in crowded and unsanitary conditions, seemed to be mainly responsible, though there were signs of other problems such as scurvy. *The Republican* identified conditions ripe for the rise of the dreaded disease. "To the filth and dirt about town—to the putrid carcasses of animals which were permitted to rot all over it—to the decayed and decaying matter in the streets and corrals, and private places, which if permitted to go on must necessarily affect the town, and probably corrupt the water." They went on to say that "the whole soil is nothing but an amalgam of putrid matter, which in warm weather will give forth an effluvia both disagreeable and sickly."[1]

Most Americans believed the claims of O'Sullivan in his article on Manifest Destiny. He claimed that they were advancing democracy and civilization with their conquest of lands like New Mexico. *The Republican* reflected that spirit when it reported that conditions improved tremendously shortly after the treaty which recognized the land as part of the United States. By the spring of 1848 new, better constructed houses replaced the old dilapidated structures people called home before the peace. The end of war and the impact on the spending of the army no doubt boosted the economy, but the newspaper claimed that "not a street in the place presents the appearance it did this time two years ago, and if things continue, in one year more the whole appearance of the city will be changed." The fields were cultivated and materials and army supplies began to flow down the Santa Fe Trail so that the paper claimed

Three. New Mexico Territory

"Santa Fe never saw the same spirit manifested, nor the same hum of every kind of business it does at present."[2]

We have little to tell us about the role that John Adams played in all that transpired in New Mexico, only what we can deduce from the records that confirm his presence and extrapolate based on what records we do have on his life in general. He did not operate in a vacuum and to know his life we must know the stage on which he lived it.

First, we will study the big picture for both the United States and the future state of New Mexico. Second, we will take a look at the original inhabitants of the land; after all, it is they who were the reason Adams and the army remained in the land. Third, since we do not have much information on Adams' personal experiences, we must make some assumptions on the conditions as they existed for all American military stationed there during that part of his life. Only then will we be able to proceed to the fourth stage and use what we do know about the man and try to draw a picture of the part he played.

The thinking of most historians today is that the conquered Mexican lands that came with the Treaty of Guadalupe Hidalgo fueled the debates over the expansion of slavery into the territories and thus brought about the rise of the Republican Party, which in turn sparked the Civil War. For this reason most U.S. history text books devote at least a few paragraphs to the territory of New Mexico. The Compromise of 1850 reduced the new land to the background of American history where it would remain until 1912, at which time it became the 47th state.

National Politics and the Territory of New Mexico

To understand where New Mexico fit in the national struggle, which for awhile showed promise of statehood more than sixty years sooner than actually achieved, we must take a look at those issues which most affected the national drama between 1848 and 1850. The first of three important national issues was the spread of slavery, which hinged on the Wilmot Proviso. This became the focus for the second development, the political contest between the Democratic and Whig political parties. A third question would revolve around the growing anti-immigrant or anti–Catholic sentiments which so infected the general population. This one was not as important in New Mexico as it could have been considering the large number of Mexican and Spanish Catholics.

Although much of the American public today believes that the Civil War was fought to free the slaves, the fact is that Abraham Lincoln and the Republican Party never campaigned on the issue of abolishing slavery. Every historian knows that the main platform for the new party was to halt the spread of slavery into the territories, even though most are of the opinion that slavery caused the war. The first national debate on slavery in the new territories or states came with the admission of Missouri. The Compromise of 1820 resolved the question for the time being, but it only lay dormant until the Mexican War. U.S. history textbooks have plenty of material on the controversy which led to Compromise of 1850 and what followed the treaty of Guadalupe Hidalgo, but most do not delve very deeply into the specific politics in the territory of New Mexico. Since John Adams was there and played a minor role in these events, it is necessary to take a closer look at how New Mexico fit in the bigger picture.

Mexico did not have slavery and thus New Mexico did not have slavery. Many of the Americans that arrived on the scene, even before the Mexican War began, came from the South and thus some of them were slave owners. As long as they lived in Mexico it was an issue between them and the government of that country. Once New Mexico became part of the United States, Southerners had at least a glimmer of hope that the new territory could become slave territory. Even the Compromise of 1820 with its rule about no slavery north of 36° 30' did not appear to be a barrier since most of the land lay below that line. Slave owners hoped to extend the boundary into the newly conquered lands. Neither the dry desert nor the pine covered Rocky Mountains offered the preferred climatic conditions conducive to the spread of the plantation economy that they had grown used to in the East. Nonetheless, some still hoped to see New Mexico become a slave state.

Meanwhile more and more people in the North, as well as some in the South, wanted to halt the spread of slavery even though most were not interested in abolishing it in those states where it already existed. The abolitionists would be the most radical between 1848 and 1861, but even some of the slave owners, such as Zachary Taylor, did not want to see the institution of slavery expand. On March 1, 1845, John Tyler signed the bill annexing Texas, as previously discussed. Many from the North had resisted this action out of the fear that it would lead to war with Mexico. To make a long story short, it did. Congressman David Wilmot introduced the Proviso in the United States House of Representatives on August 8, 1846, as they debated the funding for the war which mostly Southerners wanted. It passed the House and failed in the Senate. Another attempt was made again in February of 1847. Wilmot and his followers failed in another attempt, this time by attaching it to the treaty in 1848. The proposal was to prohibit the expansion of slavery in any of the territory acquired by the Mexican War.[3]

Prior to 1848 there were Northern Democrats and there were Southern Democrats, and likewise there were Northern Whigs and there were Southern Whigs. The glue that held the Whigs together was the desire to see government support the growth and expansion of American business, and thus the party did have support of many of the wealthy and progressive in both regions. There were some wealthy, mainly planters, who were Democrats. They were generally not as modern in their thinking.

The issue of slavery began to divide both parties into regional factions. The Wilmot proposal served to fuel division in the Democratic Party. The barnburners of the North became the nucleus of the Free Soil Party, dedicated to stopping the spread of slavery. Democrat Stephen Douglas from Illinois started off with a proposal to simply extend the 36° 30' line from the Missouri Compromise, but later he became a spokesman for Popular Sovereignty which would leave it up to the residents of new territories to decide for themselves. This would be used in an attempt to expand slavery to Kansas and would ultimately lead the Supreme Court to declare the 36° 30' restriction of the Compromise of 1820 unconstitutional. The Whig Party too began to divide based on those who supported the Wilmot Proviso and those who opposed it. The division within both parties tended to follow regional lines. For the more radical on either end of the spectrum, neither party served their needs.

The bottom line is that by the election of 1860 the Whig party was extinct and the Democrats had split, with mainly those favoring the Proviso being in the Northern faction while most Southerners fell into the anti–Proviso faction. The Northern Whigs became the foundation for the rise of the Republican Party. Thus men like Abraham Lincoln went from the Whig Party to the newly formed Republicans.[4]

Amid the growing political frenzy and unrelated to the spread of slavery in the territories, the ancient phobia of Catholics began to increase as a result of the growing immigrant population. Though most of the nativist attacks were aimed at German and Irish Catholics, the hatred of papism has been part of the American culture since the arrival of those who wanted to purify the Church of England of its Catholic characteristics, better known as the Puritans. The American soldiers overwhelmingly came from the native Protestant stock which rioted across the country during the period between the Mexican and Civil Wars, often burning Catholic churches and even killing Catholic immigrants from Boston to Philadelphia, from Louisville to Baltimore. Catholics in New Mexico were added to the Protestant American population by conquest rather than immigration. They were neither German or Irish; however, in the mind of the xenophobic American this was made up for by the fact that many were dark skinned. To the nineteenth century white mind, European as well as American, those with darker skins were generally regarded as intellectual inferiors. It does seem that those issues related to the spread of slavery overshadowed the ethnic and religious makeup of those new Americans in New Mexico, but it did play a role. The Know-Nothing Party rose up with an anti-immigrant platform. Some Southerners had hopes of building an alliance with the Northerners in this party, but it never materialized, as it seems that most of them were supporters of the Wilmot philosophy.[5]

New Mexico at the Time of the Treaty

It is no wonder that researchers are left with many uncertainties about the population of New Mexico since we do not have a reliable census. This is further complicated by the fact that the borders of that land were also in dispute. The three main population groups were European, including American, civilized Indians, generally meaning Pueblo, and wild Indians. This latter group tended to be a problem for the first two segments of the population. It may be considered politically incorrect to refer to the Plains Indians as "wild," but that is the term

Three. New Mexico Territory

they used at the time. Those concerned about political correctness can plug in whatever term is appropriate to describe those Indians who did not consider themselves as either part of the Mexican or American political states. It is they who caused problems for the rest and are primarily the reason for military men such as Adams to remain in the territory after the war was over. In a report from 1844-45, General Mariano Martínez de Lejanza put the population at 100,064, which probably included about one-third wild Indians. This group would of course be the most difficult to number. An 1850 United States census put the population at 61,525, of which 58,415 were born in New Mexico, only 772 were born elsewhere in the United States, 22 were free Negroes and 2,151 were foreign born. Of those born in New Mexico, we do not have the percentages of Mexican, Spanish, Indian, or mixed, but regardless the Anglo or protestant American population was quite small. Those living there at the time Adams served did make a distinction between Spanish and Mexican, though we do not have a count of how many were in each group.[6]

Most U.S. history textbooks focus on the national issues over slavery in the territory; however, it is the wild Indians who caused the problems for those who settled in the towns and farms with hopes of participating in the American and world economies. Governor Donaciano Vigil wrote, "The pacification of the Indians is another necessity of the first order, for as you already know the principal wealth of this country is the breeding of livestock, and the warfare of the Indians obstructs this almost completely." The Indians made it rather difficult for the agriculturist to produce; any surplus would likely be stolen by raiding natives before it could be turned into cash in the markets.[7]

The European settlements were mainly in the Rio Grande valley with a few lesser areas. The Taos valley was about twenty-five to thirty miles in circumference, very scenic and surrounded by the Rocky Mountains. Also included were the Valley of Chamas at Abiquiu, Rayado and Morotown, and Las Vegas. Colonel McCall made an inventory in 1850 of 124,760 acres of cultivated land with another 303,240 acres he described as "cultivable, now vacant." He also said, "In looking at the past in the history of New Mexico, it is clear that the fruits of labor in the principal pursuits of life above noticed have, up to the time of the cession of the territory to the United States, been blighted by the presence of formidable tribes of Indians who still infest the country." He went on to say, "The Indians will hold us in the contempt with which they now look upon the Mexicans, whom they have wantonly robbed and murdered for two centuries."[8]

Those Americans who either visited or settled in the new land held varying views, but generally speaking did not admire the industriousness of the Mexican residents. Of course it was common for the mind of the nineteenth century white of European stock to hold those they conquered around the world in low regard. They thought the Mexican male lacked intelligence and was cowardly and slothful. They not only objected to the Catholic religion, but to some the Mexican version was even more objectionable because it was different from what they had been accustomed to. Some admired the beauty of the land and found the people friendly and exotic, whereas others despised all that was not American. McCall claimed that it was "with difficulty he can be kept at work longer than is requisite to earn a few dollars," to which he added "while this lasts, he indulges to the full luxury of lounging away the hours of the day with his cigarrito, and passing the evening in the more exciting amusements of the fandango and the monte table."[9]

The war, occupation, and increased population of American settlers had a major impact on the economy and thus improved financial conditions. New hotels were constructed to house the new arrivals. In the days of Mexican rule few stores offered year-round trade, as most commerce was beneath the portals of the plaza or in the plaza itself, under American rule permanent stores and shops began to appear. Some merchants targeted the army settlers, while others competed with them. Entertainment included the traditional halls of fandango, drinking, and gambling, but some expanded to include American style balls and theatrical performances.[10]

While at least some of those Americans who saw New Mexico found some things to admire, many back east grappling with the bigger national picture either objected to the acquisition of the new land or looked at the new Americans through the prism of nineteenth century racism. Congressman Truman Smith of Connecticut told his fellow lawmakers that they had cheated themselves and had invited disaster by bringing people of low morals, such as the New Mexicans, into the Union. John C. Calhoun said, "Ours, sir, is the Government of a white race." William

T. Sherman is quoted as saying that the United States ought to declare war on Mexico and make it take back New Mexico.[11]

Government of New Mexico Before the Compromise of 1850

When the Americans first arrived in 1846 the United States government of New Mexico was strictly military. By July of 1851 the newly created territory held its first assembly. The only role that John Adams played in the story of transition was as an officer in the military, and thus he was a mere cog in the Army bureaucracy. As noted above, the organization of the territory captured national attention so that the politicians in Washington had their own motives for discussion and final resolution to the question of statehood versus territory. A big issue would involve what territory would be included in New Mexico. The first proposal from President Zachary Taylor was to divide all the former Mexican lands between California and New Mexico. A big barrier to this plan was that Texas claimed the land east of the Rio Grande as part of their state. In the end all issues would be resolved as part of the Compromise of 1850, and that would be worked out by those in Washington. Nonetheless, a faction developed within New Mexico itself pushing for statehood while another wanted to be simply a territory.

To recap, the native population consisted of the former Mexican citizens, the Pueblo Indians who had assimilated into the Mexican society and economy, and the wild Indians who still considered the land theirs. The American population consisted of the old settlers who had been there since before the war started, those who arrived after the conquest, and of course the Army. Some of the soldiers would remain and become part of the new territory while most eventually left, whether they be those who returned to civilian life elsewhere or the professionals such as Adams who would eventually be transferred. At first the military ruled the land and tried to convince the conquered that their lives would be better under their new government. Then they needed to maintain order as the private citizens tried to exercise control over their homes. While all the politicking was taking place in New Mexico and Washington, they needed to solve the problem with the wild Indians. After the government was transferred to the civilians, the Army, including Adams, had to finish the job of conquering the original inhabitants. They would not succeed at this until well after the Civil War.

Kearney quickly departed for California, leaving Colonel Alexander Doniphan to frame a plan for a civil government. Kearney appointed Charles Bent as governor as well as other offices, and under their command a quasi-civil government began operation. Doniphan left for Mexico and in December of that year was replaced by Colonel Sterling Price. Price called for an election of a territorial legislature in late 1847, but neither the Anglo-Americans nor the natives had much interest. The Americans did not believe a true civil government could exist with such a strong military presence and the natives had little interest in a government which they had not created. In addition, most older residents were not accustomed to participating in the government.[12]

Major and Brevet Lieutenant Colonel Benjamin L. Beall assumed command when Price left at war's end in August of 1848. His rule was short, as Brevet Lieutenant Colonel John Macrae Washington assumed military command and the governorship on October 8, 1848. Once the war was over most of the volunteer military forces left and as a result the economy declined. In addition, New Mexico products lost the Mexican market, mainly the one in Chihuahua. At the same time the wild Indians continued to raid and steal from the rest. In short, there was no great reason for optimism.[13]

In October of 1849 Major and Brevet Colonel John Munroe took command of the military governorship and would rule until the civilian government created by the Compromise of 1850 took over. His main task with the civilian government was to support the elections, maintain as peaceful an environment as possible with the native population, and to police as necessary while the two factions competed for control. The struggle began with the convention of October 1848 and concluded when Congress passed the territorial act in September of 1850. The two big issues that concerned those in Washington as well as New Mexico was the question of slavery and the territorial claims of Texas.[14]

It is not clear how many delegates were selected or how they were chosen for the first convention in October of 1848. The president was Antonio José Martínez. They came up with a document that petitioned Congress for the speedy organization of a territorial civil government.

Three. New Mexico Territory

They expressed concern about any of their territory being taken by Texas, and they had no desire for slavery. No parties developed but rather two factions. One favored military rule, made up of mainly the officeholders who owed their appointments to the military. The opposition faction included Americans and natives who resented military rule. Those of the first faction identified themselves with the territorial faction.[15]

The territorial faction called for another convention to draw up a territorial constitution, which convened September 24, 1849. They were headed by Judge Joab Houghton of the territorial court. The majority called for no other form of government except territorial. They avoided all reference to slavery and they simply defined the eastern border as "the state of Texas" without an exact reference as to where that was.[16]

James S. Calhoun was sent to Santa Fe in July of 1849 supposedly as an Indian agent, but he claimed to have been sent with "secret instructions from the government at Washington to induce the people to form a state government." Calhoun did not assume the leadership role but passed it on to Richard H. Weightman, a retired army officer. With the establishment of an opposition party, both sides made promises to natives. The territorial faction seized control of the printing press, while both sides resorted to violence. In addition the Indians renewed attacks on settlements and murdered travelers almost within sight of Santa Fe. To make matters worse, the winter had the coldest temperatures in a decade and food and liquor supplies ran low. Rumors circulated of revolt among the Mexicans.[17]

It might have been unclear as to the true intent of Calhoun, not so with the arrival of Lieutenant George A. McCall on March 21, 1850. Though McCall had been sent to further President Taylor's desire to see New Mexico admitted as a state, his first report did not appear so favorable. He reported to Colonel N. W. Bliss: "Arriving here, I found politics the rage, engrossing the attention of all classes of people; the territorial party high in the ascendant — the state party down." McCall found himself explaining to Houghton that the president favored statehood in order to settle the slavery question and the Texas boundary dispute. McCall had further concluded that Weightman had negotiated to surrender parts of New Mexico to Texas in order to gain their support for statehood.[18]

Meanwhile, on April 7, Robert Neighbors, commissioner of Texas, arrived to hold elections for the region he now believed to be part of his state. While Neighbors lodged complaints with Colonel Munroe, territorial advocate Houghton advised the inhabitants to ignore all of his activities and to hold meetings to protest any claims by Texas. Neighbors fled after lodging complaints with Munroe. The military governor issued a proclamation calling for a convention to draft a proposed state constitution. Ten days later it came up with one, mainly written by Houghton. Apparently McCall had achieved some success in convincing him of Taylor's desire for New Mexico statehood. Leaders then adopted a resolution that "slavery in New Mexico is naturally impracticable, and can never, in reality, exist here." The convention also denied any claims to New Mexico territory by Texas. The elections that followed provided some victories for both factions. Weightman won one of the two senate seats and headed for Washington. He arrived to learn that the Compromise of 1850 had been passed by Congress.[19]

The death of President Taylor opened the door for passage of the Compromise of 1850, which actually involved five separate pieces of legislation. All five were signed into law by President Millard Fillmore between September 9 and September 20, 1850. First, California would be admitted as a free state. Second, the slave trade was abolished in the District of Columbia. Third, the Territory of New Mexico, which included Arizona, and the Territory of Utah, were organized under the rule of popular sovereignty. Fourth, the Fugitive Slave Act required all United States citizens to return runaway slaves. Fifth, Texas gave up its western claims in exchange for the United States assuming ten million dollars of debt. Thus ended the military rule of New Mexico; nonetheless, the Compromise of 1850 did not end the violent conflict between the two factions. The best example comes from the election of New Mexico's delegate to Congress, a nonvoting seat. Weightman ran against Captain A. W. Reynolds of the old territorial faction. Judge Sprice M. Baird, a resident of Albuquerque and ally of Weightman's, said that "a rowdy gang of twelve Americans, drunk and waving whiskey bottles, appeared at the polling place and demanded to be allowed to vote. Most of them had ridden down from Santa Fe to support their candidate." The situation was defused when the men were allowed to vote but a protest was recorded beside each name."[20]

Three. New Mexico Territory

The Indians

Despite all the drama associated with the move from military to civilian rule of the New Mexico Territory, the primary reason for Adams to be stationed there was because of the Indian situation. Some have used words such as "genocide" to describe the American treatment of those who were there when the Europeans first arrived. It is no wonder that some have believed this due to outrageous statements such as that credited to Philip Sheridan, "The only good Indian is a dead Indian."

Racism was part of nineteenth century life so that even those with good intentions often assumed an attitude of superiority. The attitude of paternalism that caused some, if not most, slave owners to treat their slaves with kindness often applied toward the Indians also. In the case of the wild Indians living in the lands ceded by the Treaty of Guadalupe Hidalgo, the United States Army tried to protect the offenders, though determined to end their raiding of the whites and peaceful Indians.[21]

The Pueblo Indians had assimilated into the agrarian life of the Spanish, and for the most part differed little from either the Mexican or American populations in that they too suffered at the hands of the wild Indians. In 1848 they probably numbered less than ten thousand, mostly along the Rio Grande. Unfortunately, there is evidence that the whites, especially those who were on their way to the California gold fields, proved to be as much a burden to the Pueblos as to the wild Indians. At times they would seize horses, mules, sheep and grain, claiming to be representatives of the United States Army or other such authorities.[22]

Colonel McCall left a good accounting of what he identified as the eight bands of wild Indians. He said the "Nabajoes and Apaches are the most formidable as enemies, the most troublesome as neighbors." He concluded that the former were the wealthiest of all, except for the Moqui, owning large stocks of horses, mules, horned cattle, and sheep. He also said, "They are said to be intelligent and industrious, and their manufactures, blankets and course cloth, in their neatness and finish go far to prove this." He then deduced that "they might with proper management be induced to settle themselves permanently as the Pueblos have done." Of the Apaches, he began by saying, "The forays which the Apaches make upon the Mexicans are incited by want; they have nothing of their own and must plunder or starve." He added, "In the first place, before anything can be done with this people, it is believed it will be indispensable to open the communication with them in their own country." He said a strong military presence would be needed and that with such, "they might give up their roving habits and settle themselves in permanent towns in the vicinity of their fields."[23]

He dismissed the Moqui as being weak in numbers and too remote to cause much of a problem. He described the Utahs as having "neither permanent villages nor cultivated fields, and subsist chiefly on game. They are warlike people and much attached to a wandering life, frequently extending their excursions to California." He said that the Cheyennes and Arapahos subsist[ing] entirely on buffalo and "are friendly to the white man." Though the Comanches struck fear in those who lived in Texas, they posed little threat in New Mexico since that is not their primary range. Likewise with the Kayuguas, who did not exceed two thousand.[24]

After evaluating the situation, McCall concluded that a strong military force would be needed in New Mexico with two main objectives. The first would be to protect the lives and property of the inhabitants. The second would be to induce the roaming bands to settle down as the Pueblo had done. In other words, he was partial to the assimilation approach. The Indian agent, not the politician, James S. Calhoun also expressed concern about the wandering tribes. He said, "The thought of annihilating these Indians cannot be entertained by an American public — nor can the Indians abandon their predatory incursions, and live and learn to support themselves by the sweat of their own brows." He did agree with McCall that more troops were needed. He did not hold the same hope for assimilation and thus was born the main policy the United States would follow until the Dawes Act of 1887. "Fragments of their tribes, must be penned up, and this should be done at the earliest possible day." In other words, put them on reservations.[25]

The Military, the Men, and the Forts

Santa Fe was of primary importance from the time of the occupation until July of 1861, not only as the center of government but also as the headquarters for the military department and general depot for military supplies. Things changed drastically in that town after Sterling Price, his staff, and the volunteers left on August 27, 1848, with a force of only 665 remaining. The local newspaper described the change, "We have not the boistrous [sic] and loud cries of the drunkard, whose abode was that of the grog shop — no loud shrill voice of the sergeant of the Guard, or that of a file of men escorting some poor wretch to the guard house." Major Beall assumed command for a short while until Major Washington arrived on October 11, 1848. With his arrival the forces had dropped below five hundred with none expected until the following summer. Two companies were stationed in Santa Fe, one in Taos and the rest spread between Albuquerque, Socorro, Tome, and Doña Ana. Major Munroe assumed command in October of 1849 when he arrived with two more companies of Second Dragoons and a detachment of Third Infantry recruits, which made a total of 885. By the summer of 1850 garrisons were stationed at Santa Fe, Albiquiu, Taos, Las Vegas, Albuquerque, Cebolleta, Socorro, Doña Ana, Coons Ranch, the Presidio of San Elizario, and at Lucien B. Maxwell's settlement on the Rayado Creek. In 1850 there was an increase to 1,188 officers and men, of which only 1,019 were present. Colonel Sumner left Fort Leavenworth on May 26, 1851, escorted by a detachment of dragoons and infantry recruits. He was not there long before Adams left the territory in February of 1852, so he saw little of the economizing Sumner did.[26]

Expense was a major concern in providing military protection in lands added to the country after the Polk presidency. Those lands existing prior to 1845 were divided into seven military departments; the newly acquired territories added four more. Department 8 was Texas, Department 9 was New Mexico, Department 10 was California and Department 11 was the Pacific Northwest, simply called Oregon. Expenditures for the 1849–50 fiscal year of $2,413,580.74 increased to $7,444,261.26 with the additional departments. From 1842 to 1846 the legal strength of the Army was 8,613 officers and men; at the close of the Mexican War it was 10,120. On November 30, 1850, the legal size was 12,927, but the actual size was only 10,763, but those who were actually at their assigned post was only 7,655, of which 3,468 were in the four new departments. In other words, the actual manpower was less than the legal army. This meant that rather than thinking of an army where entire regiments might constitute a command, most of the frontier forts would be manned by a mere company, with many even less than that.[27]

Brigadier General John Adams, CSA

Where did these men who faced the dangerous task of subduing the so-called wild Indians come from? During the 1850s two-thirds of the enlisted men were immigrants. As was the case in the country in total, most of these immigrants came from either Ireland or Germany. Remember, this is when the Know Nothing Party was campaigning to stop immigrants from entering the United States because they were considered undesirable by the established white population. The white population of America, who in those days is what one had in mind when speaking of "native Americans," had little respect for enlisted men. As one historian described them, "the riffraff of society — paupers, drunkards, reprobates, the chronically unemployed, the shiftless, and even the mentally retarded or incompetent." At least one-fourth of the enlisted men were illiterate. With such a band of brothers it should be no surprise that Adams went on many missions which involved the escorting or court-martial of prisoners. Such men often enlisted in a drunken stupor or out of acts of economic desperation. Once they found themselves in such a perilous environment many tried to prematurely resign, which of course in the military is called desertion. Those convicted could find themselves

Dr. Charles McDougall, future father-in-law of John Adams. He served as an Army surgeon in New Mexico during the time Adams served there. It is not known for certain but seems likely that this may be when Adams first met his future wife (courtesy Ann Gulbranson).

Three. New Mexico Territory

flogged with a rawhide whip, branded on the buttocks with the letter D, or losing part of an ear to cropping. Less serious crimes were punished by confinement in a small "black hole," standing in a barrel for hours, marching in a circle with weights on the legs, or working at hard labor with a ball and chain for days or weeks.[28]

The men often had inadequate housing and food. The prescribed rations included salt, twelve ounces of pork or bacon, or one pound, four ounces of salt beef, flour or hard bread, beans, coffee, sugar, salt and vinegar; however, in New Mexico only salt, beans, and insufficient quantities of flour and fresh beef were available. It is no wonder that soldiers were often reduced to eating their horses or mules. It should be no surprise that many soldiers "learned to quench thirst, subdue hunger, and otherwise obliterate their misery with whiskey."[29]

Immediately after Price's departure in 1848 there were six forts in New Mexico and another five were added by the arrival of Colonel McCall. The descriptions of these forts that follow are based on inspections made by McCall between August and October of 1850. Adams spent at least some of his time in six of these locations. Fort Marcy in Santa Fe was the main base. This fort was the headquarters for the 9th Military Department and was garrisoned by B and D Companies of the 2nd Artillery and D Company of the 3rd Infantry. It was established in 1846 by General Kearney adjacent to the Palace of the Governors, but later moved to a location on a small mesa some six-hundred yards north of the plaza. The old presidential barracks had been made comfortable for the rank and file.

Among the men stationed here was Surgeon McDougall, the future father-in-law of John Adams. He arrived on July 11, 1850. He reported the supply of medicines to be inadequate. Colonel Monroe and his acting assistant quartermaster occupied the building that was, under the Mexican government, the Palace of the Governor. The troops stayed in the former Mexican barracks while the remaining officers and quarters were rented. Albuquerque, with forty-eight men, had quarters and barracks that were in a very fair state of cleanliness. McCall did not see any need for "a larger force at this point than may be sufficient to guard a depot of forage."

Socorro is one in which Adams spent some of his service. It had fifty-four men from Company E of the 2nd Dragoons and thirty-five from Company A of the 3rd Infantry. McCall recorded that "it may be well to keep a garrison at this post, say eighty men, one half mounted, to protect the settlement and the general grazing camp of the department." Another one in which Adams spent time was Don Fernandez de Taos, which was garrisoned by Company H of the 3rd Infantry. For this one McCall said that it "may be considered a proper station for a small force, say half a company of Infantry." He added that "the inhabitants of the Valley of Taos are the most turbulent in New Mexico, and the Indians of the Pueblo of Taos, three and one-half miles north of Don Fernandez, still entertain a smothered feeling of animosity against the Americans, which is well to keep under."[30]

Two of the existing forts were south on the Rio Grande near Texas. The first was El Paso del Norte with eighty-one men in 1850. It was occupied by United States forces during the Mexican War, though the permanent post was established on the United States side September 8, 1849. McCall said, "I do not consider it important that a strong garrison should be maintained here," which explains why it was evacuated in 1851. It was reoccupied in 1854. Fort Doña Ana, with ninety-seven men, was established by Major Steen on August 1, 1849. McCall considered "this position an important one for a dragoon force. It has always been a favorite crossing place for the Apaches from the east to the west and returning."[31]

Five new posts had been established by the time of McCall's inspections. Abiquiu was occupied by Company D of the 2nd Regiment of Dragoons. No buildings belonged to the United States government with all facilities being rented. McCall said, "The locality of the town of Abiquiu has some advantages in a military point of view; it is close vicinity to the country frequented, on the north by the Utah, on the west by the Nabajo [sic] Indians." He felt that a total strength of eighty-five was enough.[32]

The post at Las Vegas was established on October 2, 1849, and was garrisoned by Company K of the 2nd Dragoons and Company G of the 3rd Infantry. In 1851 Fort Union would be constructed in Las Vegas. On March 11 the captain was placed under arrest by the commanding officer of the department. Company K arrived on June 13, 1850, while under the command of Adams. Adams had assumed command of Company K on May 15 when they were stationed in Cebolleta. There were no quarters

Three. New Mexico Territory

or other buildings at the post with all facilities for supplies, men, and work animals being rented in the town. McCall said that "a small military post, either here or at some adjacent point on the Fort Leavenworth road, is important, principally as a depot from which supplies coming from the east may be diverted." He suggested perhaps Rayado.[33]

Rayado was the home base of Adams, where Companies G and I of the 1st Dragoons were stationed under the command of Captain and Brevet Major William N. Grier. Adams was under Grier when he established the command on May 24, 1850. There were no buildings belonging to the government on this post so the men lived in tents. At the time of the inspection on September 16 the officers had quarters and it was expected that quarters for the entire command would be completed within a few weeks. This post was at the base of the Rocky Mountains on a stream of the same name, "within the country of the Apaches" on part of the land which had been part of the Maxwell Ranch, and thus very much part of the history of Kit Carson. McCall also said, "It is, thus, near the range of the Comanche and other wild tribes of the prairie." He added, "In fine, this position, in a military point of view, appears to be, in every respect, a most eligible site for a frontier post — with a garrison of at least a squadron of dragoons and a detachment of half a company of infantry."[34]

One location which was a new post for United States troops was actually very old, San Elizario. It was established as Presidio de Nuestra Señora del Pilar y Gloriosa San José by Spain in 1773. It was occupied by the United States on September 15, 1849. Portions of the old presidio or fort had been repaired and occupied by the men, which included forty-four from C Company of the 3rd Infantry. McCall believed that "one company of infantry stationed here, or at El Paso, or equally divided between the two (say forty-two men, each) would be ... a sufficient force on this section of the frontier."[35]

The town of Cebolleta was occupied and a post established on December 1, 1849, by Captain C. Ker. In October of 1850 there were fifty-six men and forty-one horses of Company H 2nd Dragoons and fifty-one men from Company I of the 3rd Infantry. Captain Ker was placed under arrest by Major Howe on May 1 and Adams was sent to assume command. It was in June that Company K was sent to Las Vegas, and they were relieved by 2nd Lieutenant J. Buford, Jr. There were no quarters or other buildings at this post. McCall said that "as a military post, Cebolleta is of some importance, in as much as two Nabajo trails pass through gorges in the mountains at a few miles distance from the post."[36]

John Adams

John Adams was on duty in New Mexico from the beginning of the Mexican War up to his transfer out in February of 1852. We ended the previous chapter with Adams still in Mexico at the end of the war. After crossing into New Mexico, on the evening of July 31, 1848, Camp Winfield Scott was established on the east bank of the Rio Grande. The next day Adams and Company I along with Companies B and G left for Santa Fe. Adams was acting quartermaster and acting commissary of subsistence. During this period he was also put in charge of a recruiting rendezvous, though the commanding officer, Major Beall, was not optimistic about the kind of men they would find in the area. During the month of October they conducted several short expeditions of little note against the Apache.[37]

Major Beall brought Adams to Taos to be adjutant for the post. While in that position he took care of correspondence and distributed orders from the headquarters to the Army. In January of 1849 he was promoted to adjutant of the dragoon detachment in New Mexico. There is no evidence of his taking an active part in either the politics going on during this period or any policing of the related violence. No doubt, in a position so close to the commanding officer, he would have been apprised of such activities.[38]

In January of 1849 Major Beall received orders from the Ninth Military Department in Santa Fe to conduct an expedition against the Kiowas searching for prisoners captured by them in Texas and New Mexico. Companies I of the 1st and Company H of the 2nd Dragoons left Taos on February 10. They crossed the mountain of Río de la Mora through deep snow toward the Arkansas River and Bent's Fort. They had been advised by the United States Indian agent for the Upper Platte that those Kiowas near the fort were "exceedingly civil, but if provoked they did have the potential of attacking the troops." The agent, Mr. Fitzpatrick, reported to Major Beall upon his arrival at the fort that those prisoners they were looking for had assimilated into the Indians' lifestyle. The women had taken Indian husbands and had many children, and the men had become "barbarised," and that the accused captors were known to be "much attached to them."[39]

Major Beall and his men, including Adams, headed for the Kiowa settlement where they also found Cheyenne and Arapaho lodges. Seeing no need for aggressive action, he called for a council of the principal chiefs he found present, which included seven Kiowa, six Arapahoes, two Cheyennes, two Apaches, and four Comanches. Though he had also been sent to look for stolen animals, he advised those present that he found none. He made sure that they were aware that the territory was under the jurisdiction of the United States, and that if they did not "stain the great road from Santa Fe with the blood of white men," then they would have nothing to fear from the soldiers and that they would have access to their hunting grounds in peace. They returned to Taos by way of Sierra Blanco passing through ten and fifteen foot snows to reach their destination on March 9, 1849.[40]

Two days after their return Adams had a week leave, which left him out of the Company's fight with the Eutaw. They lost two men while claiming fifteen to twenty of the enemy. After returning from his leave he took part in a court-martial in Socorro. He returned to Taos on April 10 and remained there most of the time until February 1850. Lieutenant Whittlesey was in command of the company except for a brief absence in May, when Adams took command. Generally his assignment was post adjutant and acting commissary.[41]

Adams remained and was left in charge in Taos while Major Grier and the rest of his company was involved in the actions that resulted from the White massacre. James M. White and his party were at a well known camping spot on the Cimarron branch of the Santa Fe Trail about eighty-nine miles northeast of Las Vegas on October 24, 1849. Another party of travelers found the body of James White and five or six others a few days later. White had been lanced and shot several times, the carriages of their party had been stripped so that all that remained was a small rocking chair that belonged to his infant daughter, Virginia. A group of Pueblo Indians told the following party that the Jicarillas had carried off Ann White, Virginia, and a black female servant. On November 4, Grier and Company I along with forty men of Captain Valdez's Mounted New Mexico Volunteers and two mountain howitzers set out across the Sangre de Cristo Mountains for a place called the Point of Rocks. They were guided by Antoine Leroux and Richard Fisher, and after they reached Rayado they were joined by Kit Carson and Dick Wootton. Pieces of Ann White's clothing, a shoe, and pages torn from a book, deliberately left on the prairie, marked the trail for them toward the canyons of the Canadian River. They caught up with the Indians in mid November and in the attack Grier was wounded. Most of the Indians escaped, but six were killed, as was Ann White. The dragoons also seemed capable of savagery. After making camp for the night a noise led them to a baby Jicarilla, less than a year old, strapped to a head board. An "old gruff soldier" stepped forward, seized the child, tied a rock to the board and threw the baby into the freezing waters. The soldier

View of the Sangre de Cristo Mountains of New Mexico. Much of the time Adams spent in the territory was in the general vicinity of Taos, Santa Fe, and Rayado (courtesy David Herrera, Albuquerque).

Three. New Mexico Territory

lamented, "I only wish I had more to treat the same way."[42]

On May 9, 1850, Adams left Taos to take command of Company K of the 2nd Dragoons following the trial and removal of the former commander Captain C. Ker. While in charge his company moved about between Santa Fe, Taos, Cebolleta, and Albuquerque. While Adams was detached from his permanent Company I, the commanding officer, Brevet Major Grier, was ordered to determine the feasibility of establishing a permanent post at the Rayado. They left Taos on May 27, instructed to note the movements of bands of predatory Indians, the nature of the roads, and the supplies that could be obtained in that area. Grier had only thirty men to defend the post from Indians and so he requested support, specifically from Adams and

Kit Carson, the famed American frontiersman. He served the United States Army on many occasions as a guide, consultant, and scout during the time that Adams served in New Mexico. They must have met on several occasions (Library of Congress).

his Company K. Colonel Alexander of the 3rd Infantry, Adams's commanding officer, decided to retain Adams after hearing of Indian activity in El Mora.[43]

Adams and twenty mounted men were accompanied by a sheriff who had warrants against several Mexicans in the area of El Mora who had made threats against the lives of Americans and friendly Mexicans. Three were arrested and five questioned about threats against others, including the alcalde. Adams concluded that rather than any insurrection, those charged were simply political enemies arising from conflicts between those who were considered Spanish and those called Mexican. He did tour other villages in the neighborhood and delivered three offenders to the sheriff to demonstrate that the American forces were there to maintain order.[44]

On June 28, Adams received orders to proceed to Rayado to assist Grier and the men of his permanent company. Two days before they had been attacked by 250 to 300 Apaches and Comanches who had driven off all the stock except their horses. The Indians had also killed several peaceful citizens in the same area. He was recalled shortly after arriving, but in response to a repeated request by Major Grier, Adams and his men returned to Rayado on July 19. After this an expedition which included Adams's Company K and Grier's Companies I and G along with a hundred Mexican volunteers traveled three days and nights before reaching the offending Indians. They killed several Indians and confiscated their stock. Another day's journey brought them to the main camp, which was evacuating after receiving a warning from one of the wounded Indians who had escaped from the earlier attacks. The men chased the fleeing Indians for two miles, killing several more Indians and capturing additional stock. They reported that in total they had retrieved sixty head of horses and mules, one hundred and fifty sheep and seventy head of cattle. Upon their return they discovered that two men who had been left in Las Vegas in charge of company funds along with other deserters had fled toward California. They were captured and court-martialed in Albuquerque the following January.[45]

Adams was caught in a tug of war between Major Grier and Colonel Alexander which resulted from the near skeleton crews that both commanders had to deal with under the shoestring military budgets. After a brief move back to Taos, Adams and Company K returned to Rayado. A brief exchange of appeals followed, but they stayed there until November, since without them Grier would be left with only twenty-five men to protect the strategic location. At that time Adams was again ordered to Las Vegas to take command of Company K of the 1st Dragoons. Adams and Grier both protested the transfer. Adams pointed out that since he joined Company I in 1846 he had spent no more than six months with his unit. In addition, they did have new recruits who needed training before they could be useful soldiers, and besides that, Adams was on the sick list. The orders stood.[46]

Three. New Mexico Territory

Adams lodged complaints during his time under Colonel Alexander in Las Vegas. He protested the use of his men, which included Company F of the 1st Dragoons, for fatigue duty. He also requested other quarters for his men due to a lack of fresh meat and vegetables or fodder for the horses. Alexander responded that the supplies could not be obtained elsewhere without paying exorbitant prices. Headquarters permitted sending half of the men to San Miguel, Anton Chico, La Questa or other points in search of additional supplies.[47]

On March 6, 1851, Adams commanded an expedition of thirty men, two non-commissioned officers and two buglers in response to Indian complaints in the vicinity of Mora. The complaints had been placed by an American named Mr. Waters. As they approached the house they ran across a shepherd with several thousand sheep, assumed to be the same sheep which had been reported stolen. After questioning the man they were told that the sheep belonged to Juan Baca. Adams was advised by his guide, Mr. Donaldson, that in his opinion Indians had not been involved at all, but rather that there had been a dispute between Waters and a Mexican who had been found dead on the ranch. When they reached the house Waters was gone, but his wife told them that some Indians had taken the sheep from Baca. A son-in-law emerged from the house and claimed that every one of Baca's sheep had been run off. Adams also questioned another American, named Mr. Mitchell, who told them that some Indians had been at his ranch, but that they were peaceful. Adams returned to Las Vegas on March 8 and stated that Indians had not been a problem but that the report had been filed for some ulterior motive.[48]

After his return he took his men in search of supplies, at which time they ran into a stroke of bad luck. They lost a wagon which fell into the Arkansas River, and Adams had an injury to his arm that prompted him to request a twenty-day leave. His request was denied on the grounds that his injury did not prevent him from exercising command of his men, who would be left without a commander since a replacement was not available.

He had recovered enough that he could lead his men in an expedition at the end of June. They were sent to investigate a report from Mr. Samson near Anton Chico that Indians were there. They arrived on June 28 and did find some Comanche, but the villagers reported that they had no fear of the Indians and a chief assured them that they were peaceful. After his return to Las Vegas, Adams was dispatched once again with Companies F and K on the complaints of Samson. On July 3 they once again reached Anton Chico to discover that Indians had passed through four days before. They had killed three calves and six goats and wounded one steer. The next day they reached La Questa and found that Comanche had taken one horse and a mule. Soon afterward, Mexicans in the plaza at La Questa complained that fourteen Indians had run off all their cattle. Adams saw that the village had at least a hundred men in the plaza, so he said, "Why don't you go bring them back. There are only fourteen Indians." Adams then announced publicly that he would use the prefect as a guide and that the person filing the complaint would be whipped if it proved to be false. At this the Mexicans said the Indians had done no harm.

The expedition went on to San Miguel, where Adams questioned a Comanche who had lived there for twenty years. The man, named Manuel, told him that the Indians had done nothing but kill cattle in La Questa. They returned to that town and stayed there until ordered to return to Las Vegas on July 17. Adams reported that such complaints made by the Mexicans were unreliable.[49]

Apparently Adams was not exempt from committing acts of excessive force against the men under his command. While on a march from Las Vegas to San Miguel to the Rio Grande, he accosted a lance corporal. He had the man's chevrons cut and had him tied to his horse and marched for ten miles. A report to Brevet Colonel Sumner charged that this was oppressive conduct. He was released on the same day as his arrest and charges suspended. It was apparently not because of innocence but more due to his being needed to resume his command.[50]

On November 13, 1851, Adams returned to his permanent assignment with Company I, which had in the meantime been moved from Rayado to Galisteo. He assumed command of the company, but he soon had to leave again for Valverde, where he was a witness in a general court-martial. While he was absent, Company I had been sent to Las Lunas or Sabinal in search of forage. Later they were sent to chastise Indians. Meanwhile, Adams was promoted to first lieutenant as of January 2, 1852, and ordered to report to Company D of the 1st Dragoons stationed at Fort Snelling, Minnesota Territory.[51]

Four
Minnesota

Almost a thousand miles separated New Mexico from Minnesota, but it was much more than distance that changed for Lieutenant Adams. Compared to the wilds of Southwest the relative peacefulness of the North must have been quite refreshing. Compared to the adobe and wood stockades, Fort Snelling must have resembled a castle from the old world. The fortress stood high above the junction of the Minnesota River with the granddaddy of American rivers, the Mississippi. Someday this would be the site of a great metropolis, but it was still in the rough when he arrived. Nonetheless, he must have been grateful to be in a land where the Indians had been mostly subdued and the countryside was not alive with stinging, biting, and horned life forms. He did not know it at the time, but his stay there would be but a temporary reprieve before returning to the deserts and mountains and canyons of New Mexico. Adams was not yet twenty-seven years old when promoted to first lieutenant, but his experience since graduation from West Point would have given him competitive advantages. By the time he arrived in Minnesota he had already experienced commanding a company and was well tested on the battlefield both against the Mexicans and Indians.

The territory of Minnesota was organized March 3, 1849, out of what was formerly Iowa Territory, and before that had been part of the Louisiana Purchase of 1803. A portion to the east had been taken from Wisconsin. The newly organized territory also included much of what later became Dakota Territory. Fort Snelling was established in 1819. The cultural ancestry of Minnesota also differed greatly from that of New Mexico, taking on a French rather than a Spanish flavor. The site of the fort had been purchased by Lieutenant Zebulon M. Pike from the Sioux in 1805.

Brigadier General John Adams, CSA

The French had been traders before the first Americans arrived in the area. Like the French, the first Yankees were also interested in furs, a typical industry in a newly established Anglo frontier. The American Fur Company sorted and put into packs, weighing about one hundred pounds, the skins of buffalo, elk, deer, fox, beaver, otter, muskrat, mink, martin, and raccoon. "Indians, Frenchmen, half-breeds, and restless wanderers from the East were always loitering about the establishment."

That first fort consisted of log cabins and a stockade, but soon Colonel Josiah Snelling began construction of the stone fort that would capture the eye of tourists, settlers, and artists for years to come. That structure was mostly completed by 1825. The farmers and their families, as was usually the case in western expansion, got their way, and through the politicians prodded the Army into subduing those who had been there first. This is what the white Americans, armed with their code of Manifest Destiny, liked to call taming the West. This task appeared to have been completed by the time Adams arrived and the castle on the bluff was approaching uselessness. There would be a relapse in 1862 with a Sioux uprising, but still the country called Minnesota was much more tamed than New Mexico.[1]

Three men are worth taking a brief look at, as they personify the conflicts within the nation as a whole during the western expansion and conquest of the continent, especially in Minnesota. The first is Lawrence Taliaferro, the federal Indian agent. The second is Henry Hastings Sibley, an early settler who would later become the first governor after statehood. The third is Alexander Ramsey, the first territorial governor.

Lawrence Taliaferro served as the Indian agent at Fort Snelling from 1820 to 1839. Though long gone by the time Adams arrived, he established the Indian policies that were just being finished up after the arrival of Adams. Taliaferro began his career in the military, but when he went to Minnesota he worked with Snelling in mediating between the American Fur Company and the Ojibwe and Dakota Indians. He generally followed the assimilation policies of Washington and Jefferson by encouraging the Indians to rely more on farming and less on hunting. He took the Dakota leaders to the nation's capital, where fair terms were negotiated for the Indians lands; however, the government was unable to keep up its end of the bargain. Taliaferro became disgusted and resigned his position and left the army. The life of the Indians was simply

Four. Minnesota

not compatible with that of the white men whether they resisted or surrendered. In most cases even those who assimilated most successfully did not do so to the degree that would be necessary to find acceptance with white Americans.[2]

Henry Hastings Sibley was born in Detroit, Michigan, in 1811. Born and raised on the frontier of the Northwest Territory, he worked as an agent for the American Fur Company. He lost out as the first territorial governor to Alexander Ramsey. Ramsey was born near Harrisburg, Pennsylvania, in 1815. Ramsey was not only a competitor with Sibley, but his lifestyle challenged that of his adversary. Sibley was descended from English aristocracy, but he identified with the frontier world where he was born and raised. He imagined himself to be one of the Indian traders, "that bold and hardy class of men, who despising the comforts and seductions of civilized life ... [were] fascinated by the unrestrained liberty of action offered men, and above all, despised the whole machinery of the law." On the other hand, Ramsey thought of the frontier as "an invitation to exploitation, a vast tract of real estate which, when cleared of its wild animals, trees, and original inhabitants, would be ripe for development." Obviously it was the men like Ramsey who molded the America we all live in today.[3]

Three main tribes occupied the area around Fort Snelling, the Ojibwe, the Sioux, and the Ho-Chunk. The Army had to deal with not only the Indians but the white men, and they did not always take the side of their white countrymen. Even though most officers shared the belief with their fellow Americans that whites were intellectual superiors as well as Christians, they felt a sense of duty to the first inhabitants. In this day of political correctness many are quick to condemn the white men, and they also seem to assume the Army to be the bad guys. Many modern liberals want to dismiss the concept of paternalism as an excuse mechanism used by the Anglo Americans to justify enslaving Africans, and forcing Christianity and modernization on the natives as well as taking most of their land. Most of the Army officers sincerely believed it their obligation to protect the Indians as if they were their own children. This is the definition of paternalism. It was real to them. In the minds of most Army officers the Indians of Minnesota shared with those of New Mexico the same level in the racial hierarchy. They were not as respected as the "civilized" tribes of the Southeast, who had been relo-

103

cated to Oklahoma, but believed them to be superior to those on the Pacific and in the mountain West.[4]

The Sioux Nation is the third largest group of Native Americans in the United States, trailing only the Navajo and Cherokee. They are divided into three main subgroups. The Lakota are those found mainly west of Minnesota, and therefore would not be the ones dealt with by John Adams. The other two, Eastern and Western Dakota, are from Minnesota. Many of the historical documents relating to the area at the time Adams was present simply refer to the Dakota, which can be confusing since this term has been applied by anthropologists and government documents to all Sioux groups. This could be due to a translation from the Ottawa from which Sioux is derived. The first records by white men of the Dakota place them at the source of the Mississippi River. By the late 17th century they had entered an alliance with the French. While Adams was present the tribe appeared to have peaceful relations with the United States; however, they attacked white farmers along the Minnesota River in August of 1862. This resulted in the Dakota War of 1862 which in turn resulted in largest mass hanging in American history. Lincoln commuted the death sentence of 284 of the Indians, but that was not until 38 others had been hanged.[5]

The Ojibwe are the fourth largest Indian group in the United States, right behind the Sioux in numbers. They are more commonly known among Anglos as the Chippewa. They are most associated with their birch bark canoes, sacred birch bark scrolls, as well as the use of cowrie shells, wild rice, and copper points. Gun technology acquired from the British enabled them to push back the Dakota Nation. They are of the Algonquian linguistic group, and apparently came from the eastern areas of the United States. By the end of the 18th century they dominated in Michigan, northern Wisconsin, and Minnesota. They allied with the French during the French and Indian War.

The Trail of Tears is well known today, an event associated with the removal of the Cherokee; however, the United States government tried to force all of the native people west of the Mississippi River. Like the more infamous Cherokee relocation, many died resisting what has been called the Sandy Lake Tragedy. After that tragedy the government agreed to let them settle on reservations in their former lands now considered white territory. The conflicts with these people directly resulted from

Four. Minnesota

the unquenchable hunger the whites had for the Indians' land, as was the case in most wars with the first inhabitants. Some were even subjected to the removals of the 1830s which sent them as far west as Kansas.[6]

The Ho-Chunk is the name the people call themselves, but they are better known by other Americans as the Winnebago. They, like other Siouan peoples, originated on the East Coast of North America. They first appeared in the reports of Jean Nicolet in 1634, when they occupied the area around Green Bay, Wisconsin. They did some corn growing, but depended more on fishing, collecting wild rice, making maple sugar, and hunting. They numbered more than 20,000 at the time of their first white contact, but by 1736 had been reduced in population to about 700. In the 19th century the government moved them to reservations in Wisconsin, Minnesota, South Dakota and even Nebraska.[7]

Calm had settled in around Fort Snelling before Adams arrived; however, the Indians were far from content. In 1848 the Ho-Chunk had been transferred to a location between the warring Sioux and Ojibwe tribes. That fall Brigadier General George M. Brooke of St. Louis chose a point opposite the Nokay River. A squadron of dragoons and the Sixth Infantry from Fort Snelling set about building a fort in that location. Halted by winter weather, they returned in the spring of 1849 and completed and occupied Fort Ripley in April. This did not keep the Ho-Chunk in line. On the first fourth of July they attacked a frontier store, "causing one gentleman to escape en dishabille [partially dressed] to the woods, where he danced to the tune of the mosquitoes during some three days and nights." A state of unrest continued among these Indians at least through 1858.[8]

Meanwhile, the Dakotas were subjected to the treaties of Traverse des Sioux and Mendota in 1851. Minnesota Territory governor Alexander Ramsey apparently well represented the white farmers, as he was largely responsible for the lopsided agreements. The Suland, as the newspapers called the lands west of the Mississippi, had been targeted and demands for its cession came from farmers, speculators, town site promoters, fur traders, mixed-bloods, and the federal government. President Taylor had appointed Ramsey the first territorial governor, but Henry Sibley had been selected to represent the territory in Congress. Sibley also represented the interests of the traders, who had money coming from the Dakotas and thus had a personal interest in seeing money coming to the Indians since that would be the only means for them to pay their debts. Luke Lea also participated in the treaties as commissioner of Indian affairs in Washington. Lea, Ramsey, and Sibley all worked in concert.[9]

Ramsey and Lea followed Sibley's advice and divided the Dakota, thus hoping to avoid the feelings of power that the Indians might have if they pictured themselves as united in resistance to the white men. First the whites settled with the Sisserton and Wahpeton. They had no greater desire to surrender their lands but felt it futile to resist. Some of those present remembered the Black Hawk War which had crushed them in Wisconsin. In July of 1851 Ramsey and Lea then met with Sisserton and Wahpeton leaders in Traverse des Sioux near present-day St. Peter. The white men had struck a good bargain for the government, as the Indians ceded all their claims south of the 1825 Dakota-Ojibwe boundary for only pennies per acre. Nonetheless, they would have been satisfied with this if they had not discovered they had been duped into signing another document in which they agreed to use the funds to pay Sibley's traders. When they realized what they had signed, they protested on deaf ears. It is generally assumed by historians that this so called "traders' paper" was behind the uprising that would come in 1862. The Mdewakanton and Wahpekute surrendered their claims to the lands with the Treaty of Mendota. The treaties did not pass the Senate until June of 1852, and was not proclaimed until February of 1853 by President Millard Fillmore, but by then the white settlers had invaded the Suland and platted town sites, including Winona, Belle Plain, and Mankato.[10]

First Lieutenant John Adams Arrives

Adams arrived on the scene after these treaties had been signed, but he was there in time to participate in their enforcement. Lieutenant Colonel Francis Lee was commander of Fort Snelling when Adams arrived in May of 1852. The commanding officer was concerned about the size of Company D, the dragoon detachment which Adams assumed command of. The company consisted of only twenty men and had insufficient horses and equipment. He also felt that more officers were needed since Adams would also be serving as post adjutant. The post

Four. Minnesota

had other logistical issues, including inadequate medicine and the lack of stationery, which was such that the adjutant could not perform his duties.[11]

Meanwhile, the lack of treaty payments was becoming obvious so that Sioux Chief Little Crow was speaking out against the falsity of the United States government. Lee described the Indians as being "in a state of disappointment, starvation and desperation." In the fall of 1852, before the relocation of the Indians commenced, the commander recognized the need for another post. Captain Dana of the quartermaster's department, escorted by a troop of dragoons, selected a suitable site on the north side of the Minnesota River a dozen miles upstream from the town of New Ulm. In February of 1853, seven privates of Company D of the 1st Dragoons, and two sergeants and thirteen privates of the 6th Infantry, were sent to start construction. In the spring of 1853 Companies C and K of the 6th Infantry, under the command of Captain James Monroe, became part of the garrison of the new Fort Ridgely. Resources at Snelling became further reduced when Governor Ramsey was successful in obtaining control of the post's only two mountain howitzers for use against the Indians.[12]

It turned out that Adams was not heavily involved in the Indian turmoil, as he was due a customary extended leave. Headquarters of the Sixth Military Department at Jefferson Barracks, Missouri, issued the orders to take effect October 1, 1852; however, Adams left on September 25 anxious to avoid winter weather which sometimes comes early in the North. He spent most of his time in Nashville, where he had relatives, but also traveled to Pulaski to visit his mother. He also spent some time in Memphis. As his leave expired, he left Nashville by steamboat for Saint Louis on May 18, 1853, and from there headed back to Fort Snelling. We have record of his activities because of monthly reports he was required to file. He returned to his new post on June 2.[13]

By the summer of 1853 he was finally established in the place that he would call home, though it would only be for one year. At this time Minnesota was still what would be considered a frontier. It had a landscape dotted with tepees, log cabins, dirt roads, and canoes. The fort itself was impressive compared to the wood stockades of New Mexico and other such western forts.

The landing was directly under the cliff that towered one hundred and six feet above. A stone wall enclosed the barracks, quarters, and storehouses. At a height nearly double that of the wall was a stone tower which served as a lookout. The barracks for the enlisted men were under the north wall and consisted of two buildings one story high. The larger of these could accommodate two companies and was divided into two sets, each having on the main floor an orderly room and three squad rooms. In the basement was a mess room and kitchen. The other barrack was designed for only one company which had all the facilities on one floor. Under the south wall and facing the barracks were two other buildings, similar in appearance. One was the officers' quarters, the place Adams would inhabit. "It was divided into twelve sets, each consisting of two rooms, the front one sixteen by fourteen feet, and the back one, eight by fifteen and a half feet." The basement contained kitchens for each set. The other building held the offices of the commanding officer, paymaster, quartermaster, and commissary. There were other buildings in the fort, including the quarters for the commanding officer, storehouses, guardhouse, and hospital.[14]

Colonel Lee was absent when Adams arrived, and he would not return until the fall. Ramsey was replaced by a new governor, Willis A. Gorman, in May of 1853. Born in Kentucky, he had lived in Indiana before coming to Minnesota, except for the time he spent in the Mexican War. He was appointed to the governor's office by Franklin Pierce. He also served as the superintendent of Indian affairs. In October he commissioned Adams a colonel in the state militia. The office did not interfere with his duties to the United States Army.[15]

The governor received reports that the Ho-Chunk had been attacking the Ojibwe and so in January of 1854 he called on Adams. On January 24 the lieutenant left with thirty-one dragoons headed for the Crow River. By the time they arrived to where the Ho-Chunk were encamped, they had the problem under control and were surprised to see the soldiers. One deaf and dumb man of their tribe had been fired upon by some Ojibwe, but the chief of those people had driven away the problem makers. Adams returned and concluded that the report had been in error.[16]

Adams was called on for only one other incident while stationed at Fort Snelling. In April of the same year news arrived at the fort that several wandering Sioux had committed murder. After a chase of seventy

Four. Minnesota

miles the guilty were apprehended and detained at Fort Snelling until orders were received to return them to their own country. Other than these minor incidents the only records of Adams' service addressed logistical problems typical of such service in a frontier fortress.[17]

Wedding Bells

Since his graduation at West Point, John Adams had been either in the Mexican War or stationed on frontier post, with the exception of the one eight month leave he had in 1853. This means that opportunities for romance were limited since his contact with the opposite sex would have been limited to mostly to Mexican or Indian women. It is assumed his attitudes would have been typical of nineteenth century Americans, who looked down on interracial marriage. This did not mean that such women could not be used to satisfy sexual urges. In one 1837 diary a missionary's wife claimed that all but two officers at Fort Snelling kept an Indian mistress. In New Mexico one officer recorded that it was "the custom when you wait upon a lady home from a party (fandango) to go in & sleep with her." Occasionally such relations resulted in formal marriage with Indian or Mexican women, but most officers would never risk the resulting ostracism. There were few single white women in such places; most of them were the daughters of the older officers.[18]

The daughters of senior officers were popular with the younger officers. Competition for their affections would have been very keen. Many opportunities existed for socializing, such as parties, dances, and picnics. Of the officers' marriages recorded in the *Army and Navy Chronicle* between 1835 and 1840, at least nineteen percent were to the daughters, nieces, or sisters of other regulars. Thus it is safe to say that John Adams was the norm when he married the daughter of a fellow officer. Dr. Charles McDougall had been stationed in New Mexico at the same time as Adams. He had opportunity to meet Georgiana during those years, and the occasion to renew the acquaintance when Dr. McDougall was transferred to Fort Snelling in April of 1853. We know that the doctor did correspond with the lieutenant while he was still on leave in Tennessee, so we know they were something more than a casual acquaintances.[19]

By the late 1830s and 1840s a distinct military subculture emerged in the United States. Today we do not think much about the class of men, and women, who pursue the military as a career. This was not always so in American society. This is a part of what Skelton is addressing in his *An American Profession of Arms*. During the period officers shared common complaints about military life: family separations, inadequate pay and slow promotion, harsh living conditions at frontier posts, and no public appreciation for their services. Such complaints may have led some to resign; however, there was a dramatic increase in the number of officers who chose to make the Army a career. "Although officers' private writings contain frequent references to economic security as a motivation for remaining in uniform, other recurring themes are a deep positive attachment to their profession and a sense of separateness from the civilian world."[20]

His marriage to Georgiana helped to secure a place for Adams as a member of this subculture. Dr. McDougall was not only a fellow officer, but part of a family which had traditional ties to the military. Their unusual family life was an important part of the subculture. More important was the kinship ties which served to increase the bonds to the Army. It would appear that these family ties, especially the Army wives, were quite often a positive force. A good example comes from Eliza Anderson, when she heard that her husband, Captain Robert Anderson, was considering resigning due to his disappointment over lack of recognition for his service in the Mexican War. She wrote, "Pray do not think of such a thing." She went on to say, "You would never be satisfied out of the army." This was apparently not just because of her concern for his well being, as she later added, "Both you and I are very much attached to the army & have been from our very childhood." What neither Dr. McDougall, Georgiana, nor John anticipated was the conflict that would arise in less than a decade when Adams would side with the Confederacy while the McDougall family would remain with the United States Army.[21]

Though the McDougalls would side with the Union when the nation divided, their background was not much different from that of Adams. They did not come from old Northern stock but rather were relative recent arrivals to America. Georgiana's grandfather was born in Dumbarton, Scotland, in 1777 and immigrated to Virginia, and then farther

Four. Minnesota

west in 1796. Whereas the Adams family, which came from Ireland, went to Tennessee, John McDougall went only slightly north to Chillicothe, Ohio. The elder McDougall valued education and occupied a public office in his adopted Ohio community. In 1818 he moved farther west, apparently with no bias against slave holding territory as he went to Missouri. Besides the father of Georgiana, he had one son who held high rank in the United States Navy and another who went to California and became that state's governor. The grandfather McDougall died in 1821.[22]

Charles, Georgiana's father, was born in Ohio in 1804, the second son of John. He began a bond with the Army subculture by his marriage to Maria Griffith Hanson, daughter of Colonel Griffith Hanson of Maryland. This was only the beginning of such an identity, as neither Colonel Hanson nor Charles were part of the West Pont elite. Charles studied medicine and started out with the Army in the Black Hawk War of 1833. He was promoted to major and surgeon in 1838. He served in the Creek and Seminole Wars between 1838 and 1841. He then went to the military academy from 1846 to 1848. He was sent west, where he remained until the start of the Civil War. Though not as bonded with the Army as some families, he was a career man. His daughter married Adams, and he had a son, Thomas, who became an Army man. He apparently took his family with him, at least most of the time, as his children were born in the West.[23]

Georgiana was born in Wisconsin on May 1, 1835. The family history says that she met John Adams at Fort Snelling, but it seems likely they met the first time in New Mexico, since her father was stationed there at the same time as Adams. Her father clearly had ties with Adams prior to Minnesota. It seems more likely that she knew her husband from before rather than accepting a proposal from someone she had known a short time. She had grown up in an Army family, and like so many of her contemporaries of like background, she married a career officer. She began her married life as an Army wife with no knowledge that the war would end her relationship prematurely. Like her mother before her, she followed her husband wherever his career took him, including assignments to the far West. The wedding took place at Fort Snelling on May 4, 1854, officiated by the Reverend M. Fisher.[24]

The wedding date had been hastened to beat the ordered departure of Adams from Minnesota. In April, Company D, commanded by John

Adams, was ordered to proceed to Fort Leavenworth, Kansas, by "the best practicable route by land." From there they would continue on to New Mexico. They did not leave until May 6, and then by steamboat. John Adams was to return to the land of the Apache and Comanche, but this time as a married man.[25]

FIVE

Return to New Mexico

A stampede was the terror of terrors on the plains, and this location was like camping on a volcano liable to erupt at any moment.

It was a perfectly bright, starlit night, and peace seemed to reign from end to end of the camp. Visiting was general among the officers, and a feeling of safety prevailed, now that we seemed to be clear of trouble with Indians. A little before nine o'clock the earth seemed to tremble as if in the violent throes of an earthquake. Like a whirlwind a stampede commenced with D Troop horses, rushing down through the extra or "led" horses and on through the mules, sweeping everything before it, barely missing officers and B Troop camp. On they went a little south of east down the river, in the mad rush trampling everything under foot, upsetting and breaking a dozen six-mule wagons by catching picket pins in the wheels as the moving mass rushed on; picket pins whizzing in the air struck an object and bounded forward like flying lances. To condense: D Troop lost two-thirds of their horses. All the string horses (600) and six hundred mules, besides some private animals, were in the mad rush of destruction. One B Troop horse, an extra, succeeded in joining the gang. Realizing the full meaning of the terrible calamity, I ordered "boots and saddles."[1]

This is the description recorded by Percival G. Lowe, who was among the caravan of pilgrims on the journey from Fort Leavenworth to New Mexico Territory, which also included John and Georgiana Adams. The threat of Indian attack was only the beginning of the potential hazards which faced those in the American West in the 1850s. They could be terrorized by hordes of insects, bitten by a rattlesnake, tortured by extreme weather, or overcome by a stampede. This phase in the life of John and Georgiana was part of the bigger tapestry of American history in two ways. First, they obviously were part of the continuing saga of relations between the white Americans and the Indians. Second, Georgiana, though not in a typical situation, lived at a time in which middle class women were influenced by the "cult of domesticity." Those who served in the military then, as those today, were dependent on wives who could understand and support their lifestyle.

Whereas Adams' first trip to New Mexico was to serve in the Mexican War and then as part of the occupying forces in the newly acquired territory, this time he arrived as part of the what the Army hoped would be a solution to the continuing problem with the Indians. To the whites, the problem was that they lost a lot of livestock, occasionally suffered destruction of their property, and in the worst cases lost their lives to raiding Indians. The Army, especially regulars such as Adams, did not always agree with the civilian population on the best way to deal with the problems. The officers spent much of their time restraining the civilian white population.

Most of the United States Army was stationed in the West. "Regulars often compared frontier whites unfavorably with the Indians in terms of order and civilization, and they usually attributed Indian-white conflicts to the greed and aggression of the frontiersmen." On one hand, many of the civilians had the opinion that the officers were part of this elite ruling class. On the other hand they liked the military expenditures which stimulated their local economy. One way in which the local communities took advantage of government spending was using their services for law enforcement, especially in the area of commerce and trade laws. Adams and his companions traveling across the prairies would arrive in the middle of significant uprisings of the first inhabitants.[2]

One of the common mistakes made today about family life of earlier Americans is that women stayed home and took care of the kids. The truth is that most European as well as American women had to work as hard as the men. It is true that the care of children was part of their job description; however, this did not compare to the soccer moms of today. In fact childhood was much shorter in the good old days, as kids were an important part of the family labor force. There was no Dr. Spock to tell parents about their child's self-esteem, and for the average citizen the American dream was to own a farm.

The period before the Civil War is known as a time for social reform as well as the technological, political, and territorial changes that occurred so rapidly. These changes did include education and the beginnings of what we call the women's movement. No doubt that with the

Five. Return to New Mexico

beginnings of industrialization, growth of the world market economy, and rapid expansion, there was a growing middle class. This growing middle class developed what we call middle class values, which incorporated education and other such reform movements. They also began to define the role of women in these changes. One popular book of the day was *Godey's Lady's Book*, which by 1860 had 150,000 subscribers. This book proclaimed "the perfection of womanhood ... is the wife and mother, the center of the family, that magnet that draws man to the domestic altar, that makes him a civilized being, a social Christian." This is the basic idea of what historians like to highlight in today's text books as the "cult of domesticity." For the most part the wives of military officers tended to fall into line in this mid-nineteenth century view of womanhood.

We do not have much information on the specifics of Georgiana's life, only that she followed her husband from post to post and bore his children. It is assumed here that she varied little from the other middle class women of Victorian America.[3]

The Journey

Two days after the wedding, John and Georgiana Adams boarded the *Minnesota Belle* for Fort Leavenworth, Kansas. They reached their destination on May 17, 1854. Adams was no stranger to this fort, as that is where he passed through on his first trip to New Mexico. This fort served as the main supply depot for all of the western activities, not only before the Mexican War and during that war, but continuing through the Indian wars. The First Dragoons had been associated with this location since its organization in 1834. Founded in 1827, it was the oldest active Army post west of the Mississippi. If anything, it became more important after the Mexican War as traffic escalated on both the Santa Fe and Oregon Trails. Its importance increased again with the passage of the Kansas-Nebraska Act of 1854.[4]

Two days after their arrival John and Georgiana departed on a leave of absence. They returned on June 17 and John immediately busied himself with preparations for not only him and his bride, but for his new command, Company D of the First Dragoons. They arrived from Fort

Snelling with Adams. Most of his men had no experience with the kind of action they would see in the Southwest. Adams and his command camped on the "blue grass" a little southwest of Merrit Lake. Company D would join Company B and they would depart on July 1 under the command of Colonel Thomas T. Fauntleroy. Fauntleroy was born in Virginia in 1796 and was commissioned a lieutenant in the War of 1812 and a major of dragoons on June 8, 1836. He was made a lieutenant colonel of the second dragoons during the Mexican War, and in 1849 assumed command of the First Dragoons.[5]

Colonel Fauntleroy, Company B and Company D, the regimental band, a large number of Army officers with an assortment of civilian family members, a large supply train and six hundred extra horses led on strings of about forty horses each set out for their new home on July 2. For the entire trip the two companies alternated with one taking the front guard and the other the rear. Percival G. Lowe of Company B, who would retire from the Army and become a prominent citizen of Leavenworth, noted that those men under Adams' command, Company D, were "composed of a fine lot of men and drilled well, but they had been stationed for some years in Fort Snelling, and did not have the long summer campaigns the B had." He mused further that they "had much to learn and to suffer before they could hope to compete with men who had traveled from fifteen hundred to three thousand miles every summer, always in an Indian country, always on the alert and obliged to move with little transportation, little or no forage save the grass that grew in abundance everywhere, and with short rations, depending largely on game which was also generally abundant." As the days passed the voyagers settled down to a routine, but that routine was doubled "as they always were on the route west."[6]

The first encounter with Indians came on Coon Creek in Edwards County, which is in southwest Kansas near the Arkansas River. A large number of Kiowas "mounted on fine horses ... cavorted about ... insolent and defiant." Company B had the advance guard and the caravan was so strung out that Company D was more than two miles to the rear. Major Chilton, one of the officers accompanying Fauntleroy, did not agree with the commanding officer's handling of the situation. "Well, if I were in command I would corral these trains and horses, and wipe these Kiowas off the face of the earth; this is no way to deal with Indians," he told the colonel. The colonel ordered the major under arrest and sent him to the rear. "The major turned, his eyes flashing, his bristling mustache looking unusually fierce, and rode to the rear."[7]

The caravan crossed the Arkansas at Cimarron Crossing, thirty miles above the present location of Dodge City. On the night of the stampede mentioned above the camp was west of the road, fully a mile up the river. D Company was at the upper end, and B, which had been the rear guard for the day, was camped just west of the road. "The wagon train, except headquarters, company and officers' transportation, was well to the front, away from the river." The horse strings were in the rear "while headquarters, officers' families, etc., were strung along the bank of the river between the two troops." The land where the horses were was sandy and soft. Lowe claimed that "it was noticed by all of our troop that the six hundred led horses were always badly picketed; that is, picket pins driven half way down and in many cases two or three lariats tied to one pin." He had even noticed men who would stick their pickets in an ant hole because they went in easier. The bottom line is that the stampede was apparently due to carelessness.[8]

The men debated the cause of the stampede, one thought being that Indians had done it, another that it was wolves. "One Indian in a wolf skin might have done it, or one horse frightened at anything running the length of his lariat and scaring a few more might bring about the whole thing." Regardless of the cause, those who still had their mounts needed to round up what they could. It was nine o'clock before they could get started, feeling their way "through the wilderness of wrecked wagons, crippled and dead horses and mules and their lariats and picket pins, met with in the first two miles, within which nearly a hundred horses and mules were found dead or injured by being pierced with flying picket pins."

They found two hundred mules within the five miles of camp and sent about a dozen men to take them back. The experienced men knew that mules calm down quicker than the horses. After collecting some of the horses they found themselves close to an Indian camp. They tried to place themselves between the horses and the camp. "In the meantime the dogs set up a terrible barking, and as we looked back the whole camp seemed to be alive, as men, women and children hustled out of their lodges." The men concluded that the camp of Kiowas and Comanches would be scouring the countryside for what horses they could gather, and so they decided to head back with what they had.⁹

In the end all mules not fatally crippled were saved. About 150 horses were dead or severely crippled, and many more not accounted for. A total of 200 missing were probably rounded up by the Indians. Since they had been able to recover so many mules and horses, they were able to move most of the wagons, except for a few which had been too badly wrecked. Two days after the stampede they were able to proceed across the river and found a safe camp on the north side.¹⁰

From there they moved off "up the north side of the Arkansas by easy marches for several days, on up the river to Bent's Old Fort, and crossed; thence south to Timpas, Water Holes, Hole in the Rock, Hole in the Prairie, crossing Purgetwa — generally pronounced Picketware — below where Trinidad now is." This was one hundred miles farther than by the Cimarron route to Santa Fe, and thus it had not been traveled since opening of the Cimarron. Due to fallen trees "it took Lieutenant Craig's pioneer party — details from B and D Troops — several days to make the road passable," but in the meantime the "animals had the finest grama grass" and improved in a very short time. One day, while they were camped, Sergeant Peel went hunting. A loud thunderstorm enabled him to shoot seventeen birds in a large flock of turkeys. It seems that they did not scatter at the gunshots, which sounded like the thunder. After getting the road open, which allowed time for the animals to improve, they "moved over the Raton Pass and camped at a pond at the foot of the mountains."¹¹

The first settlement that they reached in New Mexico was Maxwell's Ranch, on the Cimarron, and from there they proceeded to Rayado. This is when they first heard of the growing Indian troubles. Six weeks before, Company I, which was stationed at Rayado, had battled with the Apaches. They then went on to Fort Union.¹²

Fort Union was the largest post in the Southwest and was the Army headquarters of the Northern Military District of New Mexico. It had been established northeast of Las Vegas by Colonel Edwin Sumner in 1851. It had been constructed in adobe and log and was scattered over the countryside so that it looked more like a village than a fort. It was just below a mesa eight miles from the closest firewood. The nearest water supply was a spring which sometimes caused diarrhea. The Jicarilla

Five. Return to New Mexico

Fort Union, where Adams's commanding officer, General Fauntleroy, was stationed during Adams's second term in New Mexico. This is also where he joined up with other troops on missions against the Ute Indians (Wikipedia).

Apache claimed the area as their homeland. Fauntleroy turned over the command of Company D to Adams. Soon afterward he and his men departed from the rest of the party they had traveled with and headed for Fort Craig.[13]

Fort Craig was in Socorro County, on the west bank of the Rio Grande del Norte. It had been established April 1, 1854. The fort had been built for protection against the bands of Apaches that roamed the area from the Pecos to the Gila rivers. It was also meant to protect a road which ran to the lower portion of the territory on the west side. One description of the fort and its surroundings, though from 1874, probably described the same fort at the time John and Georgiana called it home. "Of wild animals, the grizzly, brown and black bears, panther, wild cat, weasel, large and small wolves are the most important. Black

119

Former officer quarters at Fort Craig. This is where Adams was stationed for most of his second assignment in New Mexico, and where his family would have lived when he went on expeditions (Plazak, Wikipedia).

and white-tailed deer, as well as antelope, are abundant in the mountain regions." They no doubt helped to feed the soldiers and their families. "Swan, pelicans, wild geese, brant and almost every species of duck abound on the river, as well as bill cranes, blue herons, bitterns and several species of snipe. At some distance from the post, and principally in the mountains, are found turkey, quail, blackbird."

The climate varied with great heat in the summer and slight frost and a little snow in the winter. "The season is disturbed by great storms of dust which blow from the west, principally over this post as well as all the lower parts of New Mexico.... This dust at times is stultifying." The fort was designed for two companies and thus had two barracks "built of adobe, in the form of a hollow square, each enclosing a placita. Each barrack consists of two dormitories fifty-one by twenty by twelve and two thirds feet, with a wide hall extending from the front of the

Five. Return to New Mexico

buildings to the enclosed court in the rear." The officers' quarters were three one-story adobe buildings with flat roofs and flooring of impure gypsum. They were at the rear of the dormitories and made part of the enclosed court. Three-quarters of the rooms had open fireplaces and were well lighted, but there were no bathrooms. The men generally went down to the river, seventy-two feet below, to bathe and fetch water. Adams had a total of sixty-four men in September of 1854. This would be home for John and Georgiana, though she would be alone there much of the time, as John was called away to settle problems with the Indians.[14]

In 1855 there were three types of mounted soldiers in the United States Army: dragoons, mounted riflemen, and cavalry. Europe had what is called heavy cavalry, which consisted of men in defensive armor and were mounted on heavy, powerful horses. All cavalry in the United States were light cavalry. Dragoons acted as either infantry or cavalry in skirmishes, though by 1855 they were pretty much limited to mounted and thus in reality the difference between the two was only in name. The United States Army at this time had two cavalry, two dragoons, and one mounted rifles. During the Mexican War dragoons were armed with musketoons, which were carried on a sling-belt, dragoon sabers of a Prussian pattern, and horse pistols. This remained unchanged for many years. Mounted rifles, on the other hand, were armed with percussion rifles and Colt's army revolvers and no sabers, while the cavalry had sabers, rifle-carbines, and Colt's navy revolvers. After the Mexican War the trimming of dragoon jackets was orange, that of rifles was green and the cavalry had yellow. Rifles and dragoons had the "Albert hat," with orange and green pompons, while the cavalry sported the cavalry hat.[15]

Indian Troubles

The generations of warfare between the United States Army and the Indians was not a continuous struggle but rather a period of uprisings and relative peace. Adams arrived in the New Mexico Territory at the tail end of Apache troubles, but became an active participant in the Ute wars of 1855. David Meriwether had become governor of the territory in May of 1853. He declared that "the Indians would either have to be fed and clothed by the federal government or chastised in thoroughgoing fashion." He complained that the policies of his predecessors had led the Indians to expect continued assistance. He was absent in March of 1854, and the starving Jicarilla and Mescalero Apache began an uprising. By the end of the summer Brigadier General Garland reported that "the Jicarilla Apaches are pretty thoroughly subdued" and were "making overtures of peace." He was convinced that he had defeated them and that "they are not safe from pursuit in the most inaccessible parts of the Rocky Mountains." Most of the militia raised by the Acting Governor Messervy had been released before their term of service had expired. Meriwether had returned in September, and Chief Chacon offered to make peace; however, he did not represent all of the Jicarillas, many of whom were not ready to give up. The federal government became involved. Congress granted $30,000 in 1854 for making treaties with the Apache, Ute, and Navajo, and $25,000 for general expenses of Indian service in New Mexico. They had a rough year, but more was to come. The New Mexico Territorial Legislature reported at the end of 1854 that during the year Indians killed 50 citizens and destroyed property worth $100,000.[16]

Meanwhile, Fauntleroy replaced Colonel Philip St. George Cooke in September of 1854, to assume command against the Jicarillas and the Utes in the spring of 1855. During that winter these two tribes needed food and objected to the continued encroachment into their lands. In November they drove off a herd of cattle and several sheep just twenty-five miles from Fort Union. Fauntleroy sent a detachment and recovered some of the livestock. The Utes had not joined in the 1854 raids but had allowed the Jicarillas to join their camps around the San Luis Valley. In December troops were sent from Los Lunas and Fort Fillmore to investigate raids along the Pecos. The Jicarilla had been joined by some of the Mescalero. On December 25 some Utes joined the Jicarilla and attacked the settlement of Pueblo on the Arkansas River, killing fourteen men, wounding two, and capturing one woman, two children, and about two hundred head of livestock. There have been many amateur and professional historians who have claimed that the United States used germ warfare against the Indians by giving them blankets intentionally infected with smallpox. This continues to be a subject of debate. It has been claimed that is why the Utes joined the war. It may be that the Indi-

Five. Return to New Mexico

ans believed this regardless of the truth. These raids sparked the plans for a major campaign that would continue until August of 1855.[17]

Colonel Fauntleroy led the campaign of United States Army and New Mexico Volunteers. Meanwhile, the raids continued. On January 11, 1855, some Mescalero attacked at Galisteo, "killed one man, wounded another, stripped a dozen women and drove off seventy mules." On January 19 Utes and Jicarillas raided Pueblo, killing four and capturing livestock. Fauntleroy led a detachment to locate those who had hit Pueblo, but returned on February 5 empty handed. On February 8 another small attack killed one man and stole more livestock; again the detachment from Fort Union had no success. On February 28 Kit Carson reported that Utes and Jicarillas "have been committing thefts, robberies and murders upon the stock and inhabitants of this northern portion of the Territory."[18]

Fauntleroy commanded men from Fort Union, Fort Massachusetts, and Cantonment Burgwin as well as six companies of volunteers under the command of Lieutenant Colonel Ceran St. Vrain. The New Mexico militia got its supplies at Fort Union. Meanwhile the Jicarillas and Utes increased their attacks along Ocate Creek, the Canadian River near Las Vegas, and in the San Luis Valley. On February 20 Fauntleroy left Fort Union and traveled to Taos where he made additional preparations for the campaign. In early March they proceeded on to Fort Massachusetts where he completed his detachment of five hundred men, which included two companies of dragoons, four companies of mounted volunteers, and thirty spies under the command of Captain Lucien Stewart from Taos, and Kit Carson, who was valuable as a scout.[19]

Fort Massachusetts was established June 22, 1852, in what is today Colorado, on the west bank of the Ute Creek, about eighty-five miles north of Taos. Its primary function was to protect travelers in the San Luis Valley from Indian attack. It was described as "a well-built stockade of pine logs, ten feet in height, and enclosing very comfortable quarters for one hundred and fifty men." It was located at an altitude of eight thousand feet in a region where the growing season was very short and the winters very cold. Grass was so short in supply that it was recommended to carry supplies in with pack mules rather than oxen. It was a poor location, but the best in the region. There were large stands of pine forest, and good water supply, but the short season made it difficult to grow food for the troops. In 1858 the men would be moved to Fort Garland.[20]

On March 14, Fauntleroy led his troops into the San Luis Valley to punish the Indians led by the Ute Chief Blanco and the Jicarilla Chief Huero, believed to be the ones responsible for the attack in Pueblo. After traveling about one hundred miles northwest they had an engagement on March 19 near Saguache Pass. Seven or eight Indians were killed before the remainder scattered into the mountains, making it impossible for the troops to pursue all of them. This is typical of the guerrilla tactics the Indians used which allowed them to survive for so many years before they could be rounded up and herded onto reservations, the policy that the United States would follow after the late 1850s. The troops followed the largest group under Chacon to a camp on the headwaters of the Arkansas River. They did capture many of the horses before being forced to return by way of the Mosca Pass to Fort Massachusetts for additional supplies.[21]

They were stranded in the fort for several weeks, as many of the troops were disabled by their long trek into the mountains, and their horses were likewise not ready to go any farther. Kit Carson returned to Taos and Adams requested a leave to return to Fort Craig, where his wife was expected to deliver their first child. It was April 9 before the leave was granted, and it was the 12th before he got underway. By the time Adams reached Fort Craig he found that his first son had beat him there. The boy was named Charles McDougall Adams, after his maternal grandfather. Fauntleroy was reprimanded for allowing Adams to leave, but apparently no penalty was enforced.[22]

Adams missed the biggest attack against the wayward Indians. Fauntleroy headed back to the San Luis Valley looking for the Utes, and St. Vrain led the remainder of the forces over the Sangre de Cristo trying to locate Jicarillas who were in Colorado. Fauntleroy identified the trail of Chief Blanco and his Moache Utes, and he followed them to a camp near the Arkansas River about twenty miles from Pencha Pass. The Indians had been up all night celebrating with a scalp dance, which gave the soldiers a big advantage when they attacked on April 28. One of his soldiers reported they "swept the enemy like chaff before the wind." They killed about forty Utes, wounded many more, and captured six children, about thirty-five horses as well as other livestock, and six rifles, five pis-

Five. Return to New Mexico

tols, twenty-five bows with arrows, and an assortment of buffalo robes and pack saddles. They lost one solder and one was wounded, with another killed pursuing those who got away.

Chief Blanco escaped so there were two more attacks on May 1 and 2. Soldiers killed two more Indians and captured fifteen more horses. Chief Blanco remained at large when Fauntleroy returned to Fort Massachusetts. They headed back into New Mexico and Adams rejoined them in Taos on May 15. From Taos they moved out to Una de Gata on May 29, where they were to join up with the volunteers. They never connected so they moved on to the Point of Rocks, where they located some peaceful Comanches. They then returned to Fort Union, where Fauntleroy assumed command on July 20.[23]

Meanwhile, the volunteers under St. Vrain followed the trail of the Jicarilla in Colorado. They attacked on Bear Creek, a tributary of the Cucharas River, killing and wounding thirteen. They followed the Indians to the Purgatoire River, where they killed four more and took some women and children captive. During this battle one of St. Vrain's volunteers brought him a scalp which was so long and full he accused the soldier of scalping a woman. The man returned to the dead Indian "and castrated him and brought the parts to the colonel, tied to a stick, and the colonel was satisfied although surprised at such an unusual method of proving the dead Indian was a man." They searched along the Canadian River without success and then returned to Fort Union for supplies. They then headed back into Colorado where they killed another six, captured seven as well as some more horses. One party of Indians did attack and kill eight to ten in the mountains of New Mexico between Cantonment Burgwin and Mora. Those guilty of the attacks escaped punishment. The volunteers were released in July, as their six month term had expired.[24]

Apparently the Indians were so destitute after the campaign, having been reduced to eating their mules, that they met with Meriwether in August. A treaty was signed with the Moache Utes on September 11 and with the Jicarillas on September 12. In addition to a protected reserve, they received rations, blankets, clothing, household utensils, farming tools and seed. They had basically agreed to follow the American policy of forced assimilation. The treaties were not ratified by Congress and many of the locals thought the Indians too close. One band under the

Apache Chief Negro refused to accept the terms and continued to raid near Mora and Rayado until March of 1856. Though the whites never made the treaty official, the Indians continued to stay near their agencies at Abiquiu and Taos. They did not receive a permanent reservation until 1887, after the wars against Geronimo.[25]

Adams departed company with the troops to be a witness at a general court-martial, leaving Fort Union on June 30. One day after his return, on July 10, his command of seventy-three men were sent to Rayado to the aid of Major George Blake, who was combating Indians in that area. After reaching Rayado they headed into the mountains near Embuda looking for the trouble-causing Apache, but all that they found were some Pueblos. From there they went into the Jicarilla Mountains near Santa Barbara Cañon. After only finding peaceful Indians, they returned to Fort Union, and then returned to Fort Craig. Adams assumed command of the post for at least half of the time between August of 1855 and May of 1856. He had only one other minor expedition against the Gila and Mongollon in February of 1856, mainly as the result for the call of a massive movement by the Indian agent, Dr. Michael Steck. Fauntleroy and his men did head toward Maxwell's Ranch from Fort Union in response to raids by the Comanche. Those Indians eventually retreated back into their normal location, so that all was peaceful through the winter of 1855 to 1856.[26]

Adams's time remaining in New Mexico was limited to routine and paper work. He was rewarded for his work in the campaign when the Army brevetted him a captain in March of 1856, and he received a letter of resolution and commendation from the Department of New Mexico. On March 12 he got orders to report to general recruiting service. He was to report to Brevet Colonel Charles A. May at Carlisle Barracks, Pennsylvania, by July 15. He was relieved of his command at Fort Craig on May 5. He left for Santa Fe on May 15, where he made arrangements for an escort of fifteen or more soldiers to Fort Leavenworth.[27]

Recruiting Duty

The journey back east was fairly uneventful, despite the fact that the Indians were not completely resigned to their agricultural white man's life. On July 14, Adams reported to Carlisle Barracks. Carlisle Bar-

Five. Return to New Mexico

racks is located in Carlisle, Pennsylvania, and is still a location for the United States Arms Training and Doctrine Command, and the site of the United States Army War College. Much different from the place they left, this base dated back to 1757, although at that time it too was on the frontier. Construction began during the Revolution, and later was a center during the Whiskey Rebellion under George Washington. It was Washington who recommended the location for the construction of the military academy, but it lost out to West Point in New York.[28]

Charles A. May, the man Adams was to report to, spent most of his career in the Second Regiment of Dragoons. He too served in the Mexican War, having command of a squadron during Zachary Taylor's expedition. He was born in Washington, D.C., coming from a prominent Baltimore family. He also spent time on the frontier, in California, New Mexico, and Texas. He had just been promoted to major in March of 1855. From Carlisle, Adams was sent to Baltimore to what was called in recruiting service the rendezvous. The recruiting party usually consisted of an officer, a non-commissioned officer, two privates, a drummer and a fifer. They would set up in a house or building chosen by the officer and then interview and lodge potential recruits. Adams, as commanding officer, would be in charge of all finances and would file monthly reports to the adjutant general's office, and the quartermaster general, and the ordnance department. Adams would swear in the new soldiers, have them checked by an Army surgeon, and administer the oath of allegiance to them. He would also begin their instruction, see that they were dressed properly, and read the rules and articles of war to them. He would send a batch of new recruits from the depot every ten days.[29]

Adams worked at recruiting between July 1856 and July of 1858. His success rate varied from a low of five for the month to a high of 18 in one month. In February of 1857 he was considered for promotion, and on March 21, 1857, he accepted a commission as captain. It was in the same month that he became ill with a "slight fever and debility with loss of flesh being the principal symptoms." It has been assumed by some to be "National Hotel disease." This is an illness named after the National Hotel in Washington, D.C. Some medical experts have concluded it was the result of an attempt to poison some of the residents, which began in January of 1857. The symptoms have been described as sudden prostration along with nausea. Tongues of patients have indicated an inflam-

The National Hotel as it appeared about the turn of the century. The hotel was built in 1826 and demolished in 1942. It is the location of the outbreak of National Hotel disease, believed to be the illness that Adams had which delayed his departure to California (Library of Congress).

mation of the mucous membranes of their stomachs, with diarrhea and vomiting occurring after the diarrhea stopped.

Among various theories of the causes, poisoning was a popular one. Some believed it was intentional, and others unintentional. A committee looked into it and found no evidence of water poisoning, food poisoning, or arsenic poisoning, the latter being a theory based on the discovery of a poisoned rat in the water supply. It subsided in February, but returned in full force in March, the same month as the inauguration of President James Buchanan. Since Adams was living in Baltimore, not far from Washington, and he became ill in the month of March, and the illness required only a visit to the dining facilities and not necessarily an overnight stay, it seems quite possible that whatever inflicted Adams was "National Hotel disease."[30]

Five. Return to New Mexico

Regardless of the nature of his illness, the fact remains that when Adams received his orders to report to California he was unable to do so. The Army gave him an official leave of absence to recuperate in August, but it was only for ten days. He did continue to report to duty in his recruiting exercise. In May of 1858 his unit began to organize an expedition to California under Colonel Fauntleroy. The plan called for them to group in Memphis, and from there they would continue to Fort Smith in Arkansas on the border of Indian Territory, then to New Mexico and on to California. Adams was to conduct a detachment of recruits from Carlisle Barracks to Memphis. Adams, his father-in-law Surgeon McDougall, and Surgeon Randall all protested this order due to his illness. The Army finally backed down on June 1, 1858, at which time he was then granted a five month sick leave to be taken at Fort Monroe, Virginia, beginning August 1. He ended his recruiting duty in July and was to report to his company in California upon his return to service. He sent a letter November 4 stating that he was prepared to resume his duties. On November 20, 1858, he and his family sailed for California. By that time they had two more sons so that a family of five boarded the ship bound for the West Coast of the United States. One son, Thomas Patton, was born in Baltimore on November 19, 1856, and another, John, was born in Washington on May 15, 1858.[31]

Six

California

General Rowe appeared, after the young sprigs of heathendom, eight in number, varying from two to twelve years old, were brought into Court, for what purpose, does not appear, as the poor brats could not understand a word of what was going on, but sat in a huddle of helpless silence, stolidly eyeing the tonguey lawyers, gazing in undisguised admiration at the inexhaustible repertoire of McQuaid's gesticulation. The poor little creatures were clad in four sacks, open at each end, with their arms thrust through holes in the sides, and though these flowers of the forest were shrivelled-legged, pot-bellied and dirty, one could see that they had intelligence and were susceptible to education. After a wordy explication from the lawyers, and sundry bitches, the Judge decided that the prisoners were not legally held by the Sheriff of Yuba county, and ordered their discharge, no evidence appearing in the return made that any charge was brought against them. Their counsel told them that they were at liberty, but the Deputy Sheriff of Sutter said that he had a claim upon them; whereupon McQuaid said that he had no right to arrest them in Yuba County; Deputy didn't care, and McQuaid defied him to do it, and told his clients to "git," but they were not willing to take his word for their freedom and reluctantly and slowly went out, followed by the deputies, lawyers and eight little Indian boys—and girls. After much parleying, the culprits looking on sheepishly, McQuaid trying to urge them off, the aborigines hustled together on the Court House steps, the Deputy Sheriff of Yuba arrested the men, as though the affair was begun de novo, and so the matter rests until their counsel takes further steps in the case.[1]

This newspaper article that appeared in the *Marysville Appeal* in October of 1861 reflects well the conditions of Indian children in California, as well as the attitudes of the white people of that state toward the first inhabitants. With the gold rush of 1849, 100,000 Americans flooded the newly conquered Mexican territory with a greater hunger for wealth and fame than even their predecessors had been in displacing the original inhabitants so that they could claim their land. The policy

Six. California

of the United States government toward the Indians had shifted toward putting them on reservations, but lust for gold made it more difficult in California. Even that land which held no value for farmers or ranchers could have held the gold they sought. People were hesitant to surrender a portion of the state which could be their chance to stake a claim to their share of that wealth. While some cared little for the Indians, others could see that the treatment of those who had already lost so much was not a Christian thing to do. While some debated whether the natives were even human, others saw in them the same light that burns in the souls of all men. Fewer yet understood that many Indians simply wanted to live the way their fathers had done before them. Most white liberals thought in terms of civilizing the poor savages. With education, soap, and some spiritual guidance, these dirty barbarians could be turned into good Americans.

John Adams had witnessed the treatment of the Indians in New Mexico and Minnesota, but what he was to see in California would make the plight of the Apache or Lakota appear fortunate. Whereas many had no concern at all for the welfare of those who came before them, thanks to a California law passed in 1850, others looked at these people as a chance for cheap labor. This applied to mainly children such as those above, who could be made slaves for all of their childhood, and some even beyond.

Between his arrival in San Francisco in December 1858 and his departure in July 1861, Captain Adams was to be carried by two major currents in the flow of American history. The first was his part in the handling of the Indians. In the second, his entire future, as that of the nation as a whole, would be dramatically altered by the politics of the day. Arguments still rage as to the causes of the Civil War, but regardless of individual opinions, the bottom line is that following the election of Abraham Lincoln in November of 1860, the states of the South would start down the road to dissolution. The young captain, like so many of his comrades in the Army, would be forced to choose between the land of his birth, Tennessee, which would go with the new Confederate States of America, or to remain loyal to the land he had served since he entered adulthood, the United States of America. The division was perhaps even more of a burden for Georgiana, as her family would choose to stay with the Union while her husband sided with the Confederacy.

Brigadier General John Adams, CSA

The California Indians Before 1849

We have only estimates of the population in America before 1790, white or Indian. It is even more difficult to know the population before 1492, but it is commonly believed that about 310,000 people lived in California before the first Europeans arrived. In the Northwest, that part of California where Adams would be stationed, included the Tolowa, Shasta, Karok, Yurok, Hupa Whilidut, Chilula, Chimarike and Wiyot tribes. This was a temperate rainforest. Most of these Indians inhabited the many rivers, lagoons and coastal bays. They used overland trails, but the most efficient way for them to get around was by canoe. Unlike most of the Indians throughout the Americas, these did attach importance to private property and thus had personal ownership of oak groves and fishing areas. Those tribes in the Northeast would also be in the general area of Adams' command. This included the Modoc, Achumawi, and Atsugewi tribes. To the east side of the mountains the rainfall diminished so much that much of the land was high desert. There instead of acorn and salmon, the people depended on grass seeds, tuber berries, rabbit and deer.[2]

The Spanish did not begin colonization of California until the mid eighteenth century. As was the case with the arrival of Europeans in others parts of the Western hemisphere, the introduction of new disease took the greatest toll on the first inhabitants. Some have applied the word "genocide" when explaining the rapid decline of the native population, but this does not seem likely when we consider the main objective of colonies was to make money. The Spanish had priests and monks, especially Franciscans, who saw an opportunity to find converts to Christianity, but this did not eliminate the prospect of using them for labor. The men of the robe were accompanied by soldiers who saw that the Indians provided the labor needed to tend the livestock and nurture the orchards and other crops. "Spain's Indian policy at the time of the invasion of California was a mixture of economic, military, political, and religious motives," one history book claimed. "Indians were regarded by the Spanish government as subjects of the Crown and human beings capable of receiving the sacraments of Christianity." Even those not herded into crowded and filthy labor camps found it more difficult to survive, as the introduction of European livestock and seed took a heavy toll on the aboriginal game and plants. "In 1818, Governor Vicente de

Six. California

Sola reported that 64,000 Indians had been baptized, and that 41,000 were dead."[3]

Life did not improve for the first inhabitants when California became part of the independent nation of Mexico in 1823. The Mexican government allocated additional land grants, and the populations of British and Americans increased in the far west. This generated a greater demand for horses which the Mexican ranchers capitalized on. The epidemics also continued. One plague alone claimed more than 20,000 Miwok, Yokuts, Wintun, and Maidu Indians in the Central Valley. One traveler said that "from the head of the Sacramento to the great bend and slough of the San Joaquin we did not see more than six or eight live Indians; while large numbers of the skulls and dead bodies were seen under almost every shade tree near the water, where the uninhabited and deserted villages had been converted into grave yards."

In 1837 Jose Maria Amador led a party which had been invited by the Indians to a feast of "pinole and dried meat ... the troops, the civilians, and the auxiliaries surrounded them and tied them up." As they herded about 100 "Christians ... at every half mile or mile we put six of them on their knees to say their prayers, making them understand that they were about to die. Each one was shot with four arrows.... Those that refused to die immediately were killed with spears." He went on to say, "We baptized all the Indians (non–Christians) and afterward they were shot in the back."

Frances Anne Cooper, who arrived in California with her family in 1846, said that "the Spanish vaqueros used to go up to what is now Ukiah and ride in among the Indian rancherias and drive out the boys and girls, leaving the mothers behind and killing the bucks if they offered any resistance. Then they would herd the captives down like so many cattle and sell them to the ranchers. About $100 was the standard price." Between the Spanish and Mexicans the Indian population of California had been reduced from about 310,000 to 100,000.[4]

The Americans Arrive

Frances Anne Cooper said, "The shameful treatment of the Indians by the Spanish was never equaled by the whites." Some would object to the claim. One Oustemah Nisenan named Betsy recalled, "A life of ease and peace was interrupted when I was a little girl with the arrival of the white men. Each day the population increased and the Indians feared the invaders and great consternation prevailed ... as gold excitement advanced, we were moved again and again, each time in haste." She added, "Indian children ... when taken into town would blacken their faces with dirt so the newcomers would not steal them." Regardless of which was the worse, the arrival of the Americans and the rapidly increasing population which accompanied the gold rush of 1849 brought a new phase of development to the first inhabitants. One California historian described it as "the savages were in the way; the miners and settlers were arrogant and impatient; there were no missionaries or others present with even the poor pretense of soul saving or civilizing. It was one of the last human hunts of civilization, and the basest and most brutal of them all."

The unintentional harm caused by the Spanish continued with the Americans. "The Indians had a precisely balanced relationship with the food supply. Soon after the arrival of the Americans serious depletion of the supply began to occur: mining operations adversely affected salmon fishing and destroyed fish dams." We will see that Captain Adams as well as other Army men recognized this as a big part of the problems they would have to deal with.[5]

It was nearly universal agreement by the United States Army that the Indians at the bottom of the scale were the "technologically primitive, loosely organized hunting and gathering peoples of California and the Rocky Mountains." One captain described the Indians at the mouth of the Eel River, in the general area which Adams would call home, "as low on the scale of humanity as possible to conceive, of brutish habits, hideous repulsive features, and loathsome from disease." The United States government dealt with these Indians as they did others, appointing agents, making treaties, allocating funds, and then failing to ratify said treaties.[6]

It was the same year that the gold rush began, 1849, that control of Indian affairs was transferred from the War Department to the Department of the Interior. Of five superintendents, only one was full time. Due to the invasion of fortune seekers on April 3, 1849, the Department of State appointed Thomas Butler King as special agent for California. The Department of the Interior had transferred one agent, John Wilson,

Six. California

to Salt Lake City, but the Compromise of 1850 had set the border of California much farther west, so Wilson had nothing to do with the Indians in that state. On the same day Adam Johnston had been made a subagent of the San Joaquin and Sacramento Valleys. He did not arrive until November. In his first report made in January of 1850, he said that the Mission Indians "had been unlawfully deprived of their lands and suggested that a commission be appointed to investigate and settle land titles affecting these tribes." Meanwhile, in November, the secretary of the interior had transferred the Sacramento Valley to John Sutter, the man whose mill had contained the first discovered nugget of gold. Sutter declined the position but did make some recommendations, sharing his experience in California with the government. It was September of 1850 before Congress authorized the funds and appointment of three agents. These new representatives quickly concluded that it was going to be a difficult job because of the large number of tribes scattered over the entire state. "The tribes differed greatly in economic conditions, language, manners, customs, and degree of civilization."[7]

The gold rush brought a much more varied assortment of whites than the previous Manifest Destiny had delivered to newly conquered lands. "While the mining population was made up primarily of honest men with restless and adventurous spirits, it also included a significant number of brutal and lawless individuals seeking 'easy money.' Among those were gamblers, saloon keepers, thieves, and opportunists of every type." Thus their attitudes toward the natives varied. "Some feared and others despised the Indians, and few felt that they had any rights which a white man was bound to respect." Georgiana's uncle, John McDougall, was governor in 1851, at which time he quickly chastised the Indians after the first hostilities in the Mariposa district. On March 3, 1852, Congress established an independent superintendent, Edward F. Beale. Beale continued to have problems with Congress in both obtaining funds to operate and with the ratification of treaties. In June of 1854 Beale was replaced by Thomas J. Henley. In July the Indian Appropriations Act provided for three reservations in California, but only the one at Tejon was in operation. In 1855 two more were authorized. In April of 1858, only eight months before Adams would arrive, investigations into Henley were begun; he would eventually be dismissed for misappropriation of Indian funds.[8]

Brigadier General John Adams, CSA

The most remarkable thing about the treatment of the California Indians was the Act for the Government and Protection of Indians passed on April 22, 1850, which more or less allowed the Indians to be turned into slaves. It employed euphemisms such as the "apprenticing" of Indian children, or that the "vagrant" Indians would be "hired" out to the highest bidders. This law allowed for any white person to go before the justice of the peace for the removal of Indians from white lands. The justice of the peace would also decide whether compulsory means were used to obtain children, could authorize the care of children, and could decide if an Indian would be required to work to pay off a fine. These laws were such that whites were tempted to steal Indian children. They often killed the parents in the process, or else killed parents who attempted to retrieve their stolen children. These rules of slavery were expanded in 1860. One example of the rational for such legislation was that "the children are much better off where they are, and that their removal has been beneficial to the community, since if they had remained they must have starved, unless the Indians had killed stock for them to live upon."[9]

This practice of slavery in California was in many ways worse than descriptions we have of the black slaves of the South. One study looked at 110 who were indentured, ranging in ages from two to fifty. Some were listed as "taken in war" or "prisoners of war." Ten married couples with children were listed. There were those who objected to this practice at the time. One newspaper stated, "One of the most infamous practices known to modern times has been carried on for several months past against the aborigines of California." It continued, "It has been the custom of certain disreputable persons to steal away young Indian boys and girls, and carry them off and sell them to white folks for whatever they could get." What made this practice worse than slavery in other parts of the country was that "in order to do this, they are obliged in many cases to kill the parents, for low as they are on the scale of humanity, they have that instinctive love of their offspring which prompts them to defend them at the sacrifice of their lives."[10]

The attitude of white Californians can best be summed up by their decision to deny the vote to the first Californians. As has been previously stated, there were some who believed that the Indians were not only human but should be considered citizens of the United States. The minority felt that they should extend the same right to the Indians that

Six. California

the Mexican government had, especially to those who would be taxed. The Constitution of the United States established a tradition that those Indians who were taxed were American citizens. The majority got their way with the argument that there were those who would march hundreds of ignorant Indians to the polls to vote the way they wanted them to. Thus the Indians of California retained the non-voting rights of other Indians in the United States which lasted until the Citizenship Act of 1924.[11]

In 1850 the state of California created a militia which would be used frequently against the Indians, and would also prove to be a challenge for affairs that Captain Adams would have to deal with during his post command in that state. The structure of this militia was not significantly different than in other states. The state constitution called for a militia "to execute the laws of the State, to suppress insurrections, and to repel invasions." in January of 1851 Governor Peter H. Burnett noted that by the time he took office there had been repeated calls for the militia "to resist and punish the attacks of the Indians upon the frontier." He said that "a war of extermination will continue to be waged between the races, until the Indian race becomes extinct ... while we cannot anticipate this result but with painful regret, the inevitable destiny of the race is beyond the power or wisdom of man to avert." The motivation of the governor seemed to be simply what he thought was the best economic advantage for the new state. He believed that "had it been once known to our fellow citizens east of the Rocky mountains, that the Indians were most hostile and formidable on the latter and more difficult portion of the route," it would deter future migration into the state.[12]

Captain John Adams Arrives

John and Georgiana and their family docked in San Francisco on December 15, 1858. They were accompanied by 145 recruits. These soldiers traveled on the same ship with Adams, but were not traveling with him or under his command. Five of the men were missing at the time of their arrival, typical of the problem with desertion of enlisted men. Adams guessed that they had gotten hold of civilian clothes and left the ship as private citizens. Many of the common soldiers came from the lower classes who had two months to think about their situation; however, they may have simply joined the army as a way to get to the gold fields of California. The recruits remained at the presidio of San Francisco as Adams and his family headed north toward their final destination, Fort Crook. They found themselves delayed in Red Bluff because of five foot snows. It was January 17, 1859, before the men could open a trail.[13]

Fort Crook had been established on July 1, 1857, by Capt. John W. T. Gardiner of the 1st Dragoons. He had been ordered to establish a post on the Pit River, at or near the mouth of the Fall River. It was originally named Camp Hollenbush, but was later changed to honor the lieutenant who had been wounded by a poison arrow. Crook would later become a general in the Union Army during the Civil War. This post was part of the plan to protect the new arrivals into California by way of Oregon. When Adams arrived he assumed command of companies A and F of the 1st Dragoons, numbering 99 men.

Crook offers us an example of the skills and equipment of these men as he talked about a raid he participated in that first year. "Both companies were mounted on mules, with improvised rigging, some with ropes, and others with equally, if not worse, makeshifts to fasten the saddles on the mules, and all did not have cruppers." He described the men themselves, "Many of our men were drunk, including our commander. Many of the mules were wild, and had not been accustomed to being ridden, while the soldiers generally were poor riders." Adams retained a Muchacho Indian named Richard Pugh as a guide. The collection of log buildings with adobe chimneys and hearths was set amid a pine forest and surrounded by a log stockade.[14]

Adams inherited a number of problems, including lack of supplies, less than reliable men, and a history of problems between the whites and the Indians in the area. There was even a dispute as to the property lines for the fort. Adams concluded that the problems with the Indians resulted from inadequate food supplies which caused some of the natives to kill the cattle of the whites, which in turn caused the whites to attack the Indians. No doubt the 1850 legislation which allowed for the enslavement of some of the Indians further aggravated the situation. Adams described the Indians as peaceful, friendly, and helpful, and grateful for the rations they received from the Army. He advised the government

Six. California

that it would be cheaper to continue to provide the rations rather than putting natives on the reservation. He saw the natives as being in greater danger at the hands of the whites rather than the other way around. He said, "There seems to prevail among the majority of white men in the valley and on the road to Red Bluffs a decided feeling of hostility against the Indians, so great as to render it very dangerous for the Indians to go any distance from the post."[15]

He found the buildings of the fort in good shape, but insufficient quarters for the officers. He requested the supplies to expand the living space as well as lumber to build additional bunks for the enlisted men. He also requested additional harness leather, clothing, pack saddles, rope, horse medicine, and iron. The snow continued to pile up through the winter, reaching up to fifteen feet in places. This impacted the food supplies for both the Indians and the soldiers. Rations for the natives was reduced to one quarter, while the men had an outbreak of scurvy due to the lack of vegetables. The order to prohibit loitering about the supplies reflects both the desperation and reliability of the men.[16]

In May a report was made to Adams that during the winter Indians had killed a man from Big Valley. First Lieutenant Milton Carr was sent to Hat Creek with fifteen men to search for the killers. When the inspector general visited Fort Crook he was not impressed with Carr, who had been acting commander of Company A as well as quartermaster and commissary officer of the post. The inspector's criticism was aimed at Carr's record keeping, though there was no comment on whether it was due to fraud or simply incompetence. The first outing produced no results, so Carr led a second expedition consisting of twenty men on June 4. They headed up the Pit River to Beaver Creek where some Indians were located. Apparently the killers were not identified, but some of the others offered to lead them to the guilty ones. Two men were captured and turned over to the sheriff of Shasta County. Adams and Carr reported to the government that the other Indians had been cooperative and helpful in the arrest.[17]

Meanwhile, Adams took care of the business of running the post. The inspector general, Joseph Mansfield, paid a visit. Mansfield, a fellow veteran of the Mexican War, had been appointed inspector general of the Army in 1853. Adams placed an order for barley and flour in July. In August additional recruits arrived from San Francisco, increasing

Adams' command to 140 men. Several of the men, under the command of Lieutenant Carr, were temporarily stationed on the Pit River at a place called Honey Lake Valley. They left on July 8 to the post called Camp Mackall to investigate the need for troops at Honey Lake. The orders came from the Department of California in response to a plea from the local residents for protection from pillaging Indians. The valley had about fifty to sixty families. In August, Carr reported that the Indians there were at the time peaceable, but prior to the arrival of the soldiers had stolen horses, mules, and oxen. He was of the opinion that the Indians had subsisted due to the presence of the Army and that they would resume their ways once the soldiers left. Those involved were Pi-utahs, Wass-utahs, and Goose Lake Indians.[18]

Back at the fort, Adams was taking steps to avoid the conflicts which would occupy the remainder of the year climaxing in February of 1860 with the slaughter of dozens of Indians. Adams and his men would play a role in what has become known as the Bald Hills War. The Army did not have control of the situation, and in fact Adams did his part to avert the problem. The war has been described as a conflict between the California Militia, California Volunteers, and the United States Army against the Chilula, Lassik, Hupa, Mattole, Nongatl, Sinkyone, Tsnungwe, Wailaki, Whilkut and Wiyot Indians.

Adams reported that those near Fort Crook were desperate for food, and he believed that the blame lay mainly with the whites. The cattle and activities of the white men ruined the hunting and fishing grounds of those who were there first, making it necessary for some to steal the cattle and other supplies to survive. This led to killing of the Indians. Adams reported that many of the whites were squatters who had not paid for the land or paid taxes, and that in fact the land had not even been surveyed. Adams predicted that the shortage of food could be relieved by rations to the Indians, otherwise the stealing would continue and could even lead to general warfare. He ended his report with "I repeat, it is a great deal more trouble to control the white men of the valley than the Indians."[19]

Adams' role in the story began with a report on the killing of a civilian by unidentified Indians on August 15, 1859. Adams sent Lieutenant R. Henry Brewer with twenty men to look for the guilty. They headed toward Hat Creek Station where they were joined by some men from the

Six. California

post at Honey Lake. As they pursued those guilty, a report came in that two more white men had been killed by Indians. Some Indians fired on the soldiers. Adams requested that the men under the command of Lieutenant Carr be returned to assist with the problems.[20]

Brewer and his men closed in on the suspects but due to the rocky soil and quicksand in the area they had difficulty reaching them. As the Indians fled Brewer ordered his men to fire on them, killing two. The soldiers camped on Hat Creek when men from McElroy's Ranch, searching for two men in a wagon, were supposedly attacked by Indians. The civilians assisted the soldiers in hauling up the wagon from the creek which produced two dead bodies. The civilians returned to the ranch while the soldiers searched Burney's Valley. Brewer suspected that the Indians were watching them, but they did not have further combat. They returned to Fort Crook.[21]

Adams then took a number of actions in an attempt to resolve the problems. He ordered Brewer to establish a temporary post at Hat Creek to guard and patrol the roads nearby. He then ordered Carr and his men to return from Honey Lake. He then sent the scout, Richard Pugh, with twenty dragoons and ten friendly Indians to form a search party to locate the suspects. He then advised the civilians in forming a volunteer group. By the time Carr arrived back at Fort Crook on September 2 the search party had returned empty handed. Meanwhile, the volunteers and other civilians of the valley had created such a ruckus that the Indians began to lay low. As Adams prepared a detachment of forty dragoons the Volunteers attacked a band of peaceful Indians on the Pit River.

Out of fear of retaliation by the Indians, Adams suspended the search party and stationed men at Roff's Ranch to protect the whites. He contacted Headquarters asking that they inform Governor Weller or the superintendent of Indian affairs of the behavior of the civilians. Adams recognized that he had no control over the savage whites. Apparently not all the whites approved of the treatment of the Indians and they encouraged the Volunteers to go home. Meanwhile, the California Militia arrived under the command of William Kibbe.[22]

Help arrived. While Carr was sent out with a patrol of nineteen men a detachment of Sixth Infantry under the command of Captain F. F. Flint was sent by Headquarters to the Pit River to protect the Red Bluffs and Yreka Road. Flint's orders had been to work with Adams in discovering and punishing the guilty tribes while taking care to not harm the peaceful Indians. By the end of the month Adams and Flint were satisfied that the roads were safe to travel, and thus Flint and his men departed for Benicia Barracks before the winter snows prohibited their travels.[23]

While the Army was convinced that the situation was under control, the Militia and Volunteers continued to raise hell. Adams described these men as "the worst remnant of the Pit River Volunteers." They arrested and murdered friendly Indians, and by the middle of October they had driven most of the others into the mountains. They then attempted to destroy the Indians' winter food supply. Adams reported to Headquarters that they "have refused protection to cattle herders whose property they have put in danger." He then went on to say, "They have driven the friendly Indians in the direction of the hostile ... they have never gone in search of the Indians who committed the murders." Kibbe and his men then forced four hundred or five hundred of the Indians, mostly women and children, to Mendocino. Adams again wrote to Headquarters claiming that all that the Militia and Volunteers had done is create an explosive situation that was likely to produce nothing but war. Civilians began to abandon their homes and farms out of the same anticipation.[24]

One citizen wrote to the editor of the San Francisco *Bulletin* confirming Adams' interpretation of the actions of the militia and volunteers, and especially General Kibbe. He began by claiming that McElroy was not the innocent victim the volunteers made him out to be. The author wrote, "I know he had killed one Indian and squaw and wounded a third, and the reason was that some Indians had stolen a deer from him." The writer addressed the food shortage which Adams had pointed out. Kibbe and his band bragged of the "caches" of roots and other Indian stores they had found. The citizen said "this can be explained, and with great credit to the Indians, in this way: Heretofore, these Indians have been subsisted through the winter by the United States Government. Early this spring, and throughout the summer, they were repeatedly assured that the Government would give them nothing this winter," as reported by Adams. "Thus, by hard work, they had ample supplies, that were destroyed."

Adams had made it clear that food for the winter was the source of the problems from the point of view of the Indians. The citizen also referred to guns loaned to Kibbe by the commanding officer of Fort

Six. California

Crook. "I have been informed they were lent to Frank McElroy with a perfect understanding, and repeated promises from himself, that he would not harm any of the valley Indians, but, on the other hand, intended co-operating with a detachment of dragoons which were just starting in pursuit of the very Indians who murdered his brother.... This same detachment, by the way, killed two or three Indians and wounded another, which were perhaps all the band which murdered McElroy."[25]

There was one particular incident which reveals the savagery of the volunteers. There were several Indians located at a place called Roff's Ranch. "There the 'bold' volunteers crept on them before day, and, without informing Roff or any of the cattle-herders thereabouts, marched on the ranch, killing about nine men, the balance escaping." The women and children remained, confident that an American would not harm them. "In this they were mistaken; for not only in the 'excitement' of the moment, but throughout the greater part of the day, they searched around among the 'haystocks' with the hatchet, and split the children's heads open. In this way there were over forty women and children butchered — the whites exceeding even the Indians in their butchery." This citizen also claimed the Indians that Kibbe and his friends hauled off were mostly women and children. "Nearly if not quite all the Indians removed by the 'General' were harmless." He also pointed out that the murdered McElroy was not mutilated as the volunteers had claimed, but that "he had a bullet hole through his head. If Kibbe was well posted he would know there is a heap of white Indians around," thus suggesting it may not have been an Indian at all who was guilty of the killing. The concerned citizen concluded, "As a taxpayer — and I have been one for five years — I sincerely hope that such gross injustice will not be committed as to call upon the people of California to meet the expenses of such a 'war.' When will California get rid of her great generals?'"[26]

We can only imagine what emotions Georgiana was feeling during these days. She was pregnant and on December 16, 1859, at the climax of all the excitement and killing, she gave birth to a son. Francis Joseph Adams was the name given to the child that began life in such a time and place. We do not know what assistance Georgiana had in her delivery, nor even if the baby was born on the post or perhaps in a safer location nearby. The child was in the household in the census taken in 1860, so we know the mother did not relocate back East.[27]

As winter set in, the post at Hat Creek had been abandoned. Adams did have trouble with his troops, which seemed to often be the case with the enlisted men. In addition to desertion some were charged with petty theft, such as vegetables and a pair of drawers. Other charges included sleeping on duty, and a corporal who neglected his prisoners. Adams reported that the recruits he had been sent were "a poor class of men, many of whom desert." He valued men who came from the recruiting station in Carlisle Barracks over those who joined up in California.[28]

These are the conditions in California when Adams served there. One infamous event took place on the coast at Humboldt Bay on February 26. There had been reports of the whites living in fear because of Indian attacks and nightly thefts and killing of livestock. Such reports, as well as those near Fort Crook, no doubt helped to inspire the attack which took place in February, though it has been claimed that the Indians there "killed nobody — neither women, children nor cattle; they troubled nobody, and nobody's property; they never were drunk nor drank liquor, and really were the most inoffensive and harmless Indians, perhaps, the world ever saw."

Even the eastern papers reported this crime, lacking the sympathy that those in the West may have had for the perpetrators. One said, "in the Atlantic and Western States, the Indians have suffered wrongs and cruelties at the hands of the stronger race. But history has no parallel to the recent atrocities perpetrated in California." One witness reported twenty-six bodies of women and children found in one spot, only a portion of the total of two hundred and forty. The killings were done with knives and hatchets so as not to attract attention from any living close by who might object. This was only one incident of many at the end of 1859 and going into early 1860. The Majority Report of a Joint Special Committee noted, "Accounts are daily coming in from the counties on the Coast Range, of sickening atrocities and wholesale slaughters of great numbers of defenseless Indians in the region.... Within the last four months, more Indians have been killed by our people than during the century of Spanish and Mexican domination." It concluded, "Either our government, or our citizens, or both, are to blame."[29]

Neither Captain Adams nor any of the men and officers of the United States Army were guilty of any mistreatment of the natives, if anything they struggled to protect the innocent with both food and in

Six. California

attempting to detain only those who were responsible for attacks against the settlers. A letter from Major G. J. Raines of the 4th Infantry to Lieutenant J. W. Cleary of the 6th Infantry was published in the San Francisco *Bulletin* confirming what Adams, as well as others, had identified as the main problem, the need for food. Raines said, "The Indians have been driven, as you say, from this part of the country, and your idea that they came to kill cattle, not from malice, but because they find it difficult to subsist, is probably correct."[30]

Adams did not participate in any way with the events in Humboldt Bay, and in fact after December the movements of the men at Fort Crook was limited by winter snows. He did receive a request from the citizens of Honey Lake, which had been previously evacuated. On May 10, 1860, Lieutenants Chapman and Brewer with twenty-six men from Company A left for Honey Lake. Meanwhile, Adams requested thirty new recruits from headquarters in anticipation of increased Indian activity.

Soon after the departure of the men from Fort Crook, Adams received word from Governor Isaac Roop of attacks at Susanville. One hundred and two volunteers had already given chase to the Indians before Roop asked for assistance from the United States Army. On May 18 Adams sent six additional men to Honey Lake with a message to Chapman for them to proceed to Susanville. Investigation by Chapman revealed that the Indians involved, about 1,500 warriors, were Paiutes from Utah Territory who had crossed over into California. Adams notified the Department of California that his numbers were too few to be effective on the plains which were part of the Utah Territory at the time.[31]

The Paiute War, also known as the Pyramid Lake War, took place in what is today part of Nevada, about forty miles northeast of Reno, but at the time was Utah Territory. The troubles were sparked by the same problems the white settlers in California had been dealing with, the disruption of the Indians' food supply. This included the cutting of Pinyon groves, monopolization of water, and the results of cattle grazing complicated by excessive snows in the winter of 1859 and 1860, in addition to the death of the respected chief Winnemucca. On May 6 Williams Station was burned and three Americans killed. One hundred and five men, poorly armed and completely unorganized, attacked. Seventy-six of the men were killed, though the number of Indians was probably no more than five hundred rather than the 1,500 reported by Chapman.

Department headquarters decided to use forces from other post and ordered Chapman and his men back to Fort Crook.[32]

Lieutenant Chapman began his return on May 26. In the meantime Adams ordered Lieutenant Mercer and eleven men to carry messages to the friendly Indians. Due to the hostilities he was concerned that the innocent may be killed or injured, and therefore he ordered them to stay off the roads. About the same time some of those who had been hauled off by Kibbe and his militia began to return. They announced to Adams that they could not live in Mendocino.[33]

Sergeant John Filmer and a private named Alexander Guise were attacked by Indians in another incident. The men had been sent to collect samples of natural history near Rhett and Klammath Lakes. They had stopped at a farmhouse occupied by a small family when Indians attacked. They killed two of the attackers as well as capturing twenty of their horses. They rode back to Fort Crook and reported the attack. As a result, Headquarters made plans for a post near Klammath.[34]

Meanwhile, those Indians in the Canon on the Pit River began to create a disturbance again. Adams did not have the resources to do anything about these Indians, as forty of his men had been ordered to Pyramid Lake. Thus Mercer and Brewer left Fort Crook on June 20, 1860. They remained there until August, when Chapman and a detachment were sent there as a permanent assignment. On the same day that Chapman and Company A departed, Company E of the Sixth Infantry arrived at Fort Crook from Benicia Barracks.[35]

Troubles continued as whites again attacked an innocent Indian couple who ended up being saved by more rational whites. With the arrival of the infantry, Adams was able to send a detachment to Hat Creek and Roff's Ranch. Mercer was sent to patrol the roads as well as map the area. At the end of November all the detachments were ordered in for the winter. Adams closed out his assignment to Fort Crook by taking care of routine business, which included the courts-martial of wayward recruits. Most were the typical cases of drunkenness and being absent without official leave. We do not know how much the men at Fort Crook paid attention to the national election that same month. They were in a state inhabited by settlers from the North and the South, and there were men in the fort from both the North and the South. It was the election, not the Indians, that would terminate Adams' assignment to California.[36]

Six. California

We do not know how much the election of Abraham Lincoln in November affected Adams. There is no doubt that the wilderness of northern California and the distractions created by the Indians did not keep him so far removed that he was not aware of the potential for disunion which the rest of the nation feared. President James Buchanan did not believe in secession, did not think it was right, but he did not agree with the incoming president when it came to the use of the United States Army to prevent the southern states from leaving. By the time that Lincoln was sworn in seven of the states in the Deep South had not only seceded but had formed a new nation called the Confederate States of America. Still no action.

The reasons why Lincoln and the North held on to Fort Sumter in Charleston are still debated. At the time and to this day there have been those who have argued it was so that they could claim the South started the war. The assumption was that the South could not tolerate occupation of a fort in their new sovereign nation by foreign United States troops. Regardless, the South did fire on the fort when the Navy attempted to re-provision it. With the firing and the subsequent demand for 75,000 troops, four more states joined the Confederacy and it was clear that there was going to be a war. Both sides were convinced that it would be a short war. Those in the North believed that all the Army had to do was get rid of a few fire eaters and the rest of the South would be glad to come back into the Union. Those in the South did not believe that the average Northerner would be willing to kill the former Americans rather than to allow them to go in peace. Both of these groups were wrong. In April, Major George Blake assumed command of Fort Crook. Orders were soon received from Washington requiring all officers to take an oath of allegiance again. On May 31, Adams tendered his resignation. It was not accepted until July 18.[37]

Conclusions

Adams had been dealing with American Indians since his graduation from West Point. Though the main enemy was Mexicans during his first assignment, many of those he dealt with in New Mexico were Indian. At the end of the Mexican War he was part of the occupation forces which continued to deal with the Indians. He then served in Minnesota, where he became involved with different Indians than those of the Southwest. On his return to New Mexico the only enemy were Indians. During his service prior to being transferred to California, the soldiers in the United States Army did not appear to hate Indians, nor did they take pleasure in the killing of those they went into combat against. There are many records from the officers in the Army who advised the best way to have peace with the natives: stop killing them, taking their land, and disrupting their food supply. There are many Americans to this day who are less than proud about the way the Indians were treated by the white men. Those in California seemed to have suffered even more. Perhaps it was the additional greed sparked by the seeking of gold which generated an even more savage behavior on the part of the whites. Maybe it was because they were so far from those in power in Washington, or even their fellow Americans separated by more than a thousand miles of mountains and deserts. Some spoke out against the treatment of the natives at the time, but the more savage of the white men seemed to have gotten their way more often than those interested in fairness. Now the white men would be killing each other as the nation went to war with itself.

Seven

War Begins

> Every tie that connects me with the Army has been broken, profession, kin, all the associations of my life have been given up — and not, suddenly, impulsively, but conscientiously — and after due deliberation — I was the senior major of my Regt. at the time — and the youngest man in the army for my position, and am twenty years in advance of my contemporaries— what my future may be I cannot tell. I have no expectations, I only know, I sacrifice more to my principles, than any other officer in the Army can do.[1]

These words of Edmund Kirby Smith give us a good idea of what most, if not all, of the West Point graduates and professional soldiers felt who chose to side against the flag that they had been trained to defend. Not all of the three hundred and six West Point graduates who supported the Confederacy were still in the Army in 1861, but for those men like Smith and Adams who had continued to serve their country up to the arrival of the most catastrophic event in American history, the feelings must have been even more intense. Whereas some of their classmates had found new vocations, men like Adams not only abandoned their country but also their chosen careers. This was expressed well by Richard S. Ewell, "By taking up the side of the South I forfeited a handsome position, fine pay and the earnings of twenty years hard service. All the pay I drew in four years in the South was not as much as one year's pay in the old army." They were not like laborers who gave up a job, but they gave up a profession and with it a big part of their identity.

William B. Skelton claimed that "between the Revolution and the Civil War, a military profession emerged for the first time in America." Adams had been very much a part of what Skelton described as "a military subculture ... which took shape, rooted in tightly knit garrison communities on the frontier and along the seaboards." He argued that "army life assumed a pace and a tone that would persist well into the twentieth century." John Adams was a perfect example of the profession of arms which Skelton wrote about.[2]

Slavery and the Civil War

Slavery was most likely the major cause for the secession of the first seven states following the election of Abraham Lincoln in 1860. The objective here is not to discuss the causes of the Civil War, a debate which has been going on since the war, but rather to clear some of the recent academic debris that makes it more difficult to understand men like John Adams. We do not have any documentation from the man himself, so all we can do is make an educated guess as to why he decided to give up a career he had followed in the United States Army for more than fifteen years and join the Confederate cause. It seems that the trend in recent years has been to prove that the war was over slavery and at times it seems to be due to political correctness more than academic integrity.

So many historians are intent on proving the importance of slavery that it often seems they have an agenda. Gary W. Gallagher, in his book *The Union War*, said, "Much Civil War scholarship over the past four decades has diminished the centrality of Union." He continued, "Slavery, emancipation, and the actions of black people, unfairly marginalized for decades in writings about the conflict, have inspired a huge and rewarding literature since the mid–1960s." Paul D. Escott, one of the better known historians on the subject of slavery, pointed out that "once the conflict of arms ended, a battle of words began, as each section tried to persuade the public that its version of this shared and bloody history was correct." The North quickly claimed that the emancipation of the slaves justified their participation. In his book *What Shall We Do with the Negro?*, Escott provides documentation that suggests "focusing on how Americans addressed the future of the slaves yields a darker, more disappointing, and more convoluted picture than the triumphant national narrative about breaking the bondsmen's chains." He then says that "this other picture, though less flattering and less inspiring, is more accurate and more useful for understanding our nation's history." Perhaps the most famous Southern historian, C. Vann Woodward, claimed that "the South has long served the nation in ways still in great demand. It has been a moral lightning rod, a deflector of national guilt." Mary-Susan Grant used this Woodward quote in her book *North Over South*, and then noted, "The Republicans expanded the portrayal of the South as a section antithetical to the North to one antithetical to the nation."[3]

At the vanguard of this trend are James W. Loewen and Edward H. Sebesta. In recent years they have produced the books *The Confederate and Neo-Confederate Reader: The "Great Truth" About the Lost Cause* and *Neo-Confederacy: A Critical Introduction*. The political motivation for these books is to discredit what they call neo–Confederates. They claim that "the fact that most teachers still misteach secession shows the extraordinary influence of neo–Confederate ideas even today." These men are active in the Southern Poverty Law Center and have declared that the neo–Confederates are responsible for much of the racism which remains in America today.

There is an organization, the Abbeville Institute, which has been formed to defend alternative views to Confederate history. Their own explanation for why they were founded is that "in a healthy society, education is the thoughtful enjoyment of a cultural inheritance." They go on to say we are in a culture war in which "if Southern tradition is mentioned at all, it is usually vilified as little more than a mask for racism." Eugene Genovese, who was "a northerner and a man of the left" for most of his career, said, "Rarely these days, even on southern campuses, is it possible to acknowledge the achievements of the white people of the South…. To speak positively about any part of this southern tradition is to invite charges of being a racist and an apologist for slavery and segregation." He said this culture war by the media and "academic elite [strips] young white southerners, and arguably black southerners as well, of their heritage, and, therefore, their identity."[4] Michael E. Woods has an excellent essay in the September 2012 edition of *The Journal of American History*. At first he confirms that the trend among professional historians is to accept the idea advocated by Loewen and Sebesta, that the war was about slavery. "By the dawn of the twenty-first century, a broad consensus regarding Civil War causation clearly reigned. Few mainstream scholars would deny that Abraham Lincoln got it right in his second inaugural address— slavery was 'somehow' the cause of the war."

He supports this position by citing James McPherson and Charles Joyner. Then he discusses some more current literature and in the end concludes, "There is not much of a consensus after all." This may signal a change in the profession that would cut down some on political correctness and put us back on an academic track. He adds, "Recent work on the topic reveals two widely acknowledged truths: that slavery was at the heart of the sectional conflict and that there is more to learn about precisely what this means, not least because slavery was always a multifaceted issue."[5]

The April 2011 edition of the *Magazine of History*, published by the Organization of American Historians, was dedicated to the origins of the Civil War. This magazine deserves our attention here not only because it reflects the latest trends among professional historians, but this publication is aimed at secondary education. Therefore it is what is promoted by the profession to be passed on to the next generation of Americans, most of whom study no more than high school level history. Matthew Pinsker says in the foreword, "What follows are a series of historical claims and counter-claims— all grounded in evidence and argued with a high degree of professionalism — without any easy consensus emerging in standard textbook fashion ... the question of what caused the war has provoked more arguments than almost any other in American history." He says of the five articles presented, "None are in full agreement about anything except perhaps the principle that good history is complicated and always requires careful attention to facts, evidence, and the ever-elusive mysteries of human behavior." It is refreshing to see that the interpretations of the causes of the war are moving back to academic rather than political. This is important if we are to understand military men such as John Adams.[6]

Many of their former classmates and countrymen would label the West Point Confederates as rebels and traitors. This no doubt made their choice that much more difficult. However, as stated by Gerard A. Patterson, "without their assistance, there is no doubt that the Confederacy could never have fielded forces of the military caliber and proficiency of the Army of Northern Virginia and the Army of Tennessee." It is hard to believe that slavery was the main concern for most of these men. Since they were in the military, very few of them had any demand for slave labor. Some came from families which did, but most did not.

One aspect of states' rights is that in 1860 many Americans thought

Seven. War Begins

of their state as their homeland. Robert E. Lee did not chose a different country than his father, the Revolutionary War General Lighthorse Harry Lee. Robert fought for the same country that his father did, their home state of Virginia. Adams, like Lee, spent most of the years after his graduation from West Point in assorted locals outside the land of his birth, but regardless, both of these men appeared to see their home state as their country. There are few today who look at the world the way these men did, which makes it difficult for us to understand their thinking. As stated by Richard Ewell, "It is hard to account for my course, except from a painful sense of duty; I say painful, because I believe few were more devoted to the old country than myself.... It was death to me." This was a big part of states' rights in 1860.[7]

Those who made up this new professional officer corps came from various parts of the United States, and therefore the individuals came into the Army with assorted regional biases. Ever since the Civil War, people from the South, as well as the North, have accepted the belief that most of the West Point graduates came from the North. There is some truth to this when one considers the percentage of the total population, but it appears to have been exaggerated. In 1860, 56 percent of West Point graduates came from the North while 43 percent came from the South, the balance being foreign born. Clearly a minority which came from the South, but when we consider that at the time only 30 percent of the white population lived in the South, then that region was well represented. When it comes to mounted soldiers there is a more unequal distribution. Sixty percent came from the South. The Confederacy definitely had a cavalry advantage.[8]

Whereas there is no doubt that many in the Deep South were motivated to secede due to their concern about the future of slavery, Adams did not come from the Deep South. He was born in the state of Tennessee, and that is where he returned after resigning his commission in the United States Army. In the beginning of the war it is in the Upper South where he participated. This is another important reason to shed some of the recent bias in academia. We will not be able to understand places such as Tennessee and Kentucky if we allow our vision to be clouded by political correctness.

A recent publication, *American Nations: A History of The Eleven Rival Regional Cultures of North America*, by Colin Woodard, helps explain the distinction between the Deep South and that land which Adams hailed from. In his introduction he began by discussing the modern division between the red states and blue states. He then points out that this is nothing new. "Americans have been deeply divided since the days of Jamestown and Plymouth. The original North American colonies were settled by people from distinct regions of the British Islands, and from France, the Netherlands, and Spain, each with their own religious, political, and ethnographic characteristics." He continued, "Throughout the colonial period, they regarded one another as competitors—for land, settlers, and capital—and occasionally as enemies." He pointed out that the colonies were being established at the time of the English Civil War "when Royalist Virginia stood against Puritan Massachusetts." He sees a total of eleven nations in what is today the United States, and though the Civil War was primarily between those in the South versus the North, there are other conflicts going on also. His thesis is that the conflicts we are in today are based on the past. "Divisions are not between red states and blue states, conservatives and liberals, capital and labor, blacks and whites, the faithful and the secular. Rather, our divisions stem from this fact: the United States is a federation comprised of the whole or part of eleven regional nations, some of which truly do not see eye to eye with one another."[9]

If Woodard is correct, this changes the way many of us look at America. This is one of the problems with the concept of American Exceptionalism. A major assumption made by believers of this is that there is a great meaning and purpose to the United States. This makes it so that the competitive nations Woodard is talking about want to believe that their set of values is what the whole nation is about. When the North won the war, they won this claim. In justifying this war on the grounds of battling slavery then, this has become an important part of the post 1865 interpretation of what the United States is all about. This is why the North is good and the South is bad. As Woodard said, "The related intra national struggle to control and define the federal government triggered the Civil War." This seems to have continued in the desire to make the war about slavery, and defining the regions in terms of being for or against the institution.[10]

If we accept Woodard's view, then debate about what the war was about, or what caused it, is not a matter of the traditional debates between slavery, or states' rights, or a struggle between Celts and Anglo-Saxons, or Roundheads and Cavaliers. It was not even a simple struggle between North and South, which he said are "two regions that, culturally and politically, didn't actually exist." He said, "The Civil War was ultimately a conflict between two coalitions. On one side was the Deep South and its satellite, Tidewater; on the other, Yankeedom. The other nations wanted to remain neutral, and considered breaking off to form their own confederations." If Woodard is correct, then it brings into question many important issues in American history today. This would include localism versus centralism, Southern identity, Northern identity, why Northerners hated Southerners, and of course the causes of the Civil War.[11]

If we can set aside ideas of American exceptionalism and look at what is going on in the rest of the Western world at the same time, then we can see that the Civil War was part of the universal struggle of centralism versus localism. The merchants of the European empires found strong central governments beneficial in world market competition. There was no unified Germany until the mid nineteenth century. Nor was there a unified Italy. Graham Robb wrote about how the various regions of France were "mapped, colonized by rulers and tourists, refashioned politically and physically, and turned into a modern state." His book *The Discovery of France* did for that country what Woodard did for the United States. France is not just one nation either. Even England was still in the process of creating Great Britain from many of the same diverse peoples who migrated to the colonies. In all of these cases there was some resistance by those who did not want to surrender their local culture to the one who would dominate the new unified nation, whether that be Berlin, Paris, Rome, or London.[12]

If one accepts Woodard's thesis, then it also goes far to address the question of Southern identity. Several of his nations, or parts of them, became part of the Confederacy, including Tidewater, Deep South, New France, Greater Appalachia, and El Norte. So, to those historians who talk about "Southern identity," it seems Woodard would agree. The war forced these nations into an alliance. The "Lost Cause Myth" would have been the result of the experience that all of these people shared as they were invaded by the Union. It would make perfect sense that the idea of "the South" did not exist until after the war. As he said, "Most people in the South shared the Deep Southerners' credo of white supremacy and their distrust of Yankees, but many disagreed with their ideal of an aristocratic republic." This also helps to explain that the Confederacy was not created all at once, and not everyone in that new nation agreed with breaking away from the Union.[13]

Likewise, the other side was not all in agreement with what Woodard labeled Yankeedom, comprised of the New England states. "Indeed, prior to the South Carolinian militia's assault of Fort Sumter, Yankeedom was isolated, lacking a single national ally in its desire to put down the Deep Southern rebellion by force." When the war was over those who had been on one side created the "Lost Cause Myth," while those who had been on the other side rallied around their new identity of the "Union."[14]

Mary-Susan Grant wrote about the rise of Northern Nationalism in her book *North Over South*. In the first chapter she argues, "Many of the current theories that prevail concerning European nationalism can be equally applied to the American case." In the second chapter she traces the development of the North between 1820 and 1860. "It uncovers the background of the northern critique of the South and shows that this, ironically, had its origins in a national outlook that, over time, became entrenched in a sectional ideology." She then points out that this ideology "was not national at all but was predicated on opposition to the South." In the third chapter she "examines the emergence of a much more vociferous northern critique of the South, showing how and why this grew in force during the 1840s in response to the Mexican War and to northern ideas about the slave power of the South." It seems she might agree with some of Woodard's views. Another way of looking at this is that the northern nationalism was based on a hatred of the South.[15]

It is after the Mexican War that the issue of slavery became more important in the struggle between the Deep South and Yankeedom in determining the future of the Union. Many of those in the other nations to the North were not as concerned as those in Yankeedom, as Woodard pointed out. By 1860 the concern about the "Slave Power" had increased. Kenneth Stampp observed that those in the other states, or what Woodard called nations, began to change after the Dred Scott case and agreed with the view in the *Cincinnati Daily Commercial*, a non-abolitionist paper, that "there is such a thing as THE SLAVE POWER." According

Seven. War Begins

to Woodard, "Yankee abolitionists argued that the Deep South and Tidewater were autocratic despotisms." As more and more of those to the north agreed with this view, slavery became more and more important. The abolitionist view, according to Stampp, was that the Slave Power had three goals, "to re-open the slave trade; to extend the institution of slavery ... ; and to remove from the free white man those constitutional and traditional guarantees of liberty which stood in the way of the exercise of control over the middle and lower classes."[16]

Grant offered a good bibliography on the development of northern nationalism and the hatred of the South. She began by discussing Patrick Gerster and Nicholas Cords, who "observed that the subject of the northern origins of the southern myth 'has seldom been given more than passing attention.'" Grant also mentioned Eric Foner, who "uncovered evidence that supported his contention that northerners—particularly Republicans—were overtly hostile toward the South." She spoke of Howard Floan in his study *The South in Northern Eyes*, and how "most antebellum northerners ... knew little about the South and cared less." New Englanders, or Yankeedom, "succeeded in convincing many antebellum northerners of the backwardness of life in the South; that image has had a pernicious influence ever since." Later Grant said, "It is evident that northerners, no less than southerners, were engaged in a quest for self-definition that ultimately led to the development of an ideology predicated not on the American nation but on the northern one." Almost sounds like something Woodard would say.

Major General Isaac Ridgeway Trimble, like Adams, had no personal investment in slavery. This man was from a Quaker family, never owned a slave, and lived most of his adult life in Baltimore. He wrote in his diary that Northerners hated the South and drove it from the Union by their "bigotry & hatred of everything southern." Even the famous carpetbagger Albion W. Tourgée realized, "That was our mistake. We tried to superimpose the civilization, the idea of the North, upon the South at a moment's warning.... It was a Fool's Errand."[17]

Slavery became an important issue in determining which nation would dominate and determine the future of the Union. Abolition was not the purpose of the war. As stated by Gallagher, "Almost all Democrats and some Republicans initially expressed strong opposition to freeing slaves and arming black men, but military events changed their attitudes." Yankeedom had convinced their allies that the Slave Power was the problem, so that "a struggle for a different kind of Union emerged, support for which sprang from related impulses to win the war, punish oligarchic slaveholders, and remove the irritant that had vexed the nation from 1787 to 1860." Secession probably started over slavery, at least for the first seven states, but the war was over union, which is the concept of nationalism.[18]

Woodard agreed, "There is no question that the Deep South seceded and fought the Civil War to defend slavery, and its leaders made no secret of this motive." That is not why the four states of the Upper South joined. To make a long story short, after Lincoln's call for 75,000 troops, Tennessee Senator A. O. P. Nicholson exclaimed, "It is no longer the Negro question but a question of resistance to tyranny." No doubt many of those in the Deep South who did not initially support the idea of secession changed their view at that time also.

Likewise, Yankeedom saw slavery as a critical issue, but "whatever qualms Americans had about slavery in the 1850s, most people living outside of Yankeedom were willing to overlook it and the issues it raised." Throughout the war there were many in the South who resisted Southern independence, and throughout the North there were those who objected to the war. In the 1864 presidential election, 45 percent voted against Lincoln, and most historians seem to agree that had Atlanta not fallen in August, McClellan probably would have won the election.[19]

Regardless of the role that slavery played in the Deep South seceding, Lincoln made it clear the war had nothing to do with slavery. Loewen and Sebesta, and many other historians, like to talk about his second inaugural where Lincoln said, "All knew that this interest was somehow the cause of the war." They seem to go out of the way to ignore what he said in his first address, "I have no purpose, directly or indirectly, to interfere with the institution of slavery in the states where it exists." He was a lawyer and knew the Constitution protected the institution. "I believe I have no lawful right to do so, and I have no inclination to do so." He told Horace Greeley, "My paramount object in this struggle is to save the Union, and is not either to save or to destroy slavery."[20]

Congress also made it clear early on that they were not fighting a war to interfere with slavery, not even those in the Republican Party. "Party members reaffirmed that stance in July 1861 when, overwhelmingly, they supported a resolution put forth by John Crittenden of Kentucky. It declared that 'this war is not prosecuted ... for any purpose of conquest or ... interfering with the rights of established institutions of those [Southern] States.'" The House approved the statement 117–2, and the Senate 30–5. So, neither the president nor the Congress were fighting a war to end slavery. At least that is what they said.[21]

As the war progressed it moved toward the abolition of slavery; shortly after the war was over the Thirteenth Amendment was passed. As Gallagher put it, "A struggle for a different kind of Union emerged, support for which sprang from related impulses to win the war, punish oligarchic slaveholders, and remove the irritant that had vexed the nation from 1787 to 1860." He later referred to what he called "the Appomattox syndrome.... The surrender of Lee's army effectively ended a war that both restored the Union and destroyed slavery: therefore, it seems logical that a war begun to save the Union had been transformed into a war for Union and emancipation as equally worthy outcomes."[22]

Regional bias existed at West Point as it did in the rest of the nation, but there does seem to have been a level of tolerance that came with being part of the same profession. J.E.B. Stuart noted, "But we are far from entertaining towards each other as marked antipathy as the times would suggest were we 'cits,' but there seems to be a sentiment of mutual forbearance, in a word, with us all is harmony." During the times of tense national conflicts efforts had to be made to maintain this harmony, but even during the critical Kansas-Nebraska crisis the men tried to maintain a neutral policy. After the election in November of 1860 up until the summer of 1861, this military regional tolerance evaporated. A total of 269 regulars, or 24.7 percent of the officer corps, chose the path that Adams did. This is far from a majority of professional officers. For those of the highest rank, that is the generals, the percentage was greater. This was also true when comparing the regions within the South. Those who came from the Deep South went with the Confederacy at a higher rate than those of the upper South.[23]

As to the officers in the field, Richard Ewell agreed with Stuart. When he received news about South Carolina, he wrote to his niece, "Every one here is on the tenter hooks of impatience to know what the Southern States will do." He continued, "Officers generally are very much averse to any thing like civil war, though some of the younger ones are a little warlike." In his view, "the truth is in the army there are no sectional feelings and many from extreme ends of the Union are the most intimate friends."[24]

Tennessee Becomes Confederate

Though the seven slave states which formed the Confederate States of America were concerned about the future of the institution of slavery, when Lincoln took office there were eight slaves states plus the Indian Territory which remained loyal to the Union. Tennessee was not one of those first seven states motivated to secede over slavery. The Confederate States did not declare war, only independence.

Lincoln took the position that the attack on Fort Sumter was an attack on the Union, and many accept this to be true today. However, even his contemporaries recognized that this fort, which was occupied by the United States Army, was in the newly independent state of South Carolina. This is why those such as John Shipley Tilley, in his book *Lincoln Takes Command*, have looked at the continued occupation of Fort Sumter, as well as a handful of other forts, as an attempt to entice the South to fire the first shot. The Union evacuated most other forts in the South, and so it does seem possible that Sumter was occupied as bait. Whether one accepts this thesis or not, the only thing about the firing on Fort Sumter that can be said for certain is that some in the South did not think that a foreign nation should occupy a fort on their soil. It is doubtful that the newly independent United States would have accepted the continued occupation of forts after declaring independence from Great Britain; why should the newly declared independent Confederate States be expected to tolerate such a thing? The attack on Fort Sumter was an attempt to get United States troops out of a Confederate Fort, but this does not mean that it was a declaration of war on the United States. There were those in the South and North who did not approve of the firing on Fort Sumter, and there can be a good case made for the claim that these first shots were the point of no return. Many have said that when the South did this, it was as an act of war, but the fact remains there is no proof that it would not have ended there if the North had simply withdrawn from the fort on Southern soil.

Seven. War Begins

All we can do is to assume that Adams' thinking was very much along the lines of others from the state of Tennessee. Therefore we need to understand what happened in that state. He did not resign his commission until after his home state joined the Confederacy, and when he went east he returned to his home state of Tennessee. In that state, some advocated secession early on, but this was not accepted by the majority of the population. It was not until after the firing on Fort Sumter and the U.S. government's subsequent demand for 75,000 troops that Tennessee seceded.

On December 20, 1860, South Carolina was the first to secede from the Union. On January 7, 1861, Governor Isham G. Harris called a special assembly of the legislature of the state of Tennessee. It is clear from his speech at that assembly that he favored secession. He referred to the "systematic, wanton, and long continued agitation of the slavery question." He proceeded to go into great detail on each and every issue he could think of in which the northern states took a stand against slavery or else the spread of slavery into the territories, from the Kansas situation to the John Brown raid. It is clear that if it were not for his concern over slavery he would not be proposing secession. However, his view was based on his interpretation of the Constitution. It is a fact that the Constitution protected slavery. It is also true, as argued by Harris, that failure to enforce the fugitive slave laws was unconstitutional. This is what agitated many in the North, especially those with a leaning toward abolition. He believed that with the attacks on slavery and failure to enforce the fugitive slave laws, the Northern states were not abiding by the Constitution. This is why he came up with a list of amendments to the Constitution which he believed would save the Union and preserve the rights of the Southern states. Each of these proposed amendments revolved around the subject of slavery, again an example of the importance of slavery. However, this does not negate states' rights. He started by pointing out that "previous to the adoption of the Federal Constitution, each State was a separate and independent government — a complete sovereignty within itself — and in the compact of union, each reserved all the rights and powers incident to the sovereignty, except such as were expressly delegated by the Constitution to the general government."

In summary, he pointed out that the Constitution protected slavery and supported fugitive slave laws, and thus the position of South Carolina and the position of Harris was that the North was not abiding by the Constitution. He also believed that the states were sovereign. That is, the issue was states' rights. It is true that he was concerned about slavery, but he was defending slavery on the principle of states' rights.[25]

Though the governor was in favor of secession, when he and his fellow secessionists called for a special vote in February of 1861, it was rejected by a margin of 54 to 46 percent. From these facts it is clear that for many people in the state of Tennessee slavery was a major reason for them to want to secede from the Union. It is a logical assumption that Harris represented a popular belief among the secessionists, since politicians win elections because they are good at voicing the opinions of their constituency. The bottom line is that even though a large number supported the idea of secession, the majority did not. It is also a fact that slavery was an important issue to secessionists such as Governor Harris; however, this does not mean that states' rights was not the overriding issue.

Although men like Harris advocated secession out of concern of the future of slavery, that is not what brought about the secession of the state of Tennessee. Tennessee, along with Virginia, North Carolina, Arkansas, and the Indian Territory did not secede until after the firing on Fort Sumter, and more importantly after Lincoln's demand for 75,000 troops. This indicates that there were other issues at stake in addition to slavery. Just as the situation changed in these four states and Indian Territory, it is safe to assume that there were others in the Deep South who later supported secession who did not do so prior to these events. Historian Daniel W. Crofts stated it clearly, "In March, Congressman Horace Maynard, the unconditional Unionist and future Republican from East Tennessee, felt assured that the administration would pursue a peaceful policy. Soon after April 15, a dismayed Maynard reported that 'the President's extraordinary proclamation' had unleashed 'a tornado of excitement that seems likely to sweep us all away.'" Crofts went on to quote Maynard that men who had "heretofore been cool firm and Union loving," had become "perfectly wild" and were "aroused to a frenzy of passion."

Over the years many have suggested that those 75 percent of Southerners who were not slave owners may have dreamed of becoming a slave owner. This may be true, and is the stuff of which historical debate is

Seven. War Begins

made. However, another possibility is that they saw the actions of Lincoln and the Northern radicals as an attack on all things Southern. Maynard went on to point out that those previous Union supporters now asked themselves what could such an Army want "but to invade, overrun, and subjugate the Southern states," so that now they felt that they should "fight for our hearthstones and the security of home." This is totally consistent with the earlier discussion about Colin Woodard and how the firing on Fort Sumter polarized the other "nations."[26]

The situation changed in Tennessee after April 15. Harris called for another meeting an April 25. The speech he made then did not mention slavery, but was dominated by discussion of Constitutional rights and defense from invasion. He referred to the "tyrannical policy of the Presidential usurper fully before us; in the face of his hordes of armed soldiery, marching to the work of Southern subjugation." In May, Governor Harris and the Tennessee General Assembly formed a military league with the Confederate States of America and took other measures to align themselves with the Confederacy. On June 8 the people of Tennessee voted in favor of secession by 69 percent to 31 percent. There were several counties in the eastern part of the state which remained Unionist and would even provide Union troops during the war, but the state in general went Confederate. There are arguments in the modern debates over the causes of the Civil War which point out the fact that there were those who opposed secession, as if it somehow proves something. It is true that all of the Southern states, even in the Deep South, had some loyal unionists in their populations. However, each of the Northern states had people who opposed Mr. Lincoln's war. The only thing this proves is that not everyone approved of the events taking place in any given state or region.[27]

As tensions increased between the election in November of 1860 and the firing on Fort Sumter in April 1861, Adams was busy with the Indian situation in California. We do not know how much, how accurate, or how timely was the news that arrived in far northern California. There is no doubt that the news reached there. With the Pony Express news about the election of Lincoln reached San Francisco seven days and seventeen hours after it hit the East Coast. We do not know how much such things were discussed or debated among the other men who served with him in the Army. We do not have any direct quotes from him or anyone in his family, so we can only assume that he was typical. All that we do know is that it was not until May 31 that he resigned his commission. This would be after the April assembly, but before the popular vote. We know for certain he did resign and join the Confederate cause. He was not a slave owner and we have no record of his concern about the future of slavery. He did not resign until after Fort Sumter and the secession of his home state, which suggest that this was his main reason. This is not proof, so we are left with only assumption as to his motivation.[28]

His career and his identity to home were very much intertwined with his family, as was the case with most of the other officers. Skelton concluded, "A look at the officers who were most prominent in bucking their sectional trends gives further confirmation of the primacy of family as an influence on officers' decisions." Skelton also believed that "for most army officers, as no doubt for most nineteenth-century Americans, the constitutional question of states' rights versus federal supremacy was less central than traditional loyalties rooted in kinship and locality." He went on to say, "When push finally came to shove during the secession winter and spring, relatively few regulars were sufficiently committed to their profession — or to the nation in the abstract — to pit themselves against their families and home communities."[29]

We do not have any documentation on the attitudes of Adams' family. We know that his brother, Thomas, who was not a professional Army man, ended up on his staff in Memphis. We know he had at least one cousin who served with him. We know that his wife's family remained loyal to the Union. His father-in-law, whom he had served with in New Mexico and Minnesota, was medical director for the Army of the Tennessee and was brevetted a brigadier-general on March 13, 1865. His brother-in-law, Thomas Mower McDougall, at the age of eighteen, was appointed second lieutenant in the 10th Louisiana Volunteers of African Descent, later redesigned the 48th Colored Infantry, a Union regiment. Therefore, every indication is that his family was pro Confederate and that his wife's family remained loyal to the Union.[30]

As the decision to leave the Union varied from one individual to another, so did the issue of a divided family. Some never spoke with the wayward relatives, while others did not let it interfere with family ties. We do not know many details on how this familial division affected

Seven. War Begins

Adams, but the facts we do have suggest that the divide was not so great as to result in the McDougall family disowning their daughter. We see that during the war she gave the family name to a newborn child, and after the war, the widow Georgiana and her children lived with her parents.

Home to Tennessee

Adams had made up his mind to fight for the Confederate cause, but since he was in California it was early August of 1861 before he arrived in the East. John, his four sons, and his pregnant wife, Georgiana, arrived on August 2. They must have gone by way of Panama since the record for sailing all the way around South America was still 89 days set by the *Flying Cloud* in 1854. On August 5, after their arrival in New York but before they reached Tennessee, Winfield Scott advised William Seward, secretary of state, that "among the persons who have just arrived at New York from California, mentioned in the newspaper slip enclosed ... I think it desirable that John Adams, a native of Tennessee, who recently resigned a captaincy in the U.S. First Regiment of Dragoons, be arrested and held a political prisoner." He went on to say, "I do not doubt that he designs to take service in the rebel army against us."

Those who had resigned their commission earlier and were already active in the Confederate Army did not have to face this challenge. The suspension of habeas corpus had been done as early as the riots in Baltimore in April; however, by August this practice had extended well beyond that city. Those arrested or threatened with arrest included military officers, political leaders, newspaper editors, and even President Franklin Pierce and Chief Justice Roger B. Taney. Estimates have ranged from 13,000 to as high as 38,000. Some have put most of the blame on Seward rather than Lincoln for this infringement of not only the Constitution of the United States but of a right protected by English law since the Magna Carta of 1215, or at least not long after that. Seward bragged to Lord Lyons, the British minister in Washington, "I can touch a bell on my right hand and order the imprisonment of a citizen of Ohio; I can touch a bell again and order the arrest of a citizen of New York; and no power on earth, except the President, can release them. Can the

Brigadier General John Adams, CSA

Winfield Scott, credited by some with the creation of the modern military. He served his country since the War of 1812, but was too aged to do much more than advise during the Civil War. Although a Southerner himself, he sided with the North. He recommended the arrest of Adams upon his arrival in New York in August of 1861 (Library of Congress).

Seven. War Begins

Queen of England do so much?" We do not know if Seward tried to follow through on Scott's recommendation. We do know that Adams reached Tennessee by August 8 without being arrested.[31]

In the beginning of the war most had interest in the East, especially after Virginia joined the Confederacy and the capital was moved to Richmond; however, after September 3, 1861, things did begin to develop in the West when Major General Leonidas Polk occupied Columbus, Kentucky. Two days later Union brigadier general Ulysses S. Grant seized Paducah, Kentucky. He then requested permission from the theater commander, Major General John C. Frémont, to attack the Confederates in Columbus.[32]

Leonidas Polk was descended from a wealthy and prominent family, and related to President James K. Polk. A West Point graduate, he resigned six months after graduation to study in the Episcopal ministry, being appointed bishop of Louisiana in 1841. Jefferson Davis, a former classmate, persuaded him to accept a commission as major general on June 25, 1861. When Polk occupied Columbus, Kentucky, on September 4, he hurt the Confederate cause in the area. On September 15 Albert Sydney Johnston replaced him.[33]

The situation in Kentucky is another good example of how the modern morality interpretations complicate the understanding of events. By looking at the Civil War as a crusade against slavery, it is easy to ignore the fact that the slave state of Kentucky not only remained loyal to the Union, but continued to have slavery until the end of the war and the ratification of the Thirteenth Amendment. If the Civil War really was a crusade against slavery the rational person would ask, "Why did the Union continue to have slaves?" Most of the slave owners in Kentucky believed the future of the institution was kept safer by remaining loyal.

On December 9, 1860, Governor Beriah Magoffin proposed a conference of the slave states. Though Kentucky's governor was pro Confederate, he endorsed an official position of neutrality of the state after the firing on Fort Sumter. Therefore, when Polk captured Columbus, he threatened Kentucky's neutrality, which upset many of those previously sympathetic. On October 29, 1861 63 delegates from 34 counties met to discuss the formation of a Confederate government, which was eventually accepted as a Confederate state; however, most in Kentucky remained Unionist and even more were alienated by Polk's invasion.

Although Kentucky is one of the stars on the Confederate flag, according to Lincoln and most historians, it remained a Union state.[34]

Meanwhile, Albert Sydney Johnston arrived in Richmond from California. Johnston had earned quite a reputation beginning with the Black Hawk War, going through the Texas Revolution and Mexican War, and the Mormon War. He was commander of the United States Army Department of the Pacific in California at the same time that Adams was there. When his adopted state of Texas seceded he marched east as a soldier with the Los Angeles Mounted Rifles, leaving May 27, 1861. Many respected Johnston's abilities, though today some do not accept Jeff Davis's claim that he was "the greatest soldier, the ablest man, civil or military, Confederate or Federal, then living." The reactions to Polk's occupation of Columbus convinced Davis it was a good idea to put Johnston in charge in the west.[35]

The Battle of Belmont was the first contest for Grant on November 7, 1861. On November 6 he traveled by riverboat from Cairo to position himself to attack Polk at Columbus. He learned the next day that the Confederates had crossed over to Belmont, Missouri, another one of the slave states that remained loyal to the Union. At first he overran the Confederates; however, they reorganized, and with reinforcements from Columbus they forced Grant back to his boats and then back to Paducah.[36]

This is what was going on when Adams joined the action. President Davis accepted Adams into the Provisional Army of the Confederate States with a commission as a captain in the cavalry. He was given command of a post in Memphis as his first assignment, being under the direct command of Leonidas Polk. At the time of his arrival, by November of 1861, the city was still peaceful, but was destined to soon be on the front. The first year of the war was very much a learning curve for both sides. Adams assumed command of men who had not yet been well trained and they were not well armed. The vast majority of the men on the side of the Union were just as green; however, the Confederate military, unlike the United States military, was brand new and lacked a developed command structure. It also lacked even the basics of supply lines.

We can see why some say that if it had not been for the experienced men such as Adams who had gone to the gray, it is likely that the war would not have lasted as long as it did. The Confederates did share with the Union Army the fact that not all of their citizens supported this war

Seven. War Begins

which was just starting to heat up; however, the Confederates would soon have to start dealing with the fact that increasingly larger chunks of their new nation would fall under enemy control. In the records of Adams' command during his stay in Memphis, we see that he was expected to do recruiting and training and forage for supplies, not only for his men but for the Confederate Army in general, provide hospital care for the wounded and take command of prisoners from the Union Army. He retained this command until April of 1862.[37]

The people of the South suffered considerably by the war's end in 1865, but they

John Adams as he appeared in the Civil War.

began sacrificing from the very start. Today the United States military is involved in operations around the world, but it has a well developed infrastructure which provides housing, food, clothing, weapons and medical care and is set up to exercise control over prisoners of war. The Confederacy was new, the Army was new, and thus their organization was new. In addition, it depended on the support of a civilian population, many of whom were not all that convinced of the cause from the start. As hardships on themselves and families increased, support for that cause declined, which was expressed in various ways such as food riots and desertion. Some not only deserted but joined the pro Union forces. It is popular today to emphasize the problems for the Confederates and lack of civilian support; however, the Union also suffered many of the same problems from the very start. Whereas the Confederates had to deal with maintaining support from the civilian population as it fell under Union occupation, the Union had to worry about the attitudes of an occupied population. Union brigadier general Albin Francisco Schoepf pointed out in a report dated November 2, 1861, "The county of Laurel will not supply forage for more than 10 to 20 days, and even now utmost dissatisfaction prevails among the inhabitants."

At this point the Union troops were in Kentucky about to begin their attacks on Forts Donelson and Henry in Tennessee. The United States Army may have been better established than the Confederate, but they too depended on local food supplies to support their troops. General Schoepf reported, "We are taking at the point of the bayonet what the citizens really need for the support of their families, without returning to them anything available therefore; thus turning against us a public sentiment which we should endeavor to cherish." So both sides had to deal with a civilian population often concerned more with personal survival or the welfare of their families.[38]

In addition to the lack of weapons and ammunition, food, clothing, and supplies, they also had to deal with issues such as sickness or lack of commanders. More soldiers died from disease than from battle wounds. On November 6, Confederate brigadier general Lloyd Tilghman reported 750 sick, "owing, I suppose, to this terrible weather." The troops were green and they lacked those of officer caliber who could train them and who could command them. Tilghman noted this lack of leadership: "I need not only more force, but I need some person besides myself to rely on in case of an accident." This is another good example of why men like Adams were so important to the Southern cause. He went on, "They are good men, but with no military knowledge. The raw troops are very raw, and it will take good handling to make them at all steady under the first fire in action." No doubt this is the kind of thing that McClellan saw in the Union Army which made him so hesitant to march his men into combat too early.[39]

Such are the conditions Adams faced setting up his command in Memphis. He started receiving prisoners in early November. At first he used a large cotton warehouse, perhaps arranged with the assistance of his brother, who was a cotton merchant in that city. He reported that "the owner of the cotton warehouse objects so much to their occupying his house that I have determined to move them as soon as possible to a more convenient and equally secure place." The building had a large yard with high thick walls.

For guards Adams only had twenty-four privates, two commis-

Seven. War Begins

sioned officers and three non-commissioned officers, all taken from the home guard. On the care of prisoners, he said that the provision would be provided by the government as well as a servant to wait on the officers. The first Union prisoners Adams received were taken at the Battle of Belmont on November 7, which consisted of 93 privates and 4 commissioned officers. Of the home guard, Adams mentioned that the they "all have families and subsist themselves." He also pointed out that "a great many of them depend upon their labor for support." A few days later he moved the prisoners to a new location due to the complaints from the cotton merchant. He found a house he described as "the only suitable one in the city." He suggested to his superiors that they relocate the prisoners to Baton Rouge, where it would be easier and less expensive to maintain them.[40]

When Johnston assumed command in the West he had 40,000 men spread throughout Kentucky, Tennessee, Arkansas and Missouri. Though men were short of arms and supplies in the West, priority continued to be given to the East. Pierre Gustave Beauregard was sent and arrived at Johnston's headquarters at Bowling Green on February 4 and was given command of Polk's forces. Beauregard, of Louisiana, "the hero of Sumter" and one of the commanders at First Manassas, was second in command to Johnston.[41]

On December 20, Grant's command was renamed the District of Cairo. He began a campaign against Forts Henry and Donelson in February of 1862 with about 27,000 men. Grant proceeded south on the Tennessee River; however, on February 6 Fort Henry surrendered to a United States flag officer, Andrew H. Foote, commander of the Western flotilla. Grant's troops continued on to Fort Henry overland where they joined up with additional troops arriving by boat. Fighting began on February 13 and by February 16 the fort on the Cumberland met Grant's terms of unconditional surrender.[42]

Following the fall of the forts to the north, Johnston chose to retreat to the south and established his command at Corinth. Davis sent some reinforcements from the coastal cities along with Braxton Bragg. Bragg was in command of the II Corps and was Johnston's chief of staff. On March 29, Johnston officially assumed command of more than 40,000 men under the name of the Army of Mississippi.

Major General Henry Halleck had overall command of the Union forces, which included Grant and his 40,000 men near Pittsburg Landing. Major General Don Carlos Buell was on his way from Nashville with another 35,000. Johnston hoped to stop them before they united and so launched his forces on April 3, 1862. At first it seemed to be working, as they overran Grant's camp on April 6, the first day of the Battle of Shiloh. Through the night Buell's forces arrived so that on April 7 the Confederates were forced back to Corinth. Many believed that the greatest loss in the action was the death of Johnston.[43]

By the end of April, General Polk expressed concern about Adams in his position in Memphis. Polk said, "I find there is strong reason for believing that Captain Adams is not filling his position as might be desired. His habits, I fear, are bad, and this leads to other things not in keeping with the best interest of the service." He clearly did not think Adams incompetent as a soldier: "The best thing for him and the service would be to have him made a colonel of a regiment, and sent to the field." He said that there are now a number of volunteer regiments. He recommended that command of the post in Memphis be turned over to Colonel Dixon of the Memphis Legion. He said that this was an old organization which could "do the military duty required in Memphis—guarding prisoners, magazines, &c."[44]

Eventually Adams would be given a field command, but he remained at his post in Memphis until April. One reason for the delay may have been his pregnant wife who was close by. Perhaps his commanding officers were sympathetic to his situation. She gave birth to a daughter, Georgiana McDougall Adams, on December 6, 1861. The fact that she used her maiden name suggest that though the union of the states had been severed, and her family had chosen a different side, the family ties had not been broken. In February, Adams received 118 prisoners after the capture of Fort Donelson. It may have been a Union victory but prisoners were taken from their side too.

On February 20 he had a total of 225 Federal prisoners. He had them confined in the Exchange Building at that time, and again made a recommendation to send them deeper into southern territory. By March 9 Adams had lost some prisoners due to escape. He then began moving the rest to Tuscaloosa, Alabama, deeper in to territory still held by the Confederacy. The Confederates also lost Island Number 10 and with it control of the Mississippi near Memphis. Union forces were clearly moving in on the city. It was becoming a race to move the sick and wounded Confederate soldiers while transporting the Union prisoners to a more secure location.[45]

Cavalry Command

Following the Battle of Shiloh, the Confederate retreat back to Corinth started what is known as the Siege of Corinth. Halleck had arrived at Pittsburg Landing in time to take command of 100,000 men. Grant had been successful at the forts to the north, but at Shiloh he received some criticism so that Halleck placed him second in command so that he could keep an eye on the future general commander of Union forces. Meanwhile the Confederates were regrouping. After Johnston's death Beauregard inherited the job. He assumed command of the 30,000 troops that were left after the battle. With the arrival of General Van Dorn, fresh from the defeat at Prairie Grove, it put the total number of Confederates at about 66,000. They were still outnumbered but had a respectable force.[46]

On April 21, Adams reported to Confederate command Headquarters in Corinth, Mississippi. He assumed command of Helm's Cavalry. The brother-in-law of Abraham Lincoln, Benjamin Helm was from Kentucky. This unit would be united with Butler's to form the Kentucky 1st Regiment of Cavalry. Adams established his headquarters near Russelville, Alabama, and took command of all forces extending from Bear Creek to Decatur. From that time on he was referred to by the rank of colonel, though it was not official. At the beginning of May, while at Camp Saunders, his brigade was made up of several independent companies.

In addition to the command of Helm, he had battalions under Colonels McClellan, Woodward, and Scott, and Terry's Texas Rangers. The rangers were organized in Houston in August of 1861 and had been under the command of Albert Sydney Johnston. Colonel Thomas M. Scott was in command of the 12th Louisiana Infantry. Thomas G. Woodward was in command of Companies A and B of the First Kentucky Cavalry, and had been commander of the First before Adams took over. Adams was also given two battalions under Colonels Biffle and Gordon, which had not reported yet. Jacob Biffle assisted in the formation of the 2nd Tennessee Battalion and later was promoted to lieutenant colonel and commander of the 9th Tennessee Cavalry Regiment, also called the 19th. George Gordon, like Adams, was born in Pulaski and would later be at the Battle of Franklin. Still later he became more famous for his role in the founding of the Ku Klux Klan.[47]

Since the days of the John Brown raid on Harper's Ferry, Southerners had heightened fears of slavery uprising, and many saw this threat increased further due to the interference of Northerners. Just as the previous objective in discussion of causes of the Civil War was not to be combative but rather to help us better understand men like Adams, the purpose here is not to debate historical issues about racism. In trying to do so it is easy to be dismissed as an apologist. It is relevant here because in the early stages of the war Adams found himself in the position of dealing with African Americans and he made comments about it in his reports.

Historians like Loewen and Sebesta try to make the reason for the existence of the Confederacy to be the defense of the institution of slavery. Their purpose is to show that the neo–Confederates, as well as their Confederate predecessors, are racist. They say that neo–Confederates see America as a white nation, and in doing so are ignoring that in the early days most Americans, North or South, believed it to be a white nation. Yes, it is clear that slavery was the major concern of those first seven states to secede. Slavery, at least as practiced in the United States in 1860, was racist. With the focus on this aspect of the war it is tempting to want to apply our current morality in judging the men who fought and died for the Confederacy. It has already been pointed that Adams did not own any slaves and had no direct interest in the future of slavery. However, he did live in a slave society and as such one of the greatest fears they would have is slave rebellion. The Roman Empire was plagued by slave rebellions. Many of those living in 1860 remembered the bloody Nat Turner Rebellion, and almost all remembered John Brown's raid in Virginia. In the beginning the Union had no desire to arm the slaves, and in fact many in the North objected to such plans. By the end of 1862 Lincoln had issued his famous Emancipation Proclamation and was in the process of sending armed freedmen against their former masters. It should be obvious why this would strike a chord with the Southern people. There is no denying that the vast majority of Confederates were racist, but in order to understand the reality of the situation it should be recognized that most Americans, North or South, were racist in 1860.

Today we like to believe that our country has always been a bastion of freedom and equality, so it is difficult for many to accept the fact that it has not always been the case. This is where Confederates have become a handy scapegoat. By making the war about slavery, then the blame can be put on the Confederates, giving the illusion that the North was not racist. The fact is that prior to 1860 the United States was a nation created by men who came from the British Isles, and the nation they created was very much a British nation.

Before 1860, 85 percent of the immigrants into the United States were German or Irish, and the latter were also from the British Isles. There were Africans, but they were not citizens, and many Americans before 1860 were not happy about the immigrants, which gave rise to the Know-Nothing Party. There have been several books written on this subject, only a few examples are discussed here. Gary W. Gallagher noted in *The Union War* that "democracy as practiced in 1860 denied women, free and enslaved African Americans, and other groups basic liberties and freedoms most white northerners routinely attributed to their republic." Lincoln himself said, "When southern people tell us they are no more responsible for the origin of slavery, than we; I acknowledge the fact." He also said, "What I would most desire would be the separation of the white and black races." In *What Shall We Do with the Negro?* Paul D. Escott said, "It was a deeply flawed question, reflecting in its language the assumptions that African Americans were objects, not equals; that they were fundamentally different and outside the community; and that white people were entitled to decide the future." Marc Egnal, in his book *Clash of Extremes*, in which he argued the economic origins of the war, said, "Overwhelmingly, white Northerners felt that blacks were inferior and not deserving of equal treatment."

These are only a few examples of what every historian knows. Yes, the Confederacy was a nation of white supremacy, but the United States was also a nation of white supremacy. This was upheld by the United States Supreme Court in 1857 with the Dred Scott decision, which stated that Africans, free or slaves, were not Americans.[48]

Adams did issue some orders relating to blacks in the Civil War, and thus the subject needs to be addressed. These orders do not necessarily reveal his personal feelings on the topic. It is military men like Adams who objected to the mistreatment of the Indians. When Adams was in California it is clear in his orders that he held the white settlers responsible for the violence he was supposed to end. It is the white male legislature, which was apparently predominantly northern since that state stayed in the Union, which passed laws tempting some to kill Indians so that they could enslave the children. However, it was the job of Adams to protect those white settlers and his actions were designed to accomplish this task. Adams' reports do not necessarily reflect racist attitudes on his part as much as the pragmatic concerns of a military officer. On May 8 of 1862 he said, "It seems to be their policy to devastate the country. They have enticed Negroes away from their masters and armed them."[49]

The morality play which some try to make of the Civil War also tends to overlook the actions of the Union soldiers. The history books have been written by the Union victors and as such often overlook the atrocities committed against the civilian population of the South. As with the treatment of blacks, this is only mentioned in this biography because Adams made note of such events. For Adams this must have been more personal, as it affected those in his home county of Pulaski. Adams reported, "The citizens of Pulaski, Athens, and all through the country where the enemy have been, report that they have committed depredations of every description, broken open smoke-houses and stables and stolen meat, forage, and horses from the citizens." Such actions could be defended since they were soldiers on the march through enemy territory in need of food and supplies; however, he went on to say that they "entered dwellings, breaking up furniture and plundering even ladies of money, plate, fine jewelry, besides threatening them with personal violence." We can see that the arming of the Negroes would add to the concerns of the civilian population of the South.

All of this speaks to the idea that regardless of the significance of the slavery issue in the initial declarations of secession, the invasion and actions of the United States forces changed the nature of the cause and what some were fighting for. Adams reported, "The feeling of the inhabitants, especially those who have heretofore been neutral or Union in sentiment, is now strong for the Southern cause. The depredations of the enemy has, I think, been beneficial to the cause." Of course just because Adams believed this, it does not necessarily mean that it was true.[50]

Seven. War Begins

The Siege of Corinth involved Halleck making plans to attack Beauregard and his Confederates. The Confederate commander knew his men were not in good shape after Shiloh and his reinforcements from the West were suffering from their defeat at Prairie Grove. Part of his strategy included leading Halleck to believe that he was in a stronger position than he really was. The train continued to move in and out of the town at will and he made use of this by having his men cheer as if more troops were being added to their forces. Deserting Confederates also filled the ears of Halleck's men with stories of how strong they were, apparently part of Beauregard's plans. The bluff held off the Union troops until May 28–29, when the Confederates withdrew to the East. The weather added another stumbling block, but it was Halleck himself who was the main reason for the hesitation. He was a recognized military authority and was convinced of the French doctrine which emphasized the necessity of field fortifications. By the time the Union forces did move into Corinth the Confederates were gone, and as the war moved east the countryside in the area around Corinth was scarred by massive fortifications constructed by both sides.[51]

While the main forces were held up at Corinth, Adams was involved in actions to the east. Again, we find reports from him that brought up the issue of race. Considering the situation previously discussed, it is understandable that Adams took the position that he did in a report dated May 10, which would be considered racist today, but to Adams it may have been nothing more than military strategy and self-preservation. In referring to Union captives, he said, "The Negroes I shall have tried by a commission, and, if it is found that they were taken with arms in their hands, it may be necessary to inflict summary punishment; otherwise I shall order them turned over to the civil authorities." This does not necessarily reflect racial hatred as much as a desire to discourage slave uprising and is perhaps a reflection of the fears that most people had who lived in a slave society.[52]

The above reports relate to what has been called the Battle at Hewey's Bridge. On May 6, Adams received word from a scout that the enemy were at Elkmont and Murfreesboro. He then planned to cut off a portion of those who were retreating from Huntsville. To do this he planned on crossing the Tennessee River at Lamb's Ferry. On May 9 scouts reported that the total Union strength was 12,000 to 14,000. He

177

first sent parties to capture Union soldiers at Bethel and Blair's Ferry. He then received word that he would have additional support from Generals Smith and Evans. After receiving word that wagon trains were on the Pulaski-Elkton turnpike, he left some of his men at Lamb's Ferry and took 850 on toward Pulaski. He changed his plans after receiving reports that the Yankees occupied the town with 2,500 men. They then encountered Union General James Negley, who had 1,500 men and an artillery battery. Rather than facing the big guns as well as being outnumbered, they retreated. Men who had been left at Lamb's Ferry moved on toward Tuscumbia, and Adams' detachment held its position through the night of the 12th. By the next morning the Union forces had moved on, so Adams went deeper into Tennessee. Adams' men became further reduced when he granted Colonel Wharton permission to make an independent command of his Texas Rangers.[53]

John A. Wharton, like Adams, was a native of Tennessee but had settled in Texas by 1846. In 1860 he served as an elector while trying to get Breckinridge elected president. As a ardent secessionist he enlisted as a captain in Company B of Terry's Texas Rangers. After his association with Adams he would be involved in the invasion of Kentucky and was promoted to brigadier general on November 18, 1862, and following his actions at Chickamauga he was promoted to major general.[54]

Adams then sought reinforcements and some artillery as he made plans to take the Yankees at Fayetteville. On May 20, Negley and his men attacked and took control of Winchester. Meanwhile, Beauregard ordered Adams and his men back to the defense of Corinth. His orders were changed so that he was to remain in Tennessee, where he received the previously requested reinforcements. He soon became involved in what is called the Battle of Sweden's Cove on June 4. Adams again faced Negley, who had about 400 men. Adams had not yet received his anticipated additional support. He and his men retreated and along with forces under Morgan were held up in Chattanooga. It was during this time that Adams' brother, Major Thomas Adams, was wounded. On June 9 Adams and his command, as well as those under Colonels Scott and Wharton, were placed under the command of Nathan Bedford Forrest. On July 16, Adams was transferred to the post at Columbus, Mississippi.[55]

Nathan Bedford Forrest is perhaps number one as a target for those who like to make the Civil War a race issue. He was a large plantation owner, slave trader, commander at Fort Pillow, and given credit for founding the Ku Klux Klan. He is admired by military enthusiasts as one of the most famous warriors in American history, though he had a complete lack of military training. While Adams was being transferred to Columbus, Forrest and Wharton went on to the First Battle of Murfreesboro, which Forrest is said to have won. A Union lieutenant colonel left us an interesting report of that battle which is a good example of why we need to be careful in applying presentism in evaluating the actions of those living in the 1860s. "The forces attacking my camp were the First Regiment Texas Rangers, Colonel Wharton, and a battalion of the First Georgia Rangers, Colonel Morrison, and a large number of citizens of Rutherford County, many of whom had recently taken the oath of allegiance to the United States Government." The next part is interesting in that many of those who promote the racism of the Confederate cause claim that it is a myth that African Americans wore the grey. "There were also quite a number of negroes attached to the Texas and Georgia Troops, who were armed and equipped, and took part in the several engagements with my forces during the day." At the time the Union did not use African American troops.[56]

Columbus, Mississippi

For the remainder of the year Colonel Adams was in command of the post at Columbus. The town was a railroad depot and following the Battle of Shiloh had become primarily a hospital town. It has been said that just about every house within the town limits was used as a hospital at some point. Thousands of soldiers, including four generals, are buried there, though most of the Union dead were removed in the years after the war. It has been said that Columbus was the first to memorialize fallen soldiers from both sides, thus giving it a claim as a birthplace of Memorial Day. Shortly after Adams assumed command, Braxton Bragg had moved toward Chattanooga, and then toward Kentucky. By early September he ordered most of the troops out of Columbus, leaving only minimal forces.[57]

On January 5, 1863, Adams was ordered to report to Jackson, Mississippi. During the short time he was in command of the post at Columbus he had prepared defenses, which included stationing pickets, scouting, and trying to induce conscripts. His unit also served as a police force over the black population. He paid $1.25 per day for some of the slaves to be used in constructing the fortifications. They had a chain of breastworks and rifle-pits over five miles in length. He reported at the time of his departure, "On the Looxapalila there are three bridges and four fords, upon all of which I have placed heavy works. The Tombigbee is a natural defense, except at two points, at which there are defenses." He was in the process of constructing defenses for the northern approaches about four miles from the city. He was also in the process of constructing outer works. At the orders of Lieutenant General Pemberton he moved most of his men as well as quartermaster and commissary stores to Jackson. All that was left in Columbus were state troops, called Minute-Men, as well as an assortment of artillery and some cavalry at strategic locations in the general neighborhood.[58]

This transfer also came with the provisional rank of brigadier general, which would not be confirmed until February 1864, but which was retroactive to December 29, 1862. The report of Union General Negley referred to the "command of Colonel (Acting Brigadier General) Adams." He was also appointed commissioner for exchanged and paroled prisoners. On January 15 the Department of Mississippi and East Louisiana was reorganized. Jackson was made the headquarters of the new Fourth Military District, and Adams was put in command.[59]

Eight

The Final Stage

> While we were trying to concentrate our minds on our books one ear was always open to the varied sounds of the fife and the rattle of drums, the clatter of horses' hoofs, and the electrifying notes of the bugle. We were allowed always to run to the front gate to see soldiers pass. If they were "our boys," we waved our bonnets and handkerchiefs—if they were yankees, and we watched Buell's army of thousands pass, we looked and felt dismayed.
>
> On an ever memorable day, the 30th of November, we assembled at school as usual. Our teachers' faces looked unusually serious that morning. The Federal couriers were dashing hither and thither. The officers were gathering in squads, and the cavalry, with swords and sabers clanking, were driving their spurs into their horses' flanks and galloping out to first one picket post and then another on the roads leading south and southwest of town. The bell called us in the chapel. We were told to take our books and go home, as there was every indication that we would be in the midst of a battle that day.[1]

This was not only the last battle for John Adams, but the last day of his life. The above was from the point of view of Frances O'Bryan, a student at the Franklin Female Institute. The South was falling under control of the invading Union troops. There had always been some in the new Confederate States of America who never wanted to leave the Union. There were others who remained indifferent. To most they persistently defended their homes from the invaders. The young girl in school could do little more than wish them the best, while more and more would be like Adams and make the ultimate sacrifice for their homeland.

After his relocation to Jackson, Adams's service can be broken down into three main phases. First was the Vicksburg campaign in which he would be part of the efforts to defend that city from conquest by Grant.

Second, after the fall of Vicksburg he would move with the Army of Tennessee into position to defend Atlanta. After the fall of that city he would continue with what was left of the Army of Tennessee back into his home state, where his fate awaited him at Franklin, not far from where his life began.

Vicksburg

In the last half of 1862, while Adams was in Columbus, Mississippi, reorganization took place in both the Union and Confederate armies. After occupation of Corinth, Halleck broke up his multi-corps organization. On June 10 he put Grant in command of Army of the Tennessee and gradually George Thomas and his division was returned to Buell's Army. Grant established his headquarters in Memphis but his troops were scattered along the Tennessee and Mississippi border area. In July, Halleck was called to Washington to serve as Lincoln's general-in-chief. On the way out he expanded Grant's command. After Halleck left, Grant moved back to Corinth and later Jackson, Tennessee. Soon four divisions were assigned elsewhere, leaving Grant in the position of playing defense with a force reduced to only 50,000. On October 25, 1862, Grant assumed command of the Department of the Tennessee. By the end of the year his Army was divided into four corps under the command of John McClermand, William T. Sherman, Stephen Hurlbut, and James B. McPherson. He began planning his attack on Vicksburg in the fall of 1862. By the time of the official start of the Vicksburg Campaign he would have a force of 150,000. The leader of the Confederate defense was General John C. Pemberton.[2]

The Confederate Army of Tennessee was created November 20, 1862, by renaming the Army of Mississippi. The first commander was Braxton Bragg, who relieved Beauregard. The troops which evacuated Corinth in late May moved to the East, as previously discussed. Whereas Adams ended up in Columbus, most of the men headed north in Bragg's invasion of Kentucky. They were at the Battle of Perryville on October 8 and at the Battle of Stones River, or Murfreesboro, on December 31, 1862. Bragg was in charge after Adams rejoined the Army and they moved into Chattanooga.[3]

Eight. The Final Stage

John C. Pemberton is another example of what we lose by insisting the war was about slavery. Not only was the man born in Pennsylvania, he came from a Quaker background. He was a West Point graduate, class of 1837. He had served against the Seminole, in the Mexican War, and at several frontier posts from New Mexico to Minnesota. It is believed that his decision to resign his commission on April 28 so that he could join the Confederate cause was because of his marriage to a woman from Virginia. Like Adams, his resignation came after that state seceded, which was not until after the firing on Fort Sumter. He was promoted to lieutenant general on October 13, 1862, and was given command of the Department of Mississippi and East Louisiana. Some have claimed that putting Pemberton in command "must rank as one of Jefferson Davis' major mistakes." Some have even suggested treason; however, there is no evidence to support this charge. Pemberton had about 12,000 men in Vicksburg, and Jackson and Major General Earl Van Dorn had about 24,000 at Grenada, Mississippi.[4] The term "Vicksburg Campaign" generally refers to the period between April 29 and July 4, 1863, but Grant started his operations in late 1862. The initial strategy involved Sherman to advance down the river with his 32,000 men while Grant took the remaining forces of 40,000 to Oxford, where he would wait for news of developments, at which time he would lure the Confederate forces out of the city. Grant's first failures came when some of Forrest's cavalry tore up sixty miles of track after Van Dorn captured Grant's base at Holly Springs. Meanwhile Sherman reported after his arrival at Chickasaw Bluffs, December 27–29, "I reached Vicksburg at the time appointed, landed, assaulted, and failed." Union troops did occupy Arkansas Post in early January of 1863.[5]

Between February and April Grant had four unsuccessful "Bayou Expeditions." Unusually high waters were on the side of the Confederates. This caused a problem with the canal he tried to construct so that he could bypass the city's batteries for a planned attack from the south. By late March this idea had to be abandoned. Other failed expeditions included the Lake Providence Expedition, which did manage to get some men on the other side of Vicksburg, but it was not enough to accomplish the objective. The Yazoo Pass and Steele's Bayou expeditions also failed. By the end of March he had a total of seven failed plans.[6]

During the time Adams had been promoted to a brigadier general and had moved from Columbus to Jackson. His duties did not vary that much from what he had been doing. Jackson was an important railroad center in the state of Mississippi, which included connections to Vicksburg. On January 15 the Department of Mississippi and East Louisiana was created and Jackson was made headquarters of the new Fourth Military District which Adams commanded. At that time the troops stationed there were only 388, consisting of the First Mississippi Battalion of state troops and cavalry company of Captain J. N. Bolan from Kentucky. In February the number went up to 1,231 with the addition of the First Mississippi (Choctaw) Battalion, the 14th Mississippi Infantry and another Kentucky cavalry company under Captain B. D. Terry. By the end of April the number of troops had increased to 2,403.[7]

Adams had charge of paroled and exchanged prisoners and had the responsibility to regulate train movements. He turned down the use of the penitentiary for the prisoners of war and used instead part of a bridge over the Pearl River. Some of the prisoners slept in tents. We find another reference to black Union troops, or in this case a sailor, who had been captured with the sinking of the Union ironclad *Indianola* back in February. Adams reported that "amongst the seamen there is one negro, who is said to be a free negro." We cannot tell from this record if he reported this due to his personal racist concerns, or whether it simply reflected the general concern about the use of blacks by the Union. In the beginning, as discussed previously, not only did Lincoln make it clear in his inaugural address, "I have no purpose, directly or indirectly, to interfere with the institution of slavery," but Congress also made it equally clear on July 25, 1861, with the Crittenden-Johnson Resolution that the war, which had started by then, was being fought to "defend and maintain the supremacy of the Constitution and to preserve the Union." So, when the war started the United States government claimed they were not a threat to slavery, and thus the official position of the United States was that they would not use the slaves against their masters.

Things changed by early 1863. With the Emancipation Proclamation it seemed as if it had become policy for the North to entice those in bonds to rebel. The proclamation did not free all the slaves, only those it had no control over. It did make slavery a war measure, while allowing for the survival of the institution in those states which were not in rebel-

Eight. The Final Stage

lion by January of 1863. Those who like Lincoln and want to believe that the war was to end slavery follow the lead of historian Eric Foner. Foner realized that the most slaves were not freed; however, as more and more slave territory came under control, they were covered so that the end result was that it did free the slaves. It never did apply to those slave states which remained loyal to the Union. Some took individual state actions and ended slavery in their own states by the end of the war. In the case of Kentucky, slavery did not end until the passage of the Thirteenth Amendment. Adams had expressed concern about African American prisoners in earlier reports, but now it was under different circumstances. Adams notified his superiors in regards to the black sailor, "I respectfully ask for instructions in his case. He is at present confined with the others." The fact that he mentioned that the man had been a "free negro" suggests a distinction from those who had been slaves.[8]

Grant's move to east of the Mississippi began on April 29 at Grand Gulf as Union ironclads subdued Confederate defenses. On the same day the Navy and Army combined attacked Snyder's Bluff to keep the Confederates there from being moved to the defense of Grand Gulf. Grant also used the cavalry of General Benjamin H. Grierson to divert Pemberton's attention from the Union crossing of the Mississippi south of Vicksburg. He had a total of 1,700 men who left La Grange, near Memphis, on April 17. Grant believed that the raid "has been one of the most brilliant cavalry exploits of the war, and will be handed down in history as an example to be imitated."[9]

The activities of Grierson began on April 17 and very much involved Adams and his men. On the 23rd Adams and seven companies of the Fifteenth Mississippi were sent to Morton Station. They were soon followed by the remaining three companies as well as the Pointe Coupée. Adams and his men camped at Lake after receiving word that the Union had been through there and were on their way to Enterprise, to the south. They also received reports of a large number of Union troops so that they were very concerned about their ability to defend the area. Adams remained at Lake after it was reported that another column of Union cavalry were advancing on Enterprise from Decatur and were expected to go through Newton Station.[10]

The next day Adams received reports that there were no signs of Union forces on the Newton-Lake railroad line, but about 800 Union troops had been sighted to the south. He telegraphed Pemberton requesting that he be allowed to remain at Lake and to send another regiment to Forest, Mississippi. Pemberton instead ordered Adams to return to Jackson, but to leave a regiment with some artillery at Lake and Forest. Pemberton also ordered General Loring to return to Jackson and for Johnston to send 2,000 cavalry. He then ordered Bruckner to send two regiments to Meridian.[11]

On May 9, Pemberton estimated the enemy to have 10,000 men. Adams was left with the Fourteenth Mississippi, Steed's Battalion, with a total of about 500, along with two ordnance pieces, which he placed on the Pearl River just west of Jackson. Skirmishing occurred at Raymond on May 12 before the invasion of Jackson on May 14. The capital had fallen with little effort and from that point on Grant turned his attention to Vicksburg. The fall of Pemberton is considered to have occurred at Champion Hill and Big Black River. The Siege of Vicksburg began shortly

Black River, Mississippi, wagons and sleds. This was part of Grierson's Raid in May of 1863. Lloyd Tilghman was killed during the battle and Adams assumed command of his brigade (Library of Congress).

Eight. The Final Stage

afterward; the city fell on July 4. After the Union occupation of Jackson, Adams was commanding a brigade of cavalry. On May 23 he was camped at Vernon, Mississippi. He moved around in the area near Mechanicsburg and eventually fell back as far as Pritchard's Cross-Roads, where he remained seven days. On June 8, orders came which called for Adams to join the division of General Loring. Adams gave up his brigade which numbered 1,678 men and assumed command of Tilghman's Brigade. Lloyd Tilghman had been killed at Big Black River on May 16.[12]

Tilghman was born in Maryland in 1817, was a West Point graduate and had served in the Mexican War. He and his brigade of less than 1,500 took a stand against an enemy 6,000 to 8,000 strong. "He fell in the midst of his brigade that loved him well, after repelling a powerful enemy in deadly fight, struck by a cannon shot." The "brigade wept over the dying hero, alike beautiful as it was touching." As recalled by Pat Henry, "When General Adams was assigned to the command of this brigade ... it was resented by officers and men. We thought that we should have had a Mississippi brigadier." Adams quickly proved himself, Henry went on to say, "but this feeling soon passed away, it being recognized that he was a fine soldier, a knightly commander, and a Christian gentleman." This new command consisted of the 6th, 14th, 15th, 20th, and 23rd Mississippi Infantry Regiments

Major General William Wing Loring was direct commander over Adams from the Atlanta Campaign until his death at the Battle of Franklin. After the Civil War Loring served nine years in the Army of Isma'il Pasha, the khedive of Egypt.

with a total of 3,638 men. Later it would include the 43rd, which had been involved with defending Vicksburg.[13]

On May 18, Johnston warned Pemberton of the danger of becoming besieged in Vicksburg. Although Grant had 70,000 men to face the Confederates' 30,000, he gave up further attempts to enter the city by fire power. He decided to settle down and starve them out. The surrender came on July 4. As a result of his victory Grant was promoted to major general effective the date of the surrender. With the fall of Port Hudson on July 9 the Confederacy was cut in half. Many have called the Vicksburg campaign not only the best of Grant, but of the war. The Army of the Tennessee rested for a while after the victory, and Grant was moved to Chattanooga.

On to Atlanta

On August 1, Adams's Brigade was camped near Forrest, Mississippi. From there it moved around considerably. It was in Newton on August 27, in Meridian on September 6, Brandon on October 1 and in Canton on October 16. On October 22 his forces were spread along the Mobile and Ohio Railroad and the Jackson Railroad. They were returned to Canton on October 27, where they remained until the middle of February 1864. Adams's family had been evacuated to Alabama when the city of Jackson first appeared to be in danger. Georgiana was pregnant again in addition to having another child who was sick. Adams chose this lull as an opportunity to request a leave in August of 1863 to visit his wife and family. In November the child was still ill and his wife was getting closer to the due date for the new baby, and so he asked for another three weeks' leave. A daughter, who was named Emma Portis, was born December 20.[14]

Meanwhile Grant and the Union Army's attention shifted east from Vicksburg. After the Confederate victory in Chickamauga in September, Braxton Bragg's forces moved to Chattanooga, where he tried to regain control of the city by laying siege to it. Grant arrived on the scene on October 23 to take charge of the situation being given command of the newly created Division of the Mississippi. After his success in Chattanooga, on March 9, 1864, Grant was promoted to lieutenant general,

Eight. The Final Stage

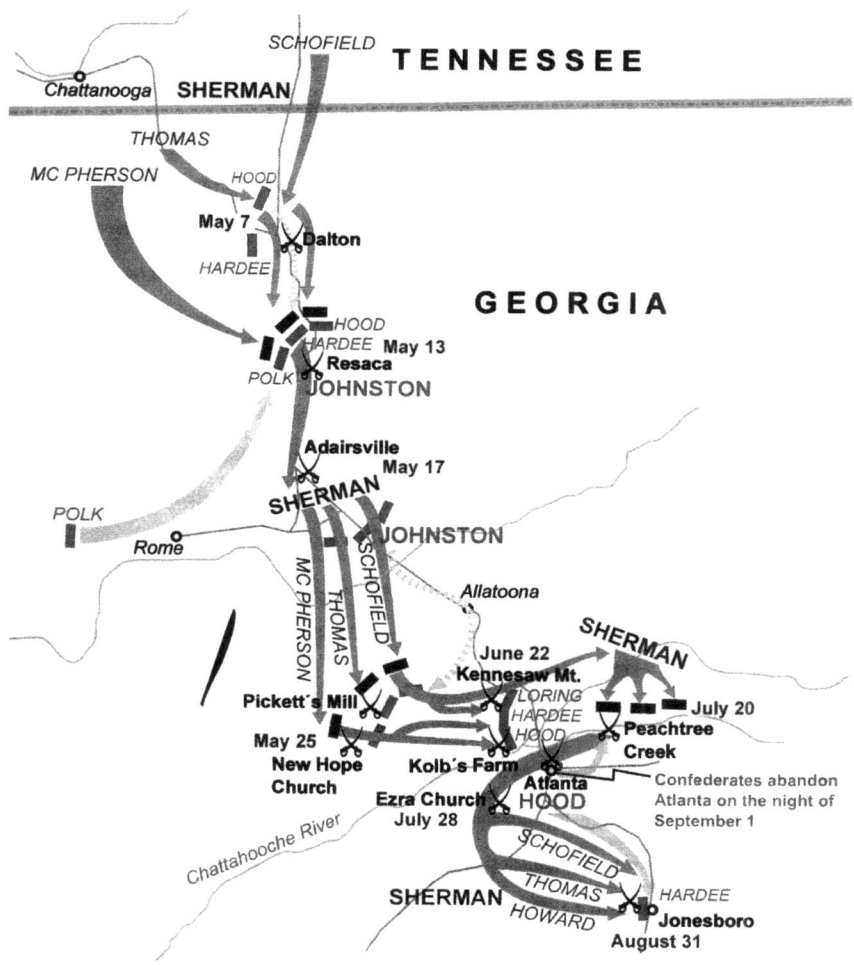

The Atlanta Campaign; Adams was in Loring's division (Andrei Nacu, Wikipedia).

a position which had previously been limited to George Washington and Winfield Scott, the latter as a brevet. On March 12 he was made general in chief of the armies of the United States. From that point he took over the strategic direction of the war. He left Sherman in charge of the western armies as they turned their sights on Atlanta. The main Union commanders in this campaign were William T. Sherman, George H. Thomas,

James B. McPherson, John Schofield and Oliver O. Howard. The opposition was under the command of Joseph E. Johnston. Under him was John Bell Hood, William J. Hardee, Leonidas Polk, and Joseph Wheeler. Adams's brigade was under Loring's division, which in turn answered to Polk. Sherman had more than 100,000 against half that number under Johnston.[15]

William Wing Loring of North Carolina is another example of a man who entered the war to defend his home, not slavery. He was not a West Point graduate, but did have experience in the Seminole War and the Mexican War. He continued his military service on the frontier and was in command of the Department of New Mexico when he resigned on May 13, 1861. He was not a secessionist and North Carolina was not one of the original seven states that created the Confederacy. He did go with his home state when it seceded following the firing on Sumter and Lincoln's demand for 75,000 troops from each state. Loring was with the Army of Northern Virginia in the beginning, but following a conflict with Jackson in early 1862 he was sent west. Pemberton blamed him for the loss at Champion's Hill.[16]

Sherman was ordered by Grant "to move against Johnston's army, to break it up, and to get into the interior of the enemy's country as far as you can, inflicting all the damage you can against their war resources." Sherman headed for the railroad center of Atlanta. Sherman launched his advance on May 7. He chose to bypass Johnston, who was holed up at Dalton. He sent McPherson on a turning movement, which is an attempt to draw the enemy out of his position. Thomas advanced frontally along the railroad, and Schofield threatened the Confederate right. This resulted in action around Rocky Face Ridge on May 5 through 9.

Rocky Face Ridge included attacks on the Confederate forces at Tunnel Hill, Mill Creek Gap, Buzzard Roost, Snake Creek Gap, Varnell's Station, and action near Dalton. Johnston occupied the ridge. The Union forces were unable to stop Johnston's retreat; however they did gain control of Dalton. Sherman's next contest occurred at Resaca.[17]

From February to May of 1864, Adams's division moved from Demopolis, Alabama, so that by May it had become part of Joseph Johnston's defense of Atlanta. They arrived in time to take part in the Battle of Resaca on May 13. The cavalry took the brunt of the assault while most of the forces took shelter behind breastworks quickly constructed

Eight. The Final Stage

by all of the men. Adams's brigade was placed on the extreme right and in the front where they were subjected to heavy shelling. Johnston's forces withdrew. Three days later Confederate forces moved south. Adams reported some skirmishing between Kingston and Cassville. On May 25, Loring's division was subjected to bombardments at New Hope Church. Sherman moved east again, forcing Johnston to abandon his position and to take up a new one. This led to the Battle of Kennesaw Mountain.[18]

Adams' brigade was stationed at the base of the mountain at the Battle of Kennesaw, on the extreme left close to Canton road. Adams and his men were charged at about four o'clock on the left and center. They were successful in holding off the attack. Fire continued against Loring's division during the evening. General Featherston, whose men were also subject to the attack, reported that "they received a severe punishment." He went on to say that Adams's "regiment acted with great coolness, courage, and determination during the engagement."[19]

By July 5, Union troops were looking at Atlanta. Polk was killed at Pine Mountain on June 14 and Johnston was replaced by John Bell Hood. Sherman had split his army into three columns for the assault on Atlanta. The two under Schofield and McPherson had moved off to the east. Hood followed the original plan of Johnston's to attack the third column under the command of George H. Thomas at Peach Tree Creek. As part of his plan on July 19 he ordered a portion of Adams's brigade for picket duty on the Chattahoochee River. On July 20 the Army of the Cumberland crossed the creek and took defensive positions. The Confederates began the attack around four o'clock in the afternoon. Confederate efforts failed to break the Union lines. Colonel Michael Farrel's 15th Mississippi took part in the main battle. Adams claimed that they had received the surrender of a Federal regiment, but that they were able to escape. Adams marched the majority of his men, who had been on picket, to the support of those at Peach Tree Creek but they did not arrive until the end of the battle.[20]

By September 1 with the Union victory at Jonesborough the Atlanta campaign was pretty much over. Hood evacuated Atlanta on the night of September 1, burning military supplies and installations and creating scenes which would become famous in the movie *Gone With the Wind*. Hood took what was left of his army and made plans to return the Army of Tennessee to its home. As they moved toward Tennessee on October

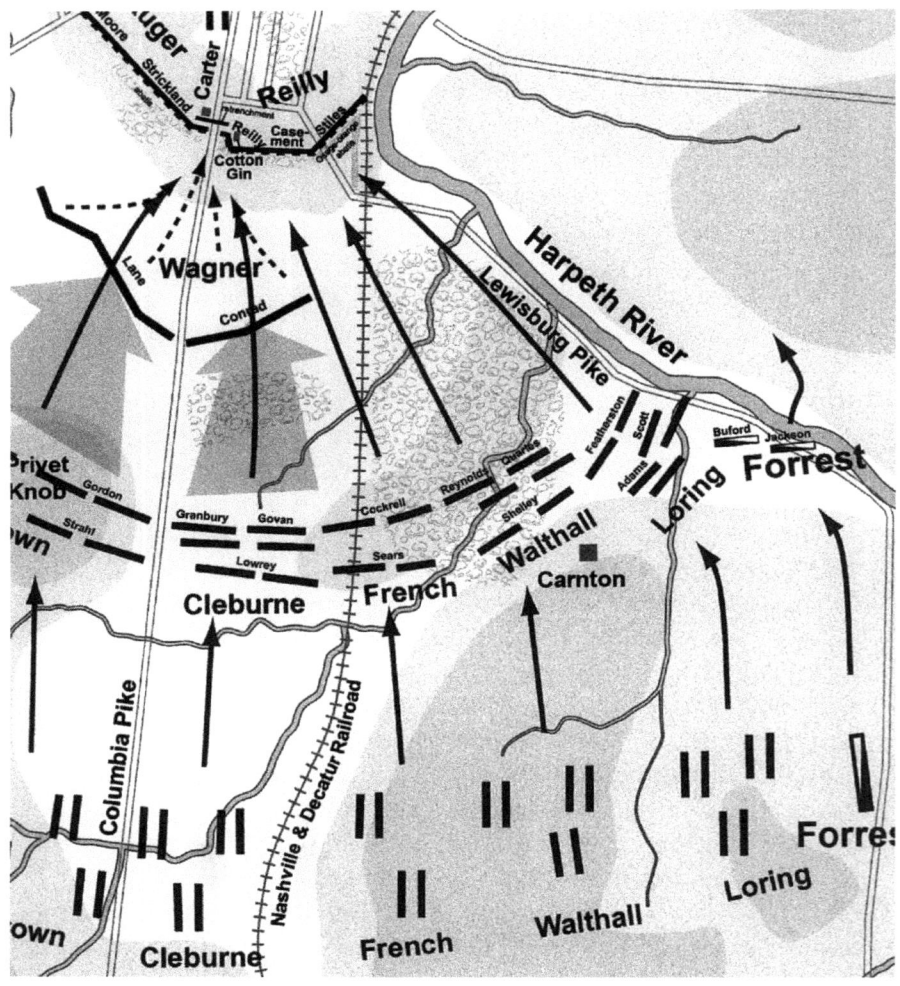

Battle of Franklin, actions about 4:00 to 4:30 P.M. Adams was in Loring's division on the right (map by Hal Jespersen, www.cwmaps.com).

4, Adams' men captured the town of Acworth located in the foothills of north Georgia. On his arrival Adams placed his brigade in position to lay siege to the town. He then sent in the inspector general to demand surrender. If the Union forces refused, Colonel Binford of the 15th Mississippi was ordered to charge the brick houses which had become a

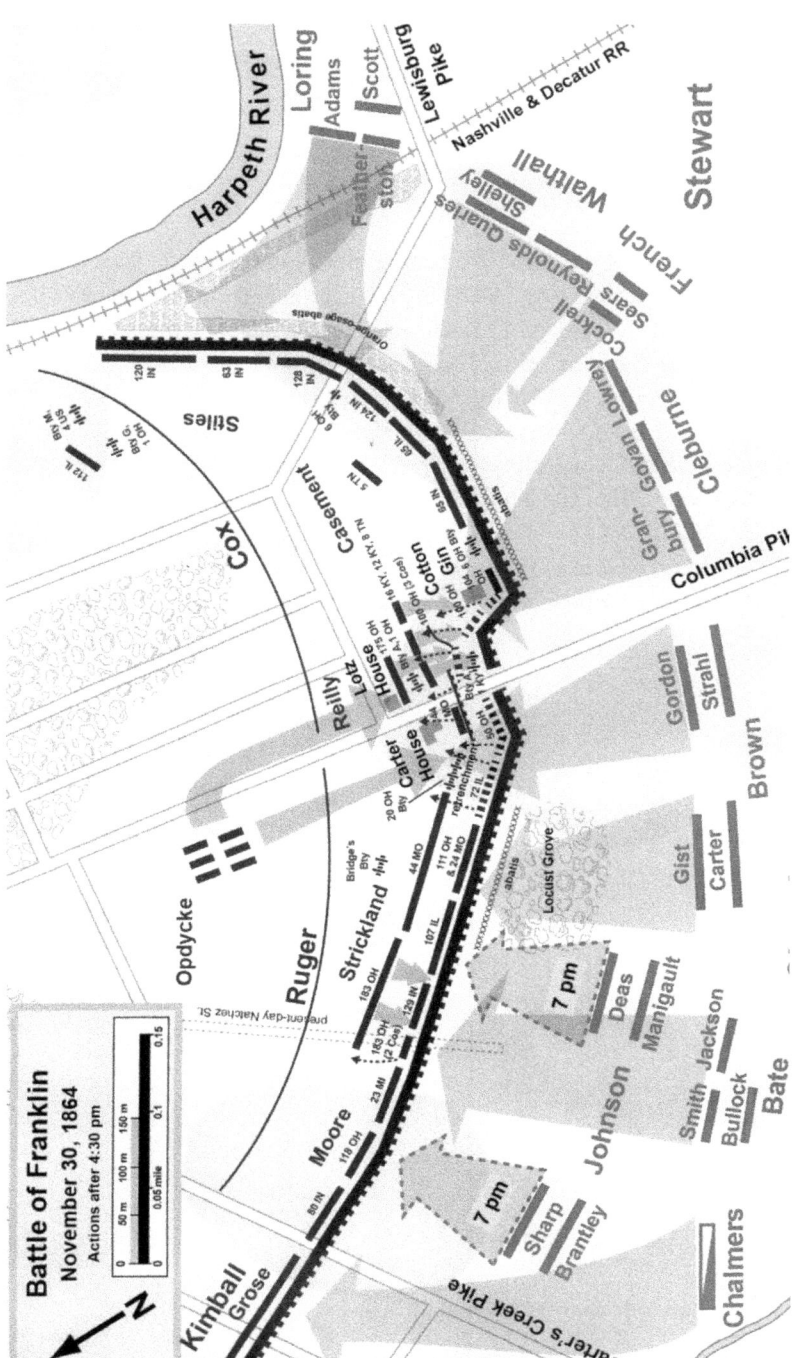

Battle of Franklin, actions after 4:30 P.M. Adams was in Loring's division, on the far right (map by Hal Jespersen, www.cwmaps.com).

Brigadier General John Adams, CSA

Union fortress. The attack was unnecessary, as the Federals surrendered 236 men complete with their horses, stores and rations.[21]

Back to Tennessee

On November 20, Adams' brigade crossed the river into Tennessee with the rest of Hood's Army. While Sherman concentrated on his march to Savannah, he sent George Thomas after the Army of Tennessee. Part of the forces of Schofield, which had been stationed at Pulaski, Adams' home, slowly retreated with the idea of meeting up with Thomas in Nashville. Hood tried to intercept Schofield, who managed to by-pass him on the night of November 29. Though combined Union forces had over 60,000 men when the armies met at Franklin, Hood had 38,000 to Schofield's 32,000.

Schofield arrived in Franklin about 6:00 A.M. and immediately began preparing defensive positions around breastworks originally constructed

General Schofield at Franklin (Library of Congress).

Eight. The Final Stage

for the First Battle of Franklin in 1863. The line was an approximate semicircle around the city, from northwest to southeast. The main obstruction for the invaders was a grove of osage hedges which had been grown by locals as a boundary fence to confine livestock. These fully mature trees were chopped off at about the four foot level giving the defenders an excellent view but affording considerable protection.

Adams in his final charge at the Battle of Franklin (courtesy Ann Gulbranson).

The cut off tops were spread out in other areas. Behind the hedges lay the main earthworks with Henderson's men and the twelve-pounder guns of Battery M, 4th United States Artillery, poised to put up a good defense. "It would be impossible to describe or even to have an adequate idea of the fearful carnage and horrors of that great battle," wrote H. P. Figuers, who was but a boy at the time. "The descending night, roar of artillery, rattle of musketry, and the Rebel yell, all conspired to form a spectacular display not often seen in the history of the world. It was at once the glory and horror of war."[22]

The Union forces were well established as the Confederates arrived and the decision made. The school girl Frances recalled, "At four o'clock that afternoon I stood in our front door and heard musketry in the neighborhood of Col. Carter's on the Columbia pike. To this day I can recall the feeling of sickening dread that came over me. As the evening wore on, the firing became more frequent, and nearer, and louder."

It was about that time that "the march was commenced toward the Federal breastworks—and death. It was a bright and beautiful day, not a cloud in the sky, an ideal autumn afternoon," Lieutenant-Colonel Edward Adams Baker of the 66th Indiana infantry recalled. "They fell by thousands, and their decimated ranks fell back to reform and come again. In this way nine separate and distinct charges were made." Loring's

Carnton Plantation, which was turned into a hospital following the battle.

brigades were separated by the hedges. Colonel Casement's men shot them down with their rifles while the artillery fired down on them at close range. After the first attack failed, roughly at 5:00 P.M., the worst was to come. The next four hours would be a nightmare for his command.

At one point Loring rode to the front amid a hail of bullets and shouted to his men to stand fast. In frustration he uttered, "Great God: Do I command cowards?" He turned alone on his horse and faced the enemy fire. "He was in full Confederate uniform. A sword belt encompassed his waist; sword and scabbard were polished and shone brightly. A large, dark plume of ostrich feathers drooped over his hat." This was but a one last act of defiance as he turned and galloped to the rear to regroup the unit. Adams and his brigade were to the far right near the Lewisburg road, through the grounds today occupied by the Confederate cemetery. The curvature of the Harpeth River and railroad had forced them to the west.[23]

Adams's brigade, which had been among the reserve, now had their go at the enemy lines. When he saw the front lines he advanced without orders. "Adams directed Captain Gibson, his cousin, to go to the right and Lieutenant Henry to stay with the left, while he went to the center,

Eight. The Final Stage

A view of the porch where the bodies of four Confederate generals, including John Adams, were laid.

remarking as he rode off 'I can be found in the center if needed.'" Earlier he had been wounded in his right arm and was urged to leave the field. His response was, "No; I am going to see my men through." Adams was well in front of his men, "turned his face ... and said in a cool, calm, deliberate tone: 'Follow me, my men,'" and spurred his gray mount, "Old Charley," even faster toward the earthworks. Colonel Stewart of the 65th Illinois shouted for his men not to fire at him even as he attempted to grasp the "old flag" from the hands of that regiment's color guard.

The Union officer Baker recalled, "Gen. Adams rode up to our works and, cheering his men, made an attempt to leap his horse over them. The horse fell dead upon the top of the embankment and the General was caught under him pierced with bullets." Baker went on to say, "as soon as the charge was repulsed our men sprang upon the works and lifted the horse, while others dragged the General from under him. He was perfectly conscious, and knew his fate. He asked for water, as all dying men do in battle as the lifeblood drips from the body." Then "one of my men gave him a canteen of water, while another brought an armload of cotton from an old gin near by and made him a pillow.... The General gallantly thanked them, and, in answer to our expressions of sorrow at his sad fate, he said, "It is the fate of a soldier to die for his country."

Pat Henry said, "Throughout it all Adams's Brigade did its whole duty, proving itself worthy of our accomplished and devoted commander." He added, "We are proud of his glorious record, for on that fated field he wrote his name among the immortals. His gallant bearing won encomiums from the enemy, among whom he fell pierced by nine wounds." Reports vary as to the number of bullets which struck Adams.[24]

Aftermath

Hood's losses were about 7,000 men, including 1,750 on the field, 4,500 wounded, and 702 taken prisoner. This would be about one-third of the infantry sent into battle. Frances, the school girl, recalled "in the afternoon, December 1st, some of us went to the battlefield, to give water and wine to the wounded. Horrors! What sights that met our girlish eyes! The dead and wounded lined the Columbia Pike for the distance of a mile." Many of the wounded had been taken to the home of Colonel Carter's house, where, she noted, "we could scarcely walk without stepping on dead or dying men. We could hear the cries of the wounded, of which Colonel Carter's house was full to the overflowing." As she entered the house she "heard a poor fellow giving his sympathetic comrades a dying message for his loved ones at home." She and her friends then passed to a locust thicket and saw "men in every conceivable position ... some with their fingers on the triggers, and death struck them so suddenly they didn't move." She then observed "trenches dug to receive as many as ten bodies." She passed around the old gin house where "men and horses were lying so thick that we could not walk. Gen. Adams's horse was lying stark and stiff upon the breastworks. Ambulances were being filled with the wounded as fast as possible, and the whole town was turned into a hospital."[25]

The fifteen-year-old Figuers noted, "The little town of Franklin then presented a sad spectacle for the Southern sympathizers and those who loved the wounded patriots that filled the town." He observed that the female institute, courthouse, every church, and many of the private

Eight. The Final Stage

houses were filled with the wounded and dying. "At the time most of the citizens were hard pressed to supply the necessaries of life for their families; but, nothing daunted, as Southern patriots they took charge of the wounded and divided with them their last morsel." They fed the soldiers a soup made of Irish potatoes, cabbage, dried beans, and turnips with plenty of red pepper. "The soldiers thought this was great diet; in fact, the best they had for more than a year." The Union Army took away all of their wounded except for those who had been captured. The wounded prisoners were kept at the Presbyterian church, "and frequently in the mornings they would bury half a dozen soldiers."[26]

Early the morning after the battle the body of the fallen General Adams was found and loaded into an ambulance. The Union officers who were with him when he died had the body removed near the cotton gin, which led those who found the body later to

Two views of the Confederate cemetery at Carnton.

believe that he had fallen in that location. His saddle had been immediately removed and presented to Colonel Casement. His watch, ring, and revolver were divided among several of the other officers. His boots, too, had been removed from the body. The watch was later given to Confederate officers and did eventually find its way to the widow Georgiana, as did the ring. Lieutenant Colonel Casement kept the saddle for many years but when he found that the widow wanted it, he delivered it to her along with a letter which reflected his respect for the fallen warrior. Adams's body lay near the remains of Major General Patrick Cleburne which made it appear as if they had been killed at about the same time, when they in fact had each fallen in distinctly different charges. They were both carried to the home of John McGavock where they joined Generals Otho Strahl and Hiram Granbury. Later some would claim that all six of the Confederate generals who had fallen in that battle were placed on that porch, but this is not true. John C. Carter was taken elsewhere and did not die until December 10. It has also been shown that General States Rights Gist had not been taken to Carnton.[27]

Those who knew Adams described him as brave and a good soldier. Pat Henry went beyond that. "I want to say that he was not only one of the bravest but one of the most conscientious and truly religious men I ever knew. He was as modest as a woman, rather retiring in his disposition, of the strictest integrity." Henry went on to say, "He scorned that which was not honorable, and lived in daily communion with his God. I rarely ever knew him to lie down at night that he did not read from his rubric and say his prayers." Others agreed that he was "ever modest, conservative, brave, and patriotic." There is no indication that he had chosen to resign his commission in the Union Army for any reason other than duty to his home, his family, and the state of Tennessee.[28]

After the War

> Furl it, brave comrade, furl it with care,
> This dear old flag, for which we bled
> That the ravages of time may never wear
> This silent epitaph of a cause that is dead.[29]

The four generals which had been laid out on the porch of the McGavock home were taken back to Columbia and buried. Later they

Eight. The Final Stage

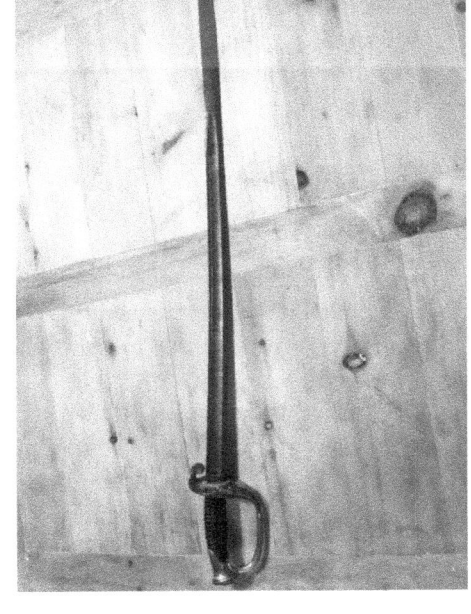

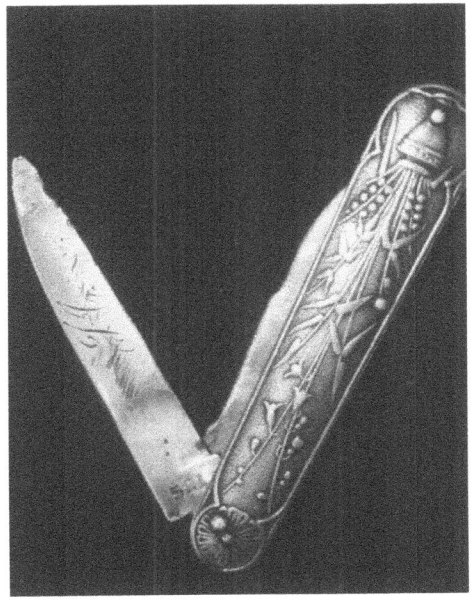

Top Left: Original family photograph of John Adams (courtesy Tamara Grabowski). ***Top Right:*** Sword of John Adams (courtesy Tamara Grabowski). ***Right:*** Pocket knife of John Adams (courtesy Tamara Grabowski).

were moved to locations near their respective homes. The final resting place for Adams was at the Maplewood Cemetery in Pulaski, Tennessee. As observed above, most of those items removed from his body found their way to his widow, Georgiana.[30]

Thomas Adams, member of the staff of his brother John, survived the battle and then served on the staff of Brigadier General Robert Lowry. He surrendered with the Army of Tennessee at Bentonville, North Carolina. He later met, at one of the many reunions of Confederate soldiers, with some of the other men who were with Adams at Franklin on that day, including Lowry, James Binford of the 15th Mississippi, Pat Henry, who had become a member of Congress, and John L. Collins. These comrades helped to describe the events on that last day in the life of their compatriot John Adams.[31]

Georgiana apparently had not damaged her relationship with her father over the fact that she and her husband went with the Confederacy while her father's family remained loyal to the Union. She and her children were living in the home of her father in St. Louis during the 1870 census, and some with him at Georgetown, Washington, D.C., in 1880. Her father, Dr. Charles McDougall, died July 25, 1885, at Fairfield, Virginia, and is buried at Jefferson Barracks National Cemetery, St. Louis. In 1900 she was living with her son, Dr. Francis Joseph Adams, in Cascade County, Montana. She died December 9, 1905, at 4152 Maryland Avenue, St. Louis, and was buried in Calvary Cemetery.[32]

The eldest son of John Adams, Charles McDougall Adams, married and worked for the Grand Island Railroad. He died about 1945 in La Jolla, California. The second son, Thomas Patton Adams, married and was an executive with the Missouri Pacific Railroad. He died in St. Louis in 1920. The third son, John, married and he also worked for the Missouri Pacific Railroad. He died October 25, 1905, in St. Louis. The fourth son, Dr. Francis Joseph Adams, married and practiced medicine in Great Falls, Montana. He died June 2, 1920, in Montana. The eldest daughter, Georgiana McDougall Adams, who was born in Memphis at the start of the war, married Conde Benoist Pallen. She died March 11, 1936, in Rochelle Park, New Jersey, but was buried in St. Louis. Emma Portis Adams, who was born while John was serving in Mississippi, married John Dickson. She was living with her sister Georgiana in New York in 1930. She died July 2, 1946, and she too was buried among family in St. Louis.[33]

NINE
Conclusions

Since the days of the Civil War there have been those who have looked to the South as defenders of a fading pre-modern age. Many a young man marched off to war imagining himself as a cavalier battling the Yankee round heads. With images of Sir Walter Scott and a sword in hand, he mounted his mighty steed, kissed his fair damsel goodbye and went to war. Margaret Mitchell wrote her book about the days which were "gone with the wind." The American public loved both the book and the movie. Serious historians, however, realize that this was not the case. The North had more industry, more railroads, and more big cities, but it is not that the South avoided such things. There were some big cities, some factories, and some railroads. When the Confederate States of America was founded it was one of the wealthiest nations in the world. The Southern people were more into agriculture, but they were mainly growing products for distribution in the world market. A businessman will look to a new enterprise with expectations of making greater gains. The planters of the South were making tremendous profits growing products to sell in the world markets, especially cotton. Why should they go into manufacturing? It is not a question of resisting modernization as much as having no reason to change from agriculture.

A biography can do little in proving or disproving historical controversy. It can be a case study, which is a close look at the life of one individual and how he or she reacted to the changing world. John Adams was a soldier, not in the tradition of a mediaeval knight but as a product of the modern world. He came from a family that did some farming, but also were merchants. He went to West Point as the American military marched forward in the modernization of America. In many ways the military academy of the early nineteenth century offered a more modern curriculum than many of the civilian colleges. While a student at Yale or Harvard studied ancient Greek or Latin, the cadet at West Point studied French and German. Which would be more useful in a modern mercantile world? The Point was as much an engineering school as a military academy. The modern soldier must know how to make use of technological advancements in order to fight the modern war. William B. Skelton saw this era as a time when the Army developed the modern officer corps that survives to this day. This is the military education that Adams received.

Upon his graduation from West Point as part of the famous class of 1846, he marched off to war and played a role in the "manifest destiny" of the United States empire. After the treaty of Guadalupe Hidalgo, he battled the first inhabitants of North America from the Apache in New Mexico to the Sioux of Minnesota to the tribes of the Northwest in California. He had to deal with the greed of the white pioneers as they encroached upon the lands of those who came first. He had a job to protect his fellow white American citizens, but as most of those in the professional Army he saw the fairness of protecting the rights of the victims.

Adams was among the first of what William B. Skelton called the "profession of arms." In the modern America of today many have family members who were born in foreign lands, not because their families are recent immigrants but because they were the offspring of those serving in the United States military. This is common today, but Adams's children were among the first to be born in lands far from the birthplace of their parents due to being born to a professional Army officer. Adams was part of the developing officer corps, married and had children while pursuing his career. His wife was the daughter of an Army officer and became an Army wife. Their children were among the first of an American class called "Army brats" today. Georgiana Adams was among the first of those called "Army wives." She lived in the time of "domesticity," and was expected to live up to the standards of the middle class Victorian lady even though she had to do so in the varmint infected deserts of New Mexico or the snow shrouded mountains of California. In her later years she was an Army widow with kids living in various locations throughout the land at a time when most Americans were more deeply rooted farm families.

The debates and discussions about the causes of the Civil War seem

Nine. Conclusions

as heated today as they were a century and a half ago. There is no way that the life of one man can resolve these issues. Many in the South today are still proud of their ancestors who served the Confederacy and feel they have a right to display that pride with the Confederate battle flag. There are others who do not see their cause as the noble "lost cause," but rather as a war to defend slavery and racism. The debates over what the war was about have thus become highly politicized, which has taken a heavy toll on objectivity. It seems that some historians today are more interested in providing information to support their position in these debates. There is no doubt that slavery played a major role in motivating Southerners to secede from the Union. A good case can be made that it is the main reason for such action. It is; however, also true that it is not the only reason, and certainly not the reason that every individual served the cause of Southern independence. The Confederate Constitution reveals some other issues, specifically tariffs, internal improvements, and the rights of the individual states.

John Adams did not own slaves, and slavery played no part in his chosen career as an Army officer. He was in California dealing with marauding state militias attacking, killing, and taking lands from Indians while the election of 1860 unfolded and led to South Carolina and six other states breaking away to form a new nation. Though Adams spent little time in his native state since his joining the United States Army, his resignation tells us that he felt a greater sense of duty to Tennessee than he did the Federal government. His home state failed to follow those first seven states despite their governor, who spoke of the danger to the institution of slavery under the leadership of the newly elected national government. In his inauguration the new president assured Americans that he had no intention of interfering with slavery, and that he had no right to do so. However, not long afterward he ordered every state to contribute in putting down the "rebellion." That is when Tennessee and three other states of the upper South seceded. It is not until after these events that Adams resigned his commission and joined the Confederate Army. He gave up his career, and eventually his life. He did not do so to defend slavery, regardless of the role it played in the unfolding events.

He was but one man who gave up but one life out of more than six hundred thousand. His role proves nothing in debating the events in the most important time in American history. The life of John Adams does remind us that those who played a part in the events were individuals, not merely statistics, who made great sacrifices for what they believed in. John Adams had spent his life in the Army of his country. He also died in the Army of his country, though it had taken on a new name. John Adams died for his country, his home, his family.

Chapter Notes

Preface

1. Col. James R. Binford, "Heroism at Franklin," *Confederate Veteran*, 10 (1902), 457–8.

Introduction

1. John L. O'Sullivan, "The Great Nation of Futurity," *The United States Democratic Review*, Vol. 6 (New York: J. and H. G. Langley, 1839), 426–30.

Chapter One

1. Richard W. Johnson, *A Soldier's Reminiscences in Peace and War* (Philadelphia: J.B. Lippincott, 1886), 10.
2. William B. Skelton, *An American Profession of Arms: The Army Officer Corps, 1784–1861* (Lawrence: University of Kansas Press, 1992), xiii-xv.
3. Stephen E. Ambrose, *Duty, Honor, Country: A History of West Point* (Baltimore: Johns Hopkins Press, 1966), 3–4.
4. Skelton, *An American Profession*, 70–71; Stephen S. Webb, "Army and Empire: English Garrison Government in Britain and America, 1569–1763," *William and Mary Quarterly*, 3rd ser. 34 (January 1977), 1–32; see also Stephen S. Webb, *The Governors-General: The English Army and the Definition of the Empire, 1569–1681* (Chapel Hill: University of North Carolina Press, 1979).
5. Skelton, *An American Profession*, 72; Lt. Col. Josiah Harmar to Henry Knox, March 18, 1787, Knox Papers.
6. Skelton, *An American Profession*, 116–117; Allan Peskin, *Winfield Scott and the Profession of Arms* (Kent, OH: Kent State University Press, 2003), 59.
7. *North American Review*, 34 (1832), 257.
8. Leonard D. White, *The Jacksonians: A Study in Administrative History 1829–1861* (New York: Macmillan, 1954), 187–90; 209–11; House Report 303, 24th Congress, 2nd sess., p. 166 (November 26, 1833); Senate Doc. 247, 23rd Congress, 1st session (March 1, 1837).
9. Skelton, *An American Profession*, 133; Francis Paul Prucha, *The Sword of the Republic: The United States Army on the Frontier, 1783–1846* (New York: Macmillan, 1969), 235–248.
10. Leslie R. Tucker, *Major General Isaac Ridgeway Trimble: Biography of a Baltimore Confederate* (Jefferson, NC: McFarland, 2005), 27; Russell F. Weigley, *The American Way of War: A History of United States Military Strategy and Policy* (Bloomington: Indiana University Press, 1977), 78–91; Peskin, *Winfield Scott*, 61–62.
11. Skelton, *An American Profession*, 19, 155–57; Edward M. Coffman, *The Old Army: A Portrait of the American Army in Peacetime, 1784–1898* (New York: Oxford University Press, 1986), 46–47; William Starr Myers, *A Study in Personality: General George Brinton McClellan* (New York: D. Appleton-Century, 1934), 12; statistical data from *Historical Register and Dictionary of the United States Army, from Its Organization, September 29, 1789, to March 2, 1903* (Washington, D.C.: Government Printing Office, 1903).
12. Thomas J. Fleming, *West Point: The Men and Times of the United States Military Academy* (New York: William Morrow, 1969), 112–113; Skelton, 155–157.
13. Ann Green, "Gulbangi Family and Genealogy Research," http://www.Gulbangi.com/5families-0/p171.htmi4269: 7–10; Rita Grace Adams, *Brigadier-General John Adams, C.S.A.: Biography of a Frontier American (1825–1864)*, Ph.D. dissertation (University Microfilm, Inc., 1964), 13.
14. Green, "Gulbangi," 4, 27; Rita Grace

Notes—Chapter Two

Adams, "Biography," 13–14; Marriage Record, Book I, 1789–1837, Davidson County, Tennessee, p. 216.

15. Green, 27; Rita Grace Adams, "Biography," 14–16; Davidson County, General Index to Deeds, 1784–1871, p. 7; Giles County, Tennessee, Census, 1840 and 1850; Giles County, Tennessee, General Index to Deeds, 1810–1859, p. 6; *The Whig Courier*, February 22, 1839; *The Whig Courier*, June 28, 1839; Claude A. Campbell, "Banking and Finance in Tennessee During the Depression of 1837," *East Tennessee Historical Society Publication*, No. 9 (1937), 23.

16. Rita Grace Adams, "Biography," 18–19; AGO, Application Papers of Cadets, Doc. No. A 6, 1841; James McCollum, *A Brief Sketch of the Settlement and Early History of Giles County, Tennessee* (Pulaski: Pulaski Citizen, 1928), 105.

17. Green, "Gulbangi," 27; AGO, Application Papers.

18. AGO, Cadets: Arranged in Order of the Respective Classes, June 1846.

19. John C. Waugh, *The Class of 1846: From West Point to Appomattox* (New York: Warner Books, 1994), 11–13, 17; Rita Grace Adams, "Biography," 20–21; Sidney Forman, *West Point: A History of the United States Military Academy* (New York: Columbia University Press, 1950), 91–92; Coffman, *The Old Army*, 47.

20. Waugh, *Class of 1846*, 7–8, 18; Ambrose, *Duty, Honor, Country*, 139–40.

21. William Dutton to Miss Lucy J. Mathews, February 18, 1843, Dutton Papers.

22. Ambrose, *Duty, Honor, Country*, 153; John Pope to Lucretia Pope, July 7, 1842, Pope Papers; Waugh, *Class of 1846*, 30; George B. McClellan to his sister, Frederica, September 10, 1842, McClellan Papers.

23. George B. McClellan to his sister Frederica, September 10, 1842, McClellan Papers; William Dutton to his brother, C. Dutton, June 19, 1846, Dutton Papers; Ambrose, *Duty, Honor, Country*, 154.

24. McClellan; Dutton; Waugh, *Class of 1846*, 30.

25. 25. U.S. Corps of Cadets, Orders, Special Orders No. 78, 1845; *Regulations Established for the Organization and Government of the Military Academy* (New York: Wiley and Putnam, 1839), 31–36, 40–43; Waugh, *Class of 1846*, 30; Ambrose, *Duty, Honor, Country*, 148, 159–64.

26. Foreman, *West Point*, 95; Ambrose, *Duty, Honor, Country*, 131–33; Waugh, *Class of 1846*, 25–30; White, *The Jacksonians*, 205–07; Richard S. Ewell to Rebecca Ewell, August 29, 1836, Ewell Papers.

27. Ambrose, *Duty, Honor, Country*, 133–34; William Dutton to his brother C. Dutton, June 19, 1842, Dutton Papers.

28. Waugh, *Class of 1846*, 18–22, Ambrose, *Duty, Honor, Country*, 152; Foreman, *West Point*, 92–95; George Derby to Mary Townsend, July 2, 1842; William Dutton to John W. Mathews, July 12, 1842, Dutton Papers; Jacob Whitman Baily, to Mrs. Jane Keely, June 27, 1829.

29. Ambrose, *Duty, Honor, Country*, 149–150; William Dutton to Lucy J. Mathews, March 11, 1843, Dutton Papers; George W. Cullum to Alfred Huidekoper, November 22, 1829, Cullum File.

30. Waugh, *Class of 1846*, 37–39.

31. James W. Sohureman, to Mary Sohureman, February 14, 1840, Tucker Papers (copy).

32. Ambrose, *Duty, Honor, Country*, 143.

33. Waugh, *Class of 1846*, 67–68; Cadets; AGO, Letters Received, Doc. No. 146 A, 1846.

34. George B. McClellan to Frederica, May 3, 1846, McClellan Papers; Ambrose, *Duty, Honor, Country*, 140; Cullum, Vol. 2, No. 1296, 275; AGO, Letters Received, Doc. No. 224 T; AGO, Letters Sent, 1846, 398; AGO, Letters Received, Doc. No. 194 A.

Chapter Two

1. Frank S. Edwards, *A Campaign in New Mexico* (Ann Arbor, MI: University Microfilms, 1966), 124–25.

2. John Edward Weems, *To Conquer a Peace: The War Between the United States and Mexico.* (Garden City, NY: Doubleday, 1974), 188.

3. Brigadier General Winfield Scott to Joel R. Poinsett, January 12, 1839, in C. P. Stacey, ed., "A Private Report of General Winfield Scott on the Border Situation in 1839," *Canadian Historical Review* 21 (December 1940), 412; Skelton, *An American Profession of Arms*, 326–47.

4. Richard Bruce Winders, *Mr. Polk's Army: The American Military Experience in the Mexican War* (College Station: Texas A&M University Press, 1997), 174–5.

5. William A. Beck, *New Mexico: A History of Four Centuries* (Norman: University of Oklahoma Press, 1962), 102–109.

6. Ibid., 110–116.

7. Ibid., 123–25; Ralph Emerson Twitchell, *The History of the Military Occupation of the Territory of New Mexico from 1846 to 1851 by*

Notes — Chapter Two

the Government of the United States (Chicago: Rio Grande Press, 1963; first published in 1909), 67.

8. Beck, *New Mexico*, 125–129; Twitchell, *Military Occupation of New Mexico*, 69.

9. George Winston Smith, *Chronicles of the Gringos: The U.S. Army in the Mexican War, 1846–1848; Accounts of Eyewitnesses and Combatants* (Albuquerque: University of New Mexico Press, 1968), 27; Richard Bruce Winders, *Mr. Polk's Army*, 55.

10. Ibid., Skelton, *An American Profession of Arms*, 210–12; James F. Sunderman, ed., *Journey Into Wilderness: An Army Surgeon's Accountant of Life in Camp and Field During the Creek and Seminole Wars, 1836–1838* (Gainesville: University of Florida Press, 1953), 3; William S. Myers, ed., *The Mexican War Diary of George B. McClellan* (Princeton, NJ: Princeton University Press, 1917), 38–9; Lieutenant Thomas Williams to John R. Williams, February 28, 1847, Williams Papers.

11. Winders, *Mr. Polk's Army*, 64.

12. Skelton, *An American Profession of Arms*, 310–11.

13. Much of the life of the Bent brothers came from A. W. Bell, "On the Native Races of New Mexico," *Journal of the Ethnological Society of London*, 1869.

14. Richard A. Fletcher, *Saint James's Catapult: The Life and Times of Diego Gelmirez of Santiago de Compostela* (Oxford: Oxford University Press, 1984), 1–25.

15. George P. Hammond and Agapito Rey, eds., *Narratives of the Coronado Expedition 1540–1542* (Albuquerque: University of New Mexico Press, 1940), 1–100.

16. A. W. Bell, "Native Races."

17. Regular Army Organization Returns, First Dragoons, October 1846. (Hereafter abbreviated RAO.)

18. Winders, *Mr. Polk's Army*, 24; Richard Smith Elliott, *The Mexican War Correspondence of Richard Smith Elliott* (Norman: University of Oklahoma Press, 1951), 225.

19. Winders, *Mr. Polk's Army*, 98–202.

20. John S. D. Eisenhower, *So Far from God: The U.S. War With Mexico 1846–1848* (Norman: University of Oklahoma Press, 1989), 205–6; Cutts, 42–43.

21. Winders, *Mr. Polk's Army*, 170–71.

22. Eisenhower, *So Far from God*, 197–8; Winders, *Mr. Polk's Army*, 171; Ralph Bieber, ed., *Marching with the Army of the West 1846–1848* (Glendale, CA: Arthur H. Clark, 1936), 317.

23. Eisenhower, *So Far from God*, 198–9.

24. Chris Emmett, *Fort Union and the Winning of the Southwest* (Norman: University of Oklahoma Press, 1965), 31; Philip St. George Cooke, *The Conquest of New Mexico and California in 1846–1848* (Chicago: Rio Grande Press, 1964; reprint, *The Conquest of New Mexico and California*, New York: G. P. Putnam's Sons, 1878), 7, 8.

25. Cooke, *The Conquest of New Mexico*, 18–26.

26. Ibid., 32; Emmett, *Fort Union*, 33–34.

27. Twitchell, *Military Occupation*, 89–93.

28. Ibid., 133–34; Emmett, *Fort Union*, 25–26. The numerous errors in the quotes are as written by Bent.

29. *Missouri Statesman*, January 30, 1844; Albert Castel, *General Sterling Price and the Civil War in the West* (Baton Rouge: Louisiana State University, 1968), 4; Emmett, 45; Adjutant General's Office, Letters Received, Doc. No. 285 A, 1846 (hereafter referred to as AGO and LR); Eisenhower, 207; Louis Pelzer, *Marches of the Dragoons in the Mississippi Valley: An Account of Marches and Activities of the First Regiment United States Dragoons in the Mississippi Valley Between the Years 1833 and 1850* (Iowa City: State Historical Society, 1917), 145.

30. Elliott, *Mexican War*, 169–70; Winders, *Mr. Polk's Army*, 137–8.

31. Elliott, *Mexican War*, 170–73.

32. Ibid., 173–4.

33. Winders, *Mr. Polk's Army*, 132–37.

34. Ibid., 126.

35. AGO, Letters Received, Doc. No. A, 1846; AGO, Post Returns, Albuquerque, February, 1847; Bieber, *Marching With*, 325; Marc Simmons, *Albuquerque: A Narrative History* (Albuquerque: University of New Mexico Press, 1982), 91, 139–40.

36. Eisenhower, *So Far from God*, 235; Blanche C. Grant, *When Old Trails Were New: The Story of Taos* (New York: Press of the Pioneers, 1934), 89–90; Colonel Henry Inman, *The Old Santa Fe Trail: The Story of a Great Highway* (Minneapolis: Ross and Haines, 1966), 115–16; Twitchell, *Military Occupation*, 122–23; 133–34.

37. Grant, *Old Trails*, 91–93.

38. Eisenhower, *So Far from God*, 235–37; Grant, *Old Trails*, 93–94; Inman, *The Old Santa Fe*, 116–120; Twitchell, *Military Occupation*, 123–128.

39. Eisenhower, *So Far from God*, 237; Post Returns, Albuquerque, January, 1847.

40. Eisenhower, *So Far from God*, 237; Inman, *The Old Santa Fe*, 124–25; Twitchell, *Military Occupation*, 128.

41. Inman, *The Old Santa Fe*, 125–26; Eisenhower, *So Far from God*, 238; Twitchell, *Military Occupation*, 128.
42. Inman, *The Old Santa Fe*, 126–28; Twitchell, *Military Occupation*, 129–32; Eisenhower, *So Far from God*, 238–9.
43. Eisenhower, *So Far from God*, 239–40; Twitchell, *Military Occupation*, 133–34; Inman, *The Old Santa Fe*, 132.
44. Eisenhower, *So Far from God*, 242.
45. Twitchell, *Military Occupation*, 98–100.
46. Eisenhower, *So Far from God*, 243–246; Elliott, *Mexican War*, 36.
47. Eisenhower, *So Far from God*, 243, 247–8.
48. Ibid., 249–50.
49. Post Returns, Albuquerque, February, 1847; June–July 1847; Regular Army, Muster Rolls, Inspection Returns, First Dragoons, Company I, August 1847; Post Returns, Albuquerque, December 1847 and January–February 1848; RAO, January 1848.
50. AGO, LR, Doc. No. 170 P, 1848; Jones to Price, November 20, 1847; Price to Jones, December 17, 1847; *Santa Fe Republican*, December 11, 1847, January 8, 15, 22, 1848; Bieber, *Marching with the Army*, 61–62.
51. AGO LR, Doc. No. 170, 1848; AGO LR, Doc. No. 565 P, 1848; RAO. Ret., 1 Drag., January–March, 1848; Bieber, *Marching with the Army*, 64.
52. AGO LR, Doc. No. 170 P, 1848; Bieber, *Marching with the Army*, 355.
53. AGO LR, Doc. No. 170 P, 1848; Bieber, *Marching with the Army*, 356.
54. AGO LR, Doc. No. 170 P, 1848; AGO LR, Doc. No. 565 P, 1848; Bieber, *Marching with the Army*, 357–58.
55. Winders, *Mr. Polk's Army*, 202–6.
56. Ibid., 17–18.
57. Emmett, *Fort Union*, 79.
58. RAO. Ret., 1 Drag., April–July, 1848.

Chapter Three

1. *The Santa Fe Republican*, October 1, 1847; November 20, 1847; Robert Walter Frazer, *Forts and Supplies: The Role of the Army in the Economy of the Southwest* (Albuquerque: University of New Mexico Press, 1983), 27.
2. *The Santa Fe Republican*, May 15, 1848; Frazer, *Forts and Supplies*, 27.
3. Joel H. Silby, *Storm Over Texas: The American Controversy and the Road to the Civil War* (New York: Oxford University Press, 2005), 123–124.
4. Based on the following sources: Eric Foner, *Free Soil, Free Labor, Free Men: The Ideology of the Republican Party Before the Civil War* (New York: Oxford University Press, 1970); William W. Freehling, *The Road to Disunion: Secessionists at Bay 1776–1854* (New York: Oxford University Press, 1990); Michael F. Holt, *The Political Crisis of the 1850s* (New York: Wiley, 1978); David M. Potter, *The Impending Crisis 1848–1861* (New York: Harper and Row, 1976).
5. Joel S. Fetzer, "Economic Self-interest or Cultural Marginality? Anti-immigration Sentiment and Nativist Political Movements in France, Germany, and the USA," *Journal of Ethnic and Migration Studies*, Vol. 26, Issue 1 (January 2000), 5–23; Ray A. Billington, *The Protestant Crusade, 1800–1860: A Study of the Origins of American Nativism* (New York: Macmillan, 1938); Tyler Anbinder, *Nativism and Slavery: The Northern Know Nothings and the Politics of the 1850s* (New York: Oxford University Press, 1997).
6. Col. George Archibald McCall, with Robert W. Frazer, ed., *New Mexico in 1850: A Military View* (Norman: University of Oklahoma Press, 1968), 26, 80.
7. Ibid., 38.
8. Ibid., 90–98.
9. Ibid., 55–58, 85–86.
10. Robert W. Frazer, *Forts and Supplies*, 20–29.
11. Marc Simmons, *New Mexico: A Bicentennial History* (New York: W. W. Norton, 1977), 133.
12. Loomis Morton Ganaway, *New Mexico and the Sectional Controversy 1846–1861* (Philadelphia: Porcupine Press, 1976), 36–7.
13. Robert W. Frazer, *Forts and Supplies*, 33–39.
14. Ibid., 39–60.
15. Ganaway, *New Mexico and the Sectional Controversy*, 37–41.
16. Ibid., 41–44.
17. Ibid., 44–46.
18. Ibid., 46–49.
19. Ibid., 49–52.
20. Ibid., 52–59; Marc Simmons, *Albuquerque: A Narrative History* (Albuquerque: University of New Mexico Press, 1982), 144–45.
21. Edward Everett Dale, *The Indians of the Southwest: A Century of Development Under the United States* (Norman: University of Oklahoma Press, 1949), 3; Skelton, *An American Profession of Arms*, 313. Sheridan has traditionally been credited with the "dead

Notes — Chapter Four

Indian" quote. I have no desire to enter a debate on the authenticity of this claim; there are many examples of such an attitude throughout American history.

22. Dale, *The Indians of the Southwest*, 13; William A. Keleher, *Turmoil in New Mexico 1846–1868* (Santa Fe: Rydal Press, 1952), 53–54.
23. McCall, *New Mexico in 1850*, 99–100.
24. Ibid., 100–104.
25. Ibid., 180–88; Odie B. Faulk, *Crimson Desert: Indian Wars of the American Southwest* (New York: Oxford University Press, 1974), 147–48.
26. Frazer, *Forts and Supplies*, 30–58; *The Republican* September 6, 1848; "Position and Distribution of Troops," 31, Cong., I sess., Sen. Exec., Doc. I, 188d; "Position and Distribution of Troops," 31, Cong., sess., Sen Exec. Doc. I, Part II, 116d.
27. McCall, *New Mexico in 1850*, 59–62.
28. James A. Bennett, Clinton E. Brooks, ed., *Forts and Forays: A Dragoon in New Mexico, 1850–1856* (Albuquerque: University of New Mexico Press, 1996), viii–ix; Edward M. Coffman, *The Old Army: A Portrait of the American Army in Peacetime, 1784–1898* (New York: Oxford University Press, 1986), 141; Regimental Returns First Dragoons, January to December 1852, AGO, Record Group 94.
29. Frazer, *Forts and Supplies*, 3–4; Bennett, *Forts and Forays*, x; Percival G. Lowe, *Five Years a Dragoon and Other Adventures on the Great Plains* (Norman: University of Oklahoma Press, 1965), 122.
30. McCall, *New Mexico in 1850*, 34, 111–123, 130–36, 153–56, 162–66; Bennett, *Forts and Forays*, xiii; Frazer, *Forts and Supplies*, 29.
31. McCall, *New Mexico in 1850*, 166–174.
32. Ibid., 123–30.
33. Ibid., 136–144.
34. Ibid., 145–153.
35. Ibid., 174–76.
36. Ibid., 157–162.
37. RAO. Ret., 1 Drag., July and August 1848; AGO LR, Doc. No. 1105 B, 1848.
38. Post Returns, Taos, November 1848 to January 1849.
39. Records of United States Army Commands, Department of New Mexico, Letters Received, Doc. No. 4 B and 10 B, 1849 (Hereafter referred to as DNM LR or LS for letters sent.)
40. *Ibid*.
41. Post Returns, Taos, March–April 1849; Inspection Returns, 1 Drag., Co. I, April 1849; DNM LR, Doc. No. 14 B, 1849.
42. Inspection Returns, 1 Drag., Co. I, November 1849; DNM LR, Doc. No. 3 G, 1849; Bennett, *Forts and Forays*, xv–xx; McCall, *New Mexico in 1850*, 104.
43. DNM LS, Vol. 6 (1850), 84; Post Returns, Rayado, May 1850; DNM LR, Doc. No. 7 A, 1850; Post Returns, Las Vegas, June 1850; McCall, *New Mexico in 1850*, 137, 157.
44. DNM LR, Doc. No. 9 A, 1850.
45. DNM LR, Doc. Nos. 11 A, 12 A, 13 A and 32 G, 1850; Post Returns, Las Vegas, June and July 1850.
46. DNM LR, Doc. Nos. 12 A, 14 A, 35 G, and 43, 1850; Post Returns, Rayado, August 1850. It is assumed that the transfer to Company K of 1st Dragoons is correct and not mistaking the Company K of the 2nd Dragoons which Adams had been with previously.
47. DNM LR, Doc. No. 2 A, 1851; DNM LS, Vol. 7 (1851), p. 51.
48. DNM LR, Doc. No. 3 A, 1851; DNM LS, Vol. 8 (1851), p. 58.
49. Inspection Returns, 1 Drag., Co. K, April 1851; Post Returns, Las Vegas, March–June 1851; DNM LS, Vol. 7 (1851), 60, 140–41, 199, 207–09; DNM LR, Doc. Nos. 12 A and 41 A, 1851.
50. 1. AGO LR, Doc. No. 212 S, 1851; Records of U.S. Army Commands, Department of the West, General and Special and Division Orders, Special Order No. 64, 1851 (hereafter abbreviated Dept. of the West).
51. Post Returns, Rayado, July 1851; Inspection Returns, 1 Drag., Co. I, November 1851; DNM LR, Doc. No. 32 B, 1851; DNM LS, Vol. 5 (1851), 102–03, 110.

Chapter Four

1. United States National Park Service, *Soldier and Brave: Historical Places Associated With Indian Affairs and the Indian Wars in the Trans-Mississippi West* (Washington: U.S. Government Printing Office, 1971), 169–71; Marcus Lee Hansen, *Old Fort Snelling, 1819–1858* (Minneapolis: Ross and Haines, 1958), xiii–xiv, 80–86.
2. Rhoda R. Gilman, *The Story of Minnesota's Past* (St. Paul: Minnesota Historical Society, 1991); Steve Hall, *Fort Snelling: Colossus of the Wilderness* (St. Paul: Minnesota Historical Society, 1987).
3. Roger G. Kennedy, *Men on the Moving Frontier* (Palo Alto, CA: American West, 1969), 56–7.
4. Skelton, *An American Profession of Arms*, 305–330.
5. Royal B. Hassrick, Dorothy Maxwell,

and Cile M. Bach, *The Sioux: Life and Customs of a Warrior Society* (Norman: University of Oklahoma Press, 1964); Thomas E. Mails, *Dog Soldiers, Bear Men, and Buffalo Women: A Study of the Societies and Cults of the Plains Indians* (New York: Prentice-Hall, 1973).

6. William W. Warren, *History of the Ojibway People* (St. Paul: Borealis Books, reprint, 1984); F. Densmore, *Chippewa Customs* (St. Paul: Minnesota Historical Society Press, 1978); E. J. Danziger, Jr., *The Chippewa of Lake Superior* (Norman: University of Oklahoma Press, 1979).

7. Paul Radin, *The Winnebago Tribe* (Lincoln: University of Nebraska Press, 1990).

8. Marcus Lee Hansen, *Old Fort Snelling*, 48–49.

9. William E. Lass, *Minnesota: A History* (New York: W. W. Norton, 1998), 108–109.

10. Ibid., 110–112; Hansen, *Old Fort Snelling*, 49; Kennedy, *Men on the Moving Frontier*, 62; Kenneth Carley, *The Sioux Uprising of 1862* (St. Paul: Minnesota Historical Society, 1976), 103–104.

11. RAO Ret., 1 Drag., May 1852; AGO LR, Doc. No. 166 L and No. 199 L, 1852.

12. Saint Paul Pioneer, May 27, 1852; AGO LR, Doc. Nos. 166 L, 199 L and 202 L, 1852; Hansen, *Old Fort Snelling*, 49.

13. AGO LR, Doc. Nos. 83 A and 32 A, 1852, Nos. 51 A and 76 A, 1853; RAO Ret., 1 Drag., September 1852 and June 1854.

14. Hensen, *Old Fort Snelling*, 74–75.

15. Dept. West, LS, Vol. 2, p. 43 (hereafter referred to as DW); Governors' Collection, Minnesota State Archives, File 27; John Adams to Governor Gorman, October 6, 1853. (Hereafter abbreviated as Gov. Col.)

16. Gov. Col., file 30. Lt. Col. F. Lee to Governor Gorman, January 24, 1854, and January 28, 1854.

17. RAO Ret., 1 Drag., April 1854; DW LR, Doc. Nos 10 L, 9 L, 11 L, 13–15 A, 18 A, 1854 and No. 6 A, 1853.

18. Skelton, *An American Profession of Arms*, 189–90.

19. Ibid.; RAO, R.G. 393, Fort Snelling, April, 1853; McCall, *New Mexico in 1850*, 119; Charles McDougall to John Adams, August 22, 1853.

20. Skelton, *An American Profession of Arms*, 203–04.

21. Ibid., 205–08.

22. "Gulbangi Family and Genealogy Research," Person Page 48, 8–10.

23. "Gulbangi Family and Genealogy Research," Person Page 48, 2–7, 19–21.

24. "Gulbangi Family and Genealogy Research, Person Page 14, 16–17.

25. DW LR, Docs. Nos. 13 A, 13 L, 14 A, 18 A, 23 A, and 101 L, 1854; DW, orders, Special Order No. 20, 1854.

Chapter Five

1. Percival G. Lowe, with an introduction by Don Russell, *Five Years a Dragoon: (49 to 54) And Other Adventures on the Great Plains* (Norman: University of Oklahoma, 1965), 131.

2. Skelton, *An American Profession of Arms*, 298–99.

3. Barbara Welter, "The Cult of True Womanhood: 1820–1860," *American Quarterly* 18 (1966), 151–174; Barbara Welter, *Dimity Convictions: The American Woman in the Nineteenth Century* (Athens: Ohio University Press, 1977); Skelton, *An American Profession of Arms*, 205.

4. DW LR, Doc. No. 22F, 1854; United States National Park Service, *Soldier and Brave: Historical Places Associated With Indian Affairs and the Indian Wars in the Trans-Mississippi West* (Washington: U.S. Government Printing Office, 1971), 145–6.

5. Lowe, *Five Years a Dragoon*, 122; DW LR, Doc. No. 37A, 1854; RAO, 1 Drag., May 1854; DW, Special Orders, Special Order No. 42, 1854, p. 38; Mark Mayo Boatner III, *Civil War Dictionary* (New York: David McKay, 1959), 276.

6. DW LR, Doc. No. 38A, 1854; Dept. West., L.S., Vol. 9 (1854), p. 67; Lowe, *Five Years a Dragoon*, 124–126.

7. Lowe, *Five Years a Dragoon*, 128.

8. Ibid., 130.

9. Ibid., 132–134.

10. Ibid., 134–135.

11. Ibid., 136–138.

12. Ibid., 138.

13. Andrew K. Gregg, *Drums of Yesterday: The Forts of New Mexico* (Santa Fe: Press of the Territorian, 1968), 7–8.

14. Ibid., 24–25; Records of U.S. Army Commands, Fort Craig, N.M., Orders, Vol. 103 (1853–1863), Orders No. 23, 25, 26, 31, 1854; AGO LR, Doc. No. 65 A, 1855.

15. Albert G. Brackett, *History of the United States Cavalry, from the Formation of the Federal Government to the 1st of June, 1863* (New York: Greenwood Press, 1968), 158–161.

16. Dale, *The Indians of the Southwest*, 51–52; *Laws of the Legislative Assembly of New Mexico*, December 27–29, 1854, 115–117, 119, 121; Garland to Thomas, June 30, July 30, Au-

gust 30, September 30, and October 31, 1854, LS, Department of New Mexico (hereafter referred to as DNM, v. 9, pp. 200–240; Post Returns, Fort Union, September 1854.

17. Nicholas to Fauntleroy, January 11, 1855, LS, DNM, v. 9, pp. 265; Morris F. Taylor, "Campaigns Against the Jicarilla Apache, 1855," *New Mexico Historical Review* (April 1970), 121.

18. Fauntleroy to Nichols, January 18 and 22, February 9, 1855, LS, FU, USAC, RG 393; Garland to Thomas, January 31, 1855, Garland to Cooper, February 2, 1855, LS, DNM, v. 9, p. 287, USAC, RG 393; Post Returns, Fort Union, January–February 1855, AGO, RG 94.

19. Garland to Meriwether, January 22, 1855, Garland to Thomas, January 31, 1855, LS, DNM, v. 9, pp. 276–282, USAC, RG 393; Special Orders No. 12, HQ DNM, February 5, 1855, DNM Orders, v. 27, p. 140, USAC, RG 393; Nichols to Fauntleroy, February 6, 1855, LS, DNM, v. 9, pp. 292–297, USAC, RG 393.

20. Frazer, *Forts and Supplies*, 67.

21. Garland to Thomas, March 31, 1855, Sen. Ex. Doc. No. 1, 34 Cong., 1 sess; Carson to Meriwether, April 11, 1855, LR (434–1855, OIA, RG 75; Taylor, "Campaigns," 119–136.

22. DNM LR, Doc. No. 19 F, 1855; DNM LS, Vol. 9 (1855), p. 331.

23. Fauntleroy to Sturgis, April 30 and May 5 and 10, 1855, and Garland to Thomas, May 31, 1855. Sen. Ex. Doc., No. 1 Cong 1 sess. (Serial 811), pt. 2, pp. 64–69; Post Returns, Fort Union, July 1855, AGO, RG 94; DNM LS, Vol. 9 (1855), p. 331-2; RAO. Ret., 1 Drag., May 1855; DNM LR, Doc. No. 35 F, 1855.

24. Jacqueline Dorgan Meketa, *Legacy of Honor: The Life of Rafael Chacon, A Nineteenth Century New Mexican* (Albuquerque: University of New Mexico Press, 1986), 103; Whittlesey to Sturgis, May 26, 1855, and Post Adjutant to Carson, September 2, 1855, L.S., F.U., USAC, GR 393; Orders No. 24, HQ, DNM, September 14, 1855, DNM Orders, v. 36, p. 342, USAC, RG 393.

25. Garland to Thomas, July 31, 1855, and March 31, 1856. LS DNM, v. 9, pp. 380–381, 467–468, USAC, RG 393; Meriwether to Manypenny, September 15, 1855, LR (535–1855, OIA, RG 75; Sen. Ex. Doc. No. 1, 34 Cong., 1 sess. (Serial 810), pt. 1, pp. 506–512.

26. DNM LR, Doc. No. 35 F, 1855; Post Returns, Fort Union, June 1855; RAO Ret., 1 Drag., July 1855; DNM LR, Doc., No. 41 F, 1855; Post Returns, Fort Union, August 1855; Post Returns, Fort Craig, August 1855 to May 1856.

27. Post Returns, Fort Craig, March 1856; Headquarters of the Army, General Order No. 2, 1856; Post Returns, Fort Craig, May 1856; DNM, LR, Doc. No. 40 A, 1856.

28. DNM, LR Doc. No. 51 A, 1856; Recruiting Service, Letters Sent, Vol. 2 (1856–1857), p. 274.

29. *Regulations for the Army of The United States, 1857* (New York: Harper and Brothers, 1857), Article XLVII, "Recruiting Service," paragraphs 1284–1350; *New York Times*, December 27, 1864.

30. *New York Daily Times*, March 23, 1857, and April 3, 1857; AGO, Register of Recruits, Vol. 7 (1853 – n.d.), pp. 267–279, 491–493; AGO, LR, Doc. No. 604 R, 1856; Headquarters of the Army, LR, Doc. No. 17 M, 1857; AGO, LR, Doc. Nos. 50 A and 142 A, 1857; AGO LR, Doc. No. 125 A, 1857.

31. Rec. Serv., LS, Vol. 3 (1858), pp. 79, 90; AGO, LR, Docs. Nos. 98 A, 107 A, 288 A, 291 A, 357 A, 364 A, 1858; "Gulbangi Family and Genealogy Research," 3, 6.

Chapter Six

1. *Marysville Appeal*, October 18, 1861.

2. Edward Everett Dale, *The Indians of the Southwest*, 25; Edward D. Castillo, "Short Overview of California Indian History," http://www.ceres.ca.gov/nahc/califindian.html (1998).

3. Castillo, "Short Overview," 4–6; Robert F. Heizer, et al., *Handbook of North American Indians*, Vol. 8 (Washington: Smithsonian Institution, 1978), 100; Jack D. Forbes, *Native Americans of California and Nevada: A Handbook* (Healdsburg, CA: National Publishers, 1969), 29.

4. Castillo, "Short Overview," 7–8; Heizer, *Handbook of North American Indians*, 105–6; *San Francisco Chronicle*, September 9, 1900.

5. *San Francisco Chronicle*, September 9, 1900; Castillo, "Short Overview," 9; Hubert Howe Bancroft, *History of California* (reprint, Santa Barbara: Wallace Hebbert, 1963–64), 474; Heizer, *Handbook of North American Indians*, 108.

6. Skelton, *An American Profession of Arms*, 311.

7. Edward Everett Dale, *The Indians of the Southwest*, 27–30.

8. Ibid., 30–40; Castillo, "Short Overview," 11.

9. Chapter 133, Statutes of California, April 22, 1850; Chapter 231, Statutes of Cali-

fornia, April 8, 1860; *San Francisco Bulletin*, March 27, 1861.

10. Robert F. Heizer and Alan F. Almquist, *The Other Californians: Prejudice and Discrimination Under Spain, Mexico, and the United States to 1920* (Berkeley: University of California Press, 1971), 53; *Alta California*, April 7, 1855.

11. Ross Browne, *Report of the Debates in the Convention of California on the Formation of the State Constitution* (Washington: John T. Tower, 1850), 64–65.

12. Peter H. Burnett, "Governor's Annual Message to the Legislature, January 7, 1851," in *Journals of the Senate and Assembly of the State of California, at the Second Session of the Legislature, 1851–1852* (San Francisco: G. K. Fitch, and V. E. Geiger, State Printers, 1852), 13–18; California Constitution of 1850, Art. VII, Sect. 3.

13. AGO, LR, Doc. No. 288 A, 1858; Fort Crook, LS, January 17, 1859; Dept. Pacific (hereafter referred to as DP) LR, December 27, 1858.

14. AGO, LR, Doc. No. 111 A, 1859; Post Returns, Fort Crook, January 1859; DP LR, January 17, 1859; Post Returns, Fort Crook, February 1859; Fort Crook, LS, June 6, 1859; Martin F. Schmitt, ed., *General George Crook: His Autobiography* (Norman: University of Oklahoma Press, 1946), 26–48.

15. Post Returns, Fort Crook, February 1859; Fort Crook, LS, January 20, March 12, May 10, and June 6, 1859.

16. Fort Crook, LS, January 12 and March 12, 1859; Fort Crook, Orders No. 12, March 21, 1859, and No. 13, April 3, 1859.

17. Fort Crook, Orders No. 20, May 17 and No. 24, June 4, 1859; Fort Crook, LS, June 6, 1859.

18. Fort Crook, LS, June 6, June 14, 1859; July 27, and August 10 and 15, 1859; Fort Crook Orders, No. 21, May 25, 1859, No. 28, July 7, 1859; DP LS, Vol. 10, p. 73; John H. and David J. Eicher, *Civil War High Commands* (Stanford: Stanford University Press, 2001), 363.

19. Fort Crook, LS, August 10, 1859; David Rich Lewis, *Neither Wolf Nor Dog: American Indians, Environment, and Agrarian Change* (New York: Oxford University Press, 1994), 85–88.

20. Fort Crook, Orders, No. 32, August 15, 1859; Fort Crook, LS, August 19 and August 22, 1859.

21. Fort Crook, LS, August 21 and August 25, 1859.

22. Fort Crook, Orders, No. 33, August 25, No. 39, August 30, 1859, and No. 42, September 19, 1859; Fort Crook, LS, August 29, September 2, September 4, 1859.

23. DP LS, Vol. 10, pp. 104 and 111, September 26, 1859.

24. Fort Crook, LS, October 14 and December 28, 1859; *Sacramento Union*, October 28, December 3, December 12, and December 17, 1859.

25. San Francisco *Bulletin*, January 21, 1860.

26. Ibid.

27. "Gulbangi Family and Genealogy Research," Person Page 14, 5.

28. Fort Crook, LS, December 28, 1859; Fort Crook, Orders, Nos. 49, 50, 51 and 52, 1859 and Orders Nos. 1–7, 1860.

29. San Francisco *Bulletin*, January 21, May 11, and June 18, 1860; "Majority Report of the Special Joint Committee on the Mendocino War," in *Appendix to Journals of the Senate, of the Eleventh Session of the Legislature of the State of California* (Sacramento: C.T. Botts, State Printer, 1860), 4–7.

30. *San Francisco Bulletin*, May 24, 1860.

31. DP LS, Vol. 10, p. 137, February 21, 1860; Fort Crook LS, March 24, April 12, and May 12, 1860; Letters received at Fort Crook, May 14, May 16, May 17 and May 18, 1860.

32. LR at Fort Crook, May 16 and May 17, 1860; William Wright (Dan DeQuille), *History of the Big Bonanza* (Hartford, CT: American Publishing Co., 1877), 118–120.

33. Fort Crook, Orders, Special Order No. 14, May 21, 1860; Fort Crook, LS, May 28, 1860.

34. Fort Crook, LS, May 28, 1860; DP LS, Vol. 10, p. 167, June 6, 1860.

35. Fort Crook, LS, June 13 and 21, and July 21, 1860; DP, LS, Vol. 10, p. 172, June 18, 1860.

36. Fort Crook, LS, September 25 and 26, October 6, November 11, and December 5, 1860; Fort Crook, Orders, Special Order No. 30, November 28, 1860, and No. 19, November 7, 1860, and No. 3, January 12, 1861.

37. Post Returns, Fort Crook, April, June 1861; AGO, LR, Doc. No. 333 A, 1861.

Chapter Seven

1. Skelton, *An American Profession of Arms*, 358.

2. Ibid., xiii; Donald C. Pfanz, *Richard S. Ewell: A Soldier's Life* (Chapel Hill: University of North Carolina Press, 1998), 121.

Notes — Chapter Seven

3. Gary W. Gallagher, *The Union War* (Cambridge: Harvard University Press, 2011), 4; Paul D. Escott, *"What Shall We Do with the Negro?": Lincoln, White Racism, and Civil War America* (Charlottesville: University of Virginia Press: 2009), 1–2; Susan-Mary Grant, *North Over South* (Lawrence: University of Kansas Press: 2000), 17.

4. "The Abbeville Institute," http://www.abbevilleinstitute.org/about.php, printed 5/22/2012 8:55 a.m.

5. Michael E. Woods, "What Twenty-First-Century Historians Have Said About the Causes of Disunion: A Civil War Sesquicentennial Review of the Recent Literature," *The Journal of American History*, 99 No. 2 (September 2012), 415–416.

6. Matthew Pinsker, "The Coming of the Civil War," *Magazine of History*, 25 (April 2011), 4–5.

7. Gerard A. Patterson, *Rebels from West Point* (Mechanicsburg, PA: Stackpole Books, 1987), xiii; Pfanz, *Richard S. Ewell*, 121.

8. Skelton, *An American Profession of Arms*, 155–157.

9. Colin Woodard, *American Nations: A History of the Eleven Rival Regional Cultures of North America* (New York: Viking, 2011), 2–3.

10. Ibid., 19.

11. Ibid., 224.

12. Graham Robb, *The Discovery of France: A Historical Geography from the Revolution to the First World War* (New York: W. W. Norton, 2007), xvii.

13. Woodard, *Nations*, 229.

14. Ibid., 230.

15. Grant, *North Over South*, 15–16.

16. Kenneth M. Stampp, ed., *The Causes of the Civil War* (New York, Simon & Schuster, 3rd revised edition, 1974) 22; Woodard, *Nations*, 226.

17. Grant, *North Over South*, 2–4; Leslie R. Tucker, *Major General Isaac Ridgeway Trimble: Biography of a Baltimore Confederate* (Jefferson, NC: McFarland, 2005), 115; Albion W. Tourgée, *A Fool's Errand* (reprint, New York: Harper's, 1961), 381.

18. Gallagher, *Union*, 77.

19. Woodard, *Nations*, 226–7; Egnal, *Clash of Extremes*, 293.

20. Robert V. Remini and Terry Golway, eds., *Fellow Citizens: The Penguin Book of U.S. Presidential Inaugural Addresses* (New York: Penguin, 2008), 167, 179; Henry Louis Gates, Jr., ed., *Lincoln on Race and Slavery* (Princeton, NJ: Princeton University Press, 2009), 243.

21. Egnal, *Clash of Extremes*, 311.

22. Gallagher, *Union*, 77–79.

23. Ibid., 348–361.

24. Pfanz, *Richard S. Ewell*, 120.

25. *Public Acts of the State of Tennessee, Passed at the Extra Session of the Thirty-third General Assembly, for the Year 1861* (Nashville: E. G. Eastman and Co., 1861).

26. Daniel W. Crofts, *Reluctant Confederates: Upper South Unionist in the Secession Crisis* (Chapel Hill: University of North Carolina Press, 1989), 334.

27. *Public Acts of the State of Tennessee Passed at the Extra Session of the Thirty-third General Assembly, April, 1861* (Nashville: J. G. Griffith, 1861), 1–11.

28. "Pony Express: Romance versus Reality" at http://www.postalmuseum.si.edu/exhibits/2a5a2_ponyexptress.html.

29. Skelton, *An American Profession of Arms*, 155–7.

30. "Maj. Thomas P. Adams," *Confederate Veteran*, Vol. 9 (September 1896), 420; *Gulbangi Family and Genealogy Research — Person Page* 35, 20; *OR*, Ser. I, Vol. 10/2, 139.

31. *OR*, Ser. II, Vol. 2, 38; *Nashville Union and American*, August 10, 1861; Charles Adams, "The Warrant to Arrest Chief Justice Roger B. Taney: A Great Crime, a Fabrication or Seward's Real Folley?'" at www.lewrockwell.com/org2/adams1.html (June 20, 2011).

32. David Nevin and the Editors of Time-Life Books, *The Road to Shiloh: Early Battles in the West* (Alexandria, VA: Time-Life Books, 1983), 46.

33. Boatner, *Civil War Dictionary*, 657–8.

34. Lowell H. Harrison, *The Civil War in Kentucky* (Lexington: University Press of Kentucky, 1975), 6–7; Kent Masterson Brown, ed., *The Civil War in Kentucky: Battle for the Bluegrass* (Mason City, IA: Savas, 2009), 83.

35. Boatner, *Civil War Dictionary*, 440.

36. Nevin, *Road to Shiloh*, 48; David J. Eicher, The *Longest Night: A Military History of the Civil War* (New York: Simon & Schuster, 2001), 142–3; Kendall D. Gott, *Where the South Lost the War: An Analysis of the Fort Henry–Fort Donelson Campaign, February 1862* (Mechanicsburg, PA: Stackpole Books, 2003), 41.

37. MSR, Doc. No. A 44, 1862; *OR*, Ser. II, Vol. 1, 182–183.

38. *OR*, Ser. I, Vol. 4, 329.

39. *OR*, Ser. I, Vol. 4, 523.

40. *OR*, Ser. II, Vol. 1, 182–183; Ser. II, Vol. 3, 744; Boatner, *The Civil War Dictionary*, 57–58.

41. Boatner, *Civil War Dictionary*, 54–55.

Notes—Chapter Eight

42. Steven E. Woodworth, *Nothing But Victory: The Army of the Tennessee, 1861–1865* (New York: Alfred A. Knopf, 2005), 65–120.

43. Boatner, *Civil War Dictionary*, 752–755.

44. *OR*, Ser. I, Vol. 3, 305.

45. "Gulbangi Family and Genealogy Research," Person Page 15, 4; *OR*, Ser. II, Vol. 3, 116, 803, 815, 826; Ser. I, Vol. 8, 815; Ser. II, Vol. 3, 843, 847–8.

46. Boatner, *Civil War Dictionary*, 176.

47. Mil. Serv. Rec., Special Orders Nos. 58, Headquarters Army of the West, Memphis, 38/8, Army of the Mississippi, Docs. Nos. A 72, A 81, A 83, and 85 1862.

48. Gallagher, *Union*, 4; Henry Louis Gates, Jr., ed., *Lincoln on Race and Slavery* (Princeton: Princeton University Press, 2009), 57, 123; Escott, *What Shall We Do*, xviii; Marc Egnal, *Clash of Extremes: The Economic Origins of the Civil War* (New York: Hill and Wang, 2009), 143.

49. *OR*, Ser. I, Vol. 52/2, 311–12.

50. Ibid.

51. Boatner, *Civil War Dictionary*, 176; John F. Marszalck, "Halleck Captures Corinth," *Civil War Times*, February 2006, 46–52.

52. *OR*, Ser. I, Vol. 10/1, 887.

53. *OR*, Ser. I, Vol. 3, ii, 311–12; Ser. I, Vol. 10/1, 895

54. John D. Winters, *The Civil War in Louisiana* (Baton Rouge: Louisiana State University Press, 1963), 361–375.

55. *OR*, Ser. I, Vol. 10, 602, 895–917; Ser. I, Vol. 16/2, 102; Ser. I, Vol. 17/2, 648.

56. *OR*, Ser. I, Vol. 16/1, 805; Brian Steel Wills, *A Battle from the Start: The Life of Nathan Bedford Forrest* (New York: HarperCollins, 1992), 66–70; Boatner, *Civil War Dictionary*, 288–89.

57. *OR*, Ser. I, Vol. 17/2, 666–7, 695, 817–18; Steven Hippersteel, "Columbus, Mississippi," www.civilwaralbum.com/misc16/columbus1.htm (June 14, 2011).

58. *OR*, Ser. I, Vol. 17/2, 740, 758, 796–98; Department of Mississippi and East Louisiana, LS, 1862, 56, 88, 146; Army of Mississippi, Department No. 2, Special Orders, 1862–64, 131–183, Special Order No. 82; War Department Collection of Confederate Records, Papers of Various Confederated Notables, Lt. Gen. John C. Pemberton, LR, November 1 and 4, 1862; Pemberton Papers, October 28, November 4 and December 21, 1862.

59. *OR*, Ser. II, Vol. 5, 807; Ser. I, Vol. 10/1, 895; MSR, Confederate Archives, File No. 86, p. 10; Department of Mississippi and East Louisiana, LS, 1862.

Chapter Eight

1. "Inside the Lines at Franklin," *Confederate Veteran*, Vol. 3 (1895), 72.

2. Boatner, *Civil War Dictionary*, 871; Smith, *Grant*, 213; General Orders, No. 159, War Dept., October 16, 1862; *O.R.*, Ser. I, Vol. 17/2, 278.

3. Boatner, *Civil War Dictionary*, 78, 642.

4. Ibid., 631.

5. Ibid., 870–71; Michael B. Ballard, *Vicksburg: The Campaign that Opened the Mississippi* (Chapel Hill: University of North Carolina Press, 2004), 46–62.

6. Boatner, *Civil War Dictionary*, 871–72; Ballard, *Vicksburg*, 46–62.

7. *OR*, Ser. II, Vol. 5, 807 and Ser. I, Vol. 24/3, 609, 611, 617, 647, 707, 807; Mil. Serv. Rec., Confederate Archives, Ch. 1, File No. 86, p. 10.

8. *OR*, Ser. II, Vol. 5, 816, 822, 855; Pemberton Papers, January 17, 1863, January 25, 1863; Dept. Miss. and E. La., LS, p. 327; Robert V. Remini and Terry Golway, eds., *Fellow Citizens: The Penguin Book of U.S. Presidential Addresses* (New York: Penguin, 2008), 167; United States Congress, July 25, 1861; Eric Foner, *The Fiery Trial: Abraham Lincoln and American Slavery* (New York: W. W. Norton, 2010), 239–42.

9. Boatner, *Civil War Dictionary*, 359–60.

10. Boatner, *The Civil War Dictionary*, 359; *OR*, Ser. I, Vol. 24, 546, 531–2; Dept. Miss. and E. La., LS, 346, 358.

11. *OR*, Ser. I, Vol. 24/3, 522, 532, 789; Dept. Miss. and E. La., LS, p. 362.

12. Boatner, *The Civil War Dictionary*, 839, 874–77; *OR*, Ser. I, Vol. 24/3, 426–441, 482, 881, 937, 955, 958, 994, 1040; Patrick Henry, "Adams' Brigade in Battle of Franklin," *Confederate Veteran*, Vol. 21 (1913), 77.

13. L.S. Flatan, "Tribute to General Lloyd Tilghman," *Confederate Veteran*, Vol. 19 (1910), 75; Pat Henry, "Adams' Brigade in Battle of Franklin," *Confederate Veteran*, Vol. 21 (1913), 77.

14. Mil. Serv. Rec., Doc. No. A 47, 1863 and Dept. of Miss. and E. La., Register, No. 1942; *OR*, Ser. I, Vol. 30/4, 558, 609, 705, 717, 751, 754.

15. Boatner, *The Civil War Dictionary*, 141–142, 149, 352–3; *OR*, Ser. I, Vol. 32/1, 333.

16. Boatner, *The Civil War Dictionary*, 492.

Notes — Chapter Eight

17. Boatner, The *Civil War Dictionary*, 705–6.
18. *OR*, Ser. I, 38/3, 874–75.
19. *OR*, Ser. I, 38/3, 876–8.
20. *OR*, Ser. I, Vol. 38/3, 876–891; Boatner, *The Civil War Dictionary*, 32.
21. James Binford, "Heroism at Franklin; Tributes to General Adams, Colonel Farrell and Rorer," *Confederate Veteran*, Vol. 10 (1902), 457.
22. Wiley Sword, *Embrace an Angry Wind: The Confederacy's Last Hurrah: Spring Hill, Franklin, and Nashville* (New York: Harper-Collins, 1992), 217; H. P. Figuers, "A Boy's Impressions of the Battle of Franklin," *Confederate Veteran*, Vol. 23 (1915), 5.
23. Ibid., 146–7; "Inside the Lines at Franklin," 72; "General John Adams at Franklin: Testimony of Union Officers to His Immutable Valor," *Confederate Veteran*, Vol. 5 (1897), 300.
24. "General John Adams at Franklin," 299–300; Henry, "Adams' Brigade in Battle of Franklin," 76; "Gens. Cleburne and Adams at Franklin," *Confederate Veteran*, Vol. 10 (1902), 155, 458; Henry, "Adams' Brigade at the Battle of Franklin," 76–77; Sword, *Embrace and Angry Wind*, 227. Some sources say Adams was hit seven times, others say nine.
25. McDonough, *Five Tragic Hours*, 157; "Inside the Lines at Franklin," 73.
26. H. P. Figures, "A Boy's Impressions of the Battle of Franklin," 7.
27. "Gen. John Adams at Franklin," 300–301; "Death and Identity of Gen. Adams," *Confederate Veteran*, Vol. 6 (1898), 264; "Gen. John Adams at Franklin," *Confederate Veteran*, Vol. 6, 208; "Gens. Cleburne and Adams at Franklin," 155; McDonough, *Five Tragic Hours*, 161; Sword, *Embrace an Angry Wind*, 227.
28. Pat Henry, "Adams' Brigade in Battle of Franklin," 77; "Heroism at Franklin," 457.
29. H. L. Blanchard, "Our Battle Flag," *Confederate Veteran*, Vol. 6 (1898), 208.
30. Figuers, "A Boy's Impressions of the Battle of Franklin," 7.
31. Capt. Thomas Gibson, "Maj. Thomas P. Adams," *Confederate Veteran*, Vol. 9 (1901), 420.
32. 1870 Census, St. Louis, Missouri, roll M593–817, Book 1, p. 685; 1880 Census DC, Roll T-9–121, p. 186A; 1900 Census, MT, Roll T623910, p. 28A; "Gulbangi Family and Genealogy," 21, 3–22 of 25, 14–16 of 32.
33. "Gulbangi Family and Genealogy," 3–22 of 25 and 14–16 of 32.

Bibliography

Primary Sources

MANUSCRIPTS AND COLLECTIONS

California Historical Society
  Statutes of California
  California State Constitution
College of William and Mary
  Ewell Papers
Confederate Military Records
  Departmental Records
    Department of Alabama, Mississippi and East Louisiana.
    Fourth Military District, Brigadier General John Adams.
    Register of Letters and Telegrams Received, 1862–1865.
  Army of Mississippi
    Letters and Telegrams, Orders and Circulars, May–June 1864.
    Special Orders, Army of Mississippi, Department No. 2 and the Army of Tennessee, 1862–1864.
  Department of Mississippi and East Louisiana.
    Letters Sent.
  Department and Army of Tennessee.
    Army of Mississippi, Lieutenant General Leonidas Polk Cooperating with General Joseph E. Johnston, Department of Tennessee.
    General Field Orders, General John B. Hood, July 24, 1864–December 1, 1864.
  Papers of Confederate Generals.
    J. B. Hood, Field Dispatches, July 27, 1864–January 17, 1865.
    J. C. Pemberton, Letters and Telegrams Received, January–December 1862.
    Leonidas Polk, Letters Received, 1861–1864.
Davidson County, Tennessee, Records:
  Census Records, 1820
  General Index to Deeds, 1784–1871
  Marriage Record, Book I, 1789–1837
Giles County, Tennessee Records:
  Census Records, 1840, 1850
  General Index to Deeds, 1810–1859
Huntington Library, San Marino, CA
  John Adams Papers
Library of Congress
  George B. McClellan Papers
National Archives, Washington, D.C.
  Application Papers of Cadets, 1841
  Letters Received, 1841–1861
  Letters Sent, 1846–1861
  Post Returns
    Albuquerque, New Mexico, 1846–1848.
    Fort Craig, New Mexico, 1954–1861.
    Fort Crook, California, 1857–1866.
    Las Vegas, New Mexico, 1850–1851.
    Fort Leavenworth, Kansas, 1854.
    Fort Massachusetts, New Mexico.
    Rayado, New Mexico, 1850–1851.
    Santa Fe, New Mexico, 1848.
    Taos, New Mexico, 1848–1850.
    Fort Union, New Mexico, 1855.
Records of United States Army Commands
  Department of New Mexico.

Bibliography

Orders, 1850.
Letters Received, 1849–1856.
Letters Sent, 1850–1856.
Department of the Pacific
  Letters Received, 1859–1861.
  Letters Sent, 1859–1861.
Department of the West
  Endorsement Book, 1853–1854.
  General and Special and Division Orders, 1851–1852.
  Letters Sent, 1853–1854.
Fort Craig, New Mexico
  Orders, February 1853–March 1863.
Fort Crook, California
  Letters Sent, 1859–1861.
  Order Books.
Regular Army
  Annual Return of Casualties in the First Regiment of Dragoons
  Inspection Returns.
  Organization Returns.
  First Dragoons, 1846–1861.
Headquarters of the Army
  General Orders.
  Letters Received, 1853–1858.
  Regulation for the Army of the United States, 1857
Recruiting Service
  Letters Sent, 1856–1860.

New Mexico Historical Society
  Laws of the Legislative Assembly

Rhode Island Soldiers and Sailors Historical Society
  Bailey Papers

University of Michigan
  Hamar Papers

West Point
  Cadets Arranged in Order of Merit in Their Respective Classes As Determined at the General Examination in June, 1846
  Cullum File
  Dutton File
  Descriptive Lists of New Cadets, 1841
  Official Register of the Officers and Cadets of the United States Military Academy, 1842–1846.
  Orders, United States Corps of Cadets, December 1839–August 1842.
  Post Orders, 1842–1846.

United States Government
  House Report 303, 24th Congress, 2nd sess., November 26, 1833.
  Senate Doc. 247, 23rd Congress, 1st Sess., March 1, 1837.

Newspapers

Alta California
Marysville Appeal
Missouri Statesmen
Nashville Union and American
New York Daily Times
New York Times
Saint Paul Pioneer
San Francisco Bulletin
San Francisco Chronicle
Santa Fe Republican
Whig Courier

Books

Battles and Leaders of the Civil War. Being the Most Part Contributions by Union and Confederate Officers. New York: T. Yoseloff, 1956.

Bennett, James A., Clinton E. Brooks, ed. *Forts and Forays: A Dragoon in New Mexico, 1850–1856.* Albuquerque: University of New Mexico Press, 1996.

Bieber, Ralph P., ed. *Marching with the Army of the West, 1846–1849.* Glendale, CA: Arthur H. Clark Company, 1936.

Browne, Ross. *Report of the Debates in the Convention of California on the Formation of the State Constitution.* Washington, D.C.: John T. Tower, 1850.

Burnett, Peter H. *Journals of the Senate and Assembly of the State of California, at the Second Session of the Legislature, 1851–1852.* San Francisco: G.K. Fitch and Co., and V. E. Geiger and Co., State Printers, 1852.

220

Bibliography

California, State of. *Journals of the Senate, of the Eleventh Session of the Legislature of the State of California*. Sacramento: C. T. Botts, State Printer, 1860.

Carleton, James Henry. *Diary of an Excursion to the Ruins of Abo, Quarra and Gran Quivira in New Mexico in 1853, Under the Command of Major James Henry Carleton*. Santa Fe: Stagecoach Press, 1965.

Confederate Veteran, 40 vols. Nashville: Confederate Veteran Association, 1893–1932.

Cooke, Philip St. George. *The Conquest of New Mexico and California: An Historical and Personal Narrative*. New York: G. P. Putnam's Sons, 1875; reprint, Chicago: Rio Grande Press, 1964.

Crook, George. Martin F. Schmitt, ed. *General George Crook: His Autobiography*. Norman: University of Oklahoma Press, 1946.

Cullum, George W. *Biographical Register of the Officers and Graduates of the U.S. Military Academy at West Point, N.Y.* Boston: Houghton, Mifflin, 1891.

Cutts, James Madison. *The Conquest of California and New Mexico, by the Forces of the United States, in the Years 1846 and 1847*. Albuquerque: Horn and Wallace, 1965.

Davies, Henry Eugene. *Ten Days on the Plains*. Dallas: DeGolyer Library, Southern Methodist University Press, 1985.

Edwards, Frank S. *A Campaign in New Mexico*. Philadelphia, Carey and Hart, 1847; reprint, Ann Arbor, MI: University Microfilms, 1968.

Elliott, Richard Smith, edited by Mark L. Gardner and Marc Simmons. *The Mexican War Correspondence of Richard Smith Elliott*. Norman: University of Oklahoma Press, 1997.

Emory, W.H. *Lieutenant Emory Reports: A Reprint of Lieutenant W. H. Emory's Notes of a Military Reconnaissance*. Albuquerque: University of New Mexico Press, 1951.

Evans, Clement Anselm. *Confederate Military History a Library of Confederate States History*. Atlanta: Confederate Publishing Company, 1899.

Grazer, Robert W., ed. *New Mexico in 1850: A Military View by Colonel George Archibald McCall*. Norman: University of Oklahoma Press, 1968.

Hammond, George P., and Agapito Rey, eds. *Narratives of the Coronado Expedition, 1540–1542*. Albuquerque: University of New Mexico Press, 1940.

Heizer, Robert Fleming, ed. *The Destruction of California Indians: A Collection of Documents from the Period 1847 to 1865 in Which are Described Some of the Things That Happened to Some of the Indians of California*. Santa Barbara, CA: Peregrine Smith, 1974.

Historical Section, Army War College. *Indian Battles and Skirmishes on the American Frontier, 1790–1898*. Reprint, New York: Argonaut Press, 1966.

Inman, Henry. *The Old Santa Fe Trail: The Story of a Great Highway*. Minneapolis: Ross and Haines, 1966.

Johnson, Richard W. *A Soldier's Reminiscences in Peace and War*. Philadelphia: J.B. Lippincott, 1886.

Lowe, Percival Green, with an introduction by Don Russell. *Five Years a Dragoon ('49 to '54) and Other Adventures on the Great Plains*. Norman: University of Oklahoma Press, 1965.

McCall, Colonel George Archibald, Robert W. Frazer, ed. and intro. *New Mexico in 1850: A Military View*. Norman: University of Oklahoma Press, 1968. Maury, Dabney Herndon. *Recollections of a Virginian in the Mexican, Indian and Civil Wars*. London: Low, Marston, 1894.

Meriwether, David. *My Life in the Mountains and on the Plains*. Norman: University of Oklahoma Press, 1965.

Myers, William S., ed. *The Mexican War Diary of George B. McClellan*. Princeton, NJ: Princeton University Press, 1953.

Bibliography

North American Review. Boston: Wells and Lily, 1832.

O'Sullivan, John L. *The United States Democratic Review*, Vol. 6 Ithaca: Cornell University Library, 1999–2009.

Pelzer, Louis. *Marches of the Dragoons in the Mississippi Valley: An Account of Marches and Activities of the First Regiment United States Dragoons in the Mississippi Valley Between the Years 1833 and 1850.* Iowa City: The State Historical Society, 1917.

Polk, James K. *Message from the President ... December 2, 1845.* Washington: Ritchie and Heiss, 1845.

Remini, Robert V., and Terry Golway, eds. *Fellow Citizens: The Penguin Book of U.S. Presidential Inaugural Addresses.* New York: Penguin, 2008.

Schmitt, Martin F., editor. *General George Crook: His Autobiography.* Norman: University of Oklahoma Press, 1946.

Smith, Winston, and Charles Judah, eds. *Chronicles of the Gringos: The U. S. Army in the Mexican War, 1846–1848: Accounts of Eyewitnesses and Combatants.* Albuquerque: University of New Mexico Press, 1968.

Sunderman, James. F., ed. *Journey Into Wilderness: An Army Surgeon's Account of Life in Camp and Field During the Creek and Seminole Wars, 1836–1838.* Gainesville: University of Florida Press, 1963.

Tennessee, State of. *Public Acts of the State of Tennessee, Passed at the Extra Session of the Thirty-Third General Assembly, for the Year 1861.* Nashville: E. G. Eastman, 1861.

Tourgée, Albion W. *A Fool's Errand.* Reprint, New York: Harper's, 1861.

United States. *Historical Register and Dictionary of the United States Army, from its Organization, September 29, 1789, to March 2, 1903.* Washington, D.C.: Government Printing Office, 1903.

_____. *Regulations Established for the Organization and Government of the Military Academy at West Point.* New York: Wiley and Putnam, 1839.

_____. *Regulations of the Army of the United States, 1857.* New York: Harper and Brothers, 1857.

_____. *War of the Rebellion: Compilation of the Official Records of the Union and Confederate Armies*, Series I and II. Washington Government Printing Office, 1880–1901.

Articles

Blanchard, H. L. "Our Battle Flag." *Confederate Veteran*, Vol. 6 (1898): 208.

Figuers, H. P. "A Boy's Impressions of the Battle of Franklin." *Confederate Veteran*, Vol. 23 (1915): 4–7.

Flatan, L. S. "Tribute to General Lloyd Tilghman." *Confederate Veteran*, Vol. 19: 75.

"General John Adams at Franklin." *Confederate Veteran*, Vol. 6 (1898): 208.

"Gen. John Adams at Franklin: Testimony of Union Officers to His Immutable Valor." *Confederate Veteran*, Vol. 5, (1897): 299–301.

"Gens. Cleburne and Adams at Franklin." *Confederate Veteran*, Vol. 10 (1902): 154–155.

Gibson, Capt. Thomas. "Maj. Thomas P. Adams." *Confederate Veteran*, Vol. 9 (1901): 420.

Gore, Tom M. "Death and Identity of Gen. Adams." *Confederate Veteran*, Vol. 6 (1898): 264.

Henry, Patrick. "Adams' Brigade in Battle of Franklin." *Confederate Veteran*, Vol. 21 (1913): 76–7.

"Heroism at Franklin." *Confederate Veteran*, Vol. 10 (1902): 457–8.

"Inside the Lines at Franklin." *Confederate Veteran*, Vol. 3 (1895): 72–73.

Secondary Sources
Books

Abinder, Tyler. *Nativism and Slavery: The Northern Know Nothings and the*

Bibliography

Politics of the 1850s. New York: Oxford University Press, 1997.

Agnew, S. C. *Garrisons of the Regular U. S. Army: New Mexico, 1846–1899.* Santa Fe: Press of the Territorian, 1971.

Ambrose, Stephen E. *Duty, Honor, Country: A History of West Point.* Baltimore: John Hopkins Press, 1966.

Atkinson, M. Jourdan. *Indians of the Southwest.* San Antonio: Naylor Company, 1935.

Ballard, Michael B. *Vicksburg: The Campaign that Opened the Mississippi.* Chapel Hill: University of North Carolina Press, 2004.

Bancroft, Hubert Howe. *History of California.* Reprint, Santa Barbara, CA: Wallace Hebbert, 1963–64.

Beck, William A. *New Mexico: A History of Four Centuries.* Norman: University of Oklahoma Press, 1962.

Billington, Ray A. *The Protestant Crusade, 1800–1860: A Study of the Origins of American Nativism.* New York: McMillian, 1938.

Boatner, Mark Mayo III. *Civil War Dictionary.* New York: David McKay Company, 1959.

Brackett, Albert G. *History of the United States Cavalry: From the Formation of the Federal Government to the 1st of June, 1863.* New York: Greenwood Press, 1968.

Brooks, N. C. *A Complete History of the Mexican War: Its Causes, Conduct, and Consequences.* Chicago: Rio Grande Press, 1965.

Campbell, James Havelock. *McClellan: A Vindication of the Military Career of General George B. McClellan.* New York: Neale Publishing Company, 1916.

Carley, Kenneth. *The Sioux Uprising of 1862.* St. Paul: Minnesota Historical Society, 1976.

Castel, Albert. *General Sterling Price and the Civil War in the West.* Baton Rouge: Louisiana State University, 1968.

Coffman, Edward M. *The Old Army: A Portrait of the American Army in Peacetime, 1784–1898.* New York: Oxford University Press, 1986.

Crofts, Daniel W. *Reluctant Confederates: Upper South Unionist in the Secession Crisis.* Chapel Hill: University of North Carolina Press, 1989.

Current, Richard N., ed. *Encyclopedia of the Confederacy.* New York: Simon & Schuster, 1993.

Dale, Edward Everett. *The Indians of the Southwest: A Century of Development Under the United States.* Norman: University of Oklahoma Press, 1949.

Danziger, E. J., Jr. *The Chippewa of Lake Superior.* Norman: University of Oklahoma Press, 1990.

Davis, William C. *The Confederate General.* National Historical Society.

Densmore, F. *Chippewa Customs.* St. Paul: Minnesota Historical Society Press, 1978.

Dorsey, George A. *Indians of the Southwest.* Chicago: Passenger Dept. Atchison Topeka and Santa Fe Railway System, 1903; Reprint, university of Michigan Libraries, 1976.

Downey, Fairfax Davis. *Indian Wars of the U. S. Army, 1776–1865.* Garden City, NY: Doubleday, 1963.

Eckenrode, H. J., and Bryan Conrad. *George B. McClellan: The Man Who Saved the Union.* Chapel Hill: University of North Carolina Press, 1941.

Eicher, David J. *The Longest Night: A Military History of the Civil War.* New York: Simon & Schuster, 2001.

Eicher, John H., and David J. *Civil War High Commands.* Stanford: Stanford University Press, 2001.

Eisenhower, John S. D. *So Far from God: The U. S. War with Mexico, 1846–1848.* Norman: University of Oklahoma Press, 2000.

Emmett, Chris. *Fort Union and the Winning of the Southwest.* Norman: University of Oklahoma Press, 1965.

Escott, Paul D. *"What Shall We Do with the Negro?" Lincoln, White Racism and*

Bibliography

Civil War America. Charlottesville: University of Virginia Press, 2009.

Faulk, Odie B. *Crimson Desert: Indian Wars of the American Southwest*. New York: Oxford University Press, 1974.

Fleming, Thomas J. *West Point: The Men and the Times of the United States Military Academy*. New York: Morrow, 1969.

Fletcher, Richard A. *Saint James Catapult: The Life and Times of Diego Gelmirez of Santiago de Compostela*. Oxford: Oxford University Press, 1984.

Foner, Eric. *Free Soil, Free Labor, Free Men: The Ideology of the Republican Party Before the Civil War*. New York: Oxford University Press, 1970.

Forbes, Jack D. *Native Americans of California and Nevada: A Handbook*. Healdsburg, CA: National Publishers, 1969.

Forman, Sidney. *West Point: A History of the United States Military Academy*. New York: Columbia University Press, 1950.

Frazer, Robert Walter. *Forts and Supplies: The Role of the Army in the Economy of the Southwest*. Albuquerque: University of New Mexico Press, 1983.

Freehling, William W. *The Road to Disunion: Secessionists at Bay 1776–1854*. New York: Oxford University Press, 1990.

Gallagher, Gary W. *The Union War*. Cambridge: Harvard University Press, 2011.

Ganaway, Loomis Morton. *New Mexico and the Sectional Controversy*. Philadelphia: Porcupine Press, 1976.

Gates, Henry Louis, Jr., ed. *Lincoln on Race and Slavery*. Princeton: Princeton University Press, 2009.

Gibson, George Rutledge, and Robert Walter Frazer. *Over the Chihuahua and Santa Fe Trails, 1847–1848*. Albuquerque: University of New Mexico Press, 1981.

Gilman, Rhoda R. *The Story of Minnesota's Past*. St. Paul: Minnesota Historical Society, 1991.

Gordon, Lesley J. *General George E. Pickett in Life and Legend*. Chapel Hill: University of North Carolina Press, 1998.

Gott, Kendall D. *Where the South Lost the War: An Analysis of the Fort Henry–Fort Donnellson Campaign, February 1862*. Mechanicsburg, PA: Stackpole, 2003.

Govan, Gilbert, and James W. Livingood. *A Different Valor: The Story of General Joseph E. Johnston, C.S.A.* Westport, CT: Greenwood Press, 1956.

Grant, Blanche C. *When Old Trails Were New: The Story of Taos*. New York: Press of the Pioneers, 1934.

Grant, Susan-Mary. *North Over South*. Lawrence: University of Kansas Press, 2000.

Gregg, Andrew K. *Drums of Yesterday: The Forts of New Mexico*. Santa Fe, NM: Press of the Territorian, 1968.

Grivas, Theodore. *Military Governments in California, 1846–1850*. Glendale, CA: A. H. Clark Co., 1963.

Hall, Steve. *Fort Snelling: Colossus of the Wilderness*. St. Paul: Minnesota Historical Society, 1987.

Hansen, Marcus Lee. *Old Fort Snelling, 1819–1858*. Minneapolis: Ross & Haines, 1958.

Hassrick, Royal B., Dorothy Maxwell, and Cile M. Bach. *The Sioux: Life and Customs of a Warrior Society*. Norman: University of Oklahoma Press, 1964.

Heidler, David S., and Jeanne T. Heidler. *Encyclopedia of the American Civil War: A Political, Social, and Military History*. Santa Barbara, CA: ABC-CLIO, 2000.

Heitman, Francis B. *Historical Register and Dictionary of the United States Army*. Washington: Government Printing Office, 1903.

Heizer, Robert F. *Handbook of North American Indians*, Vol. 8. Washington, DC: Smithsonian Institution, 1978.

———, and Alan F. Almquist. *The Other Californians: Prejudice and Discrimi-

Bibliography

nation Under Spain, Mexico, and the United States in 1920. Berkeley: University of California Press, 1971.

Holt, Michael F. *The Political Crisis of the 1850s*. New York: Wiley, 1978.

Hughes, Robert M. *Great Commanders: General Johnston*. New York: D. Appleton and Company, 1895.

Inman, Colonel Henry. *The Old Santa Fe Trail: The Story of a Great Highway*. Minneapolis: Ross and Haines, 1966.

Johnson, Allen, ed. *Dictionary of American Biography*. New York: Charles Scribner's Sons, 1928.

Jones, Evan. *Citadel in the Wilderness*. New York: Coward-McCann, 1966.

Keleher, William A. *Turmoil in New Mexico 1846–1868*. Santa Fe: The Rydal Press, 1952.

Kennedy, Roger O. *Men on the Moving Frontier*. Palo Alto, CA: American West Publishing Co., 1969.

Lass, William E. *Minnesota: A History*. New York: W. W. Norton, 1998.

Lavender, David Sievert. *Bent's Fort*. Garden City, NY: Doubleday, 1954.

Lewis, David Rich. *Neither Wolf Nor Dog: American Indians, Environment, and Agrarian Change*. New York: Oxford University Press, 1994.

Longacre, Edward G. *General William Dorsey Pender: A Military Biography*. Conshohocken, PA: Combined, 2001.

McCollum, James. *A Brief Sketch of the Settlement and Early History of Giles County, Tennessee*. Pulaski: Pulaski Citizen, 1928.

McDounough, James Lee, and Thomas L. Connelly. *Five Tragic Hours: The Battle of Franklin*. Knoxville: University of Tennessee Press, 1983.

McMurry, Richard M. *John Bell Hood and the War for Southern Independence*. Lincoln: University of Nebraska Press, 1992.

Mails, Thomas E. *Dog Soldiers, Bear Men, and Buffalo Women: A Study of the Societies and Cults of the Plains Indians*. New York: Prentice-Hall, 1973.

Meketa, Jacqueline Dorgan. *Legacy of Honor: The Life of Rafael Chacon, A Nineteenth Century New Mexican*. Albuquerque: University of New Mexico Press, 1986.

Miller, Darlis A. *The California Column in New Mexico*. Albuquerque: University of New Mexico Press, 1982.

Myers, William Star. *A Study in Personality: General George Brinton McClellan*. New York: D. Appleton–Century, 1934.

The National Cyclopedia of American Biography: Being the History of the United States. Ann Arbor, MI: University Microfilms, 1967.

Nevin, David, and the editors of Time-Life Books. *The Road to Shiloh: Early Battles in the West*. Alexandria, VA: Time-Life Books, 1983.

Oliva, Leo E. *Soldiers on the Santa Fe Trail*. Norman: University of Oklahoma Press, 1967.

Patterson, Gerard A. *Rebels from West Point*. Mechanicsburg, PA: Stackpole Books, 1987.

Pelzer, Louis. *Marches of the Dragoons in the Mississippi Valley: An Account of Marches and Activities of the First Dragoon Regiment, United States Dragoons, in the Mississippi Valley Between the Years 1833 and 1850*. Iowa City: States Historical Society of Iowa, 1917.

Peskin, Allan. *Winfield Scott and the Profession of Arms*. Kent, Ohio: Kent State University Press, 2003.

Pfanz, Donald C. *Richard S. Ewell: A Soldier's Life*. Chapel Hill: University of North Carolina Press, 1998.

Potter, David M. *The Impending Crisis 1848–1861*. New York: Harper and Row, 1976.

Prucha, Francis Paul. *Broadax and Bayonet: The Role of the United States Army in the Development of the Northwest 1815–1860*. Lincoln: University of Nebraska Press, 1953.

_____. *The Sword of the Republic: The United States Army on the Frontier,*

Bibliography

1783–1846. New York: Macmillan, 1969.

Radin, Paul. *The Winnebago Tribe*. Lincoln: University of Nebraska Press, 1990.

Rea, Ralph R. *Sterling Price: The Lee of the West*. Little Rock: Pioneer Press, 1959.

Remini, Robert V., and Terry Golway, eds. *Fellow Citizens: The Penguin Book of U.S. Presidential Inaugural Addresess*. New York: Penguin, 2008.

Richmond, Patricia Joy. *Trail to Disaster*. Denver: Colorado Historical Society, 1989.

Robb, Graham. *The Discovery of France: A Historical Geography from the Revolution to the First World War*. New York: W. W. Norton, 2007.

Robertson, James I., Jr. *Stonewall Jackson: The Man, The Soldier, The Legend*. New York: Macmillan, 1997.

Shalhope, Robert E. *Sterling Price: Portrait of a Southerner*. Columbia: University of Missouri Press, 1971.

Sifakis, Stewart. *Who Was Who in the Civil War*. New York: Facts on File, 1988.

Silby, Joel H. *Storm Over Texas: The American Controversy and the Road to the Civil War*. New York: Oxford University Press, 2005.

Simmons, Marc. *Albuquerque: A Narrative History*. Albuquerque: University of New Mexico Press, 1982.

———. *New Mexico: A Bicentennial History*. New York: W. W. Norton, 1977.

Skelton, William B. *An American Profession of Arms: The Army Officer Corps, 1784–1886*. Lawrence: University of Kansas Press, 1992.

Stampp, Kenneth, ed. *The Causes of the Civil War*. New York: Simon & Schuster, 3rd revised edition, 1974.

Stanley, F. *Fort Craig*. Pampa, TX: Pampa Print Shop, 1963.

Stanley, F. *Fort Union (New Mexico)*. Denver: World Press, Inc., 1953.

Stegmaier, Mark J. *Texas, New Mexico, and the Compromise of 1850: Boundary Dispute and Sectional Crisis*. Kent, OH: Kent State University Press, 1962.

Sword, Wiley. *Embrace an Angry Wind: The Confederacy's Last Hurrah: Spring Hill, Franklin, and Nashville*. New York: HarperCollins, 1992.

Symonds, Craig L. *Joseph E. Johnston: A Civil War Biography*. New York: W. W. Norton, 1992.

Tebbel, John William. *The Compact History of the Indian Wars*. New York: Hawthorn Books, 1966.

Trafzer, Clifford E. *The Kit Carson Campaign: The Last Great Navajo War*. Norman: University of Oklahoma Press, 1982.

Tucker, Leslie. *Major General Isaac Ridgeway Trimble: Biography of a Baltimore Confederate*. Jefferson, NC: McFarland, 2005.

Twitchell, Ralph Emerson. *The History of the Military Occupation of the Territory of New Mexico from 1846 to 1851, by the Government of the United States*. Chicago: Rio Grande Press, 1963.

United States National Park Service. *Soldier and Brave: Historical Places Associated With Indian Affairs and the Indian Wars in the Trans-Mississippi West*. Washington: U.S. Government Printing Office, 1971.

Utley, Robert M. *Fort Union National Monument, New Mexico*. Washington: U. S. Department of the Interior, National Park Service, 1962.

Wakelyn, Jon L., and Frank E. Vandiver, eds. *Biographical Dictionary of the Confederacy*. Westport, CT: Greenwood Press, 1977.

Warner, Ezra J. *Generals in Gray: Lives of the Confederate Commanders*. Baton Rouge: Louisiana State University Press, 1959.

Warren, W. *History of the Ojibway People*. St. Paul: Borealis Books, reprint, 1984.

Waugh, John C. *The Class of 1846: From West Point to Appomattox: Stonewall*

Jackson, George McClellan, and Their Brothers. New York: Warner Books, 1994.

Webb, Stephen S. *The Governors-general: The English Army and the Definition of Empire, 1569–1681*. Chapel Hill: University of North Carolina Press, 1979.

Weems, John Edward. *To Conquer a Peace: The War Between the United States and Mexico*. Garden City, NY: Doubleday, 1974.

Weigley, Russell F. *The American Way of War: A History of the United States Military Strategy and Policy*. Bloomington: Indiana University Press, 1977.

Wellman, Paul Iselin. *Death in the Desert*. New York: Pyramid Books, 1963.

White, Leonard D. *The Jacksonians: A Study in Administrative History 1829–1861*. New York: Macmillan, 1954.

Wills, Brian Steel. *A Battle from the Start: The Life of Nathan Bedford Forest*. New York: HarperCollins, 1992.

Winders, Richard Bruce. *Mr. Polk's Army: The American Military Experience in the Mexican War*. College Station: Texas A&M University Press, 1997.

Winters, John D. *The Civil War in Louisiana*. Baton Rouge: Louisiana State University Press, 1963.

Woodard, Colin. *American Nations: A History of the Eleven Rival Regional Cultures of North America*. New York: Viking, 2011.

Woodworth, Steven E. *Nothing but Victory: The Army of Tennessee, 1861–1865*. New York: Alfred A. Knopf, 2005.

Wright, William. *History of the Big Bonanza*. Hartford, CT: American Publishing Co., 1877.

Wynne, Ben. *A Hard Trip: A History of the 15th Mississippi Infantry, CSA*. Macon, GA: Mercer University Press, 2003.

Articles

Bell, A.W. "On the Native Races of New Mexico." *Journal of the Ethnological Society of London*, Vol. I, 1869: 222–274.

Campbell, Claude A. "Banking and Finance in Tennessee During the Depression of 1837." *East Tennessee Historical Society Publication*, No. 9 (1937): 19–30.

Fetzer, Joel S. "Economic Self-interest or Cultural Marginality? Anti-immigration Sentiment and Nativist Political movements in France, Germany, and the USA." *Journal of Ethnic and Migration Studies*, Vol. 26, Issue 1 (January 2000): 5–23.

Marszalck, John F. "Halleck Captures Corinth." *Civil War Times Magazine*, 45 (February 2006): 46–52.

Pinsker, Matthew. "The Coming of the Civil War." *Magazine of History*, 25 (April 2011): 4–5.

Taylor, Morris F. "Campaigns Against the Jicarilla Apache, 1855." *New Mexico Historical Review* (April 1970): 269–291.

Webb, Stephen S. "Army and Empire: English Garrison Government in Britain and America, 1569–1763." *William and Mary Quarterly*, 3rd Ser. 34 (January 1977):1–32.

Welter, Barbara. "The Cult of True Womanhood: 1820–1860." *American Quarterly* 18 (1966): 151–174.

Woods, Michael E. "What Twenty-First-Century Historians Have Said About the Causes of Disunion: A Civil War Sesquicentennial Review of the Recent Literature." *Journal of American History* 99 No. 2 (September 2012): 415–439.

Internet

The Abbeville Institute. http:www.abbevilleinstitute.org (May 22, 2012).

Adams, Charles. "The Warrant to Arrest Chief Justice Roger B. Taney: A Great

Bibliography

Crime, a Fabrication or Seward's Real Folley?" http://www.lewrockwell.com/org2/adams1.html (June 20, 2011)

Castillo, Edward D. "Short Overview of California Indian History." http://www.ceres.ca.gov/hahc/califindian.html (1998).

Green, Ann. "Gulbangi Family and Genealogy Research." http://www.gulbangi.com/5families-o/p171.htm#i4269 (February 15, 2009).

Hippensteel, Steven. "Columbus, Mississippi." http://www.civilwaralbum.com/misc16/columbus1.htm (June 14, 2011).

National Postal Museum. "Pony Express: Romance versus Reality." http://www.postalmuseum.i.edu/exhibits/2a5a2_ponyexpress.html (January 8, 2012).

Dissertation

Rita Grace Adams. "Biography of a Frontier American 1825–1864." Ph.D. dissertation, University Microfilm, Inc., 1964.

Index

Abbeville Institute 151
Abert, J.W. 56
Abiquiu, New Mexico 81, 92, 126
Achumawi Indians 132
Act for the Government and Protection of Indians 136
Acworth, Georgia 192
Adams, Ann *see* Tennant, Ann
Adams, Charles McDougall 124, 202
Adams, Emma Portis 188, 202
Adams, Francis Joseph 143, 202
Adams, Georgiana *see* McDougall, Georgiana
Adams, Georgiana McDougall 172, 202
Adams, John, Jr. 129, 202
Adams, Nathan 27–9
Adams, Thomas, Jr. 164, 178, 201
Adams, Thomas Patton 129, 202
Adams, Thomas, Sr. 28–9
Africa 14, 51
Albuquerque, New Mexico 57, 62, 65, 66, 68, 70, 86, 89, 91, 96–8
Alexander, Colonel 97–9
Algonquian Indians 104
Amador, Josep Maria 133
American Fur Company 102–3
Anderson, Eliza 110
Anglican 9
Anglo-Saxon 25
Angney's Infantry Battalion 66
Anton Chico, New Mexico 99, 100
Apache, Indians 51–3, 87, 92–5, 98, 112, 118–9, 121, 126, 131, 204
Apachean 51
Appropriations Bill 26
Arapaho Indians 51, 58
Archuleta, Diego 64
Arizona 86
Arkansas River 59, 94, 99, 116, 122, 124
Armijo, Manuel 46, 56–8, 62, 71
Army of Northern Virginia 152, 190
Army of Tennessee 152, 182, 191, 194, 202
Arroyo Hondo 65

Articles of Confederation 7
Asia 14, 51
Atlanta, Georgia or Battle of 158, 182, 187–91
Atsugewi Indians 132
Aztec Indians 57

Baca, Juan 99
Baird, Sprice M. 86
Baker, Edward Adams 195, 197
Bald Hills War 140
Baltimore, Maryland 80, 127–9, 157
Baton Rouge, Louisiana 171
Bayou Expedition 183
Beal, Benjamin 71–2, 84, 89, 94–5
Beal, Edward F. 135
Bear Creek, Alabama 173
Bear Creek, Colorado 125
Beaubien, Narcissa 65
Beauregard, Pierre Gustav 171, 173, 177–8, 182
Beaver Creek 139
Becknell, William 45
Belle Plain, Minnesota 106
Belmont, Missouri or Battle of 168, 177
Benicia Barracks 142, 146
Bennett, W.T. 31
Benny Havens 37
Bent, Charles 50–2, 59, 64–5, 68, 84
Bent, George 59
Bent, Teresina 65
Bent, William 50
Benton, Thomas Hart 70
Bentonville, North Carolina 202
Bents Fort 50, 54, 94, 118
Berlin, Germany 155
Bethel, Tennessee 178
Biffle, Jacob 173–4
Big Black River 186–7
Big Valley, California 139
Binford, James 192, 202
Black Hawk War 24, 49, 106, 111, 168
Blackfoot Indians 51

229

Index

Blair's Ferry 178
Blake, George 126, 147
Blanco, Chief 124–5
Bliss, New Mexico 85
Blunt, Charles 38
Boggs, Mr. 65
Bolan, J.N. 184
Boston, Massachusetts 21, 80
Boston Massacre 21
Bowling Green, Kentucky 171
Bragg, Braxton 171, 179, 182, 188
Brandon, Mississippi 188
Brazito, New Mexico 69
Breckinridge, John C. 178
Brewer, R. Henry 140–1, 145–6
Brook, George M. 105
Brown, John 161, 174
Bruckner 186
Buell, Don Carlos 172, 181–2
Buena Vista, Mexico 74
Buford, Lt. J., Jr. 93
Burgwin, Henry John K. 62, 66–7
Burnett, Peter H. 137
Burney's Valley, California 141
Burr, Aaron 45
Buzzard Roost, Georgia 190

Calhoun, James S. 85, 88
Calhoun, John C. 82
California 12, 16, 44, 50, 53, 59, 60, 63, 83–4, 86–9, 98, 111, 127–38, 140, 143–8, 163, 165, 168, 176, 202, 204–5
California Militia 140–1
Calvary Cemetery 202
Camp Hollenbush *see* Fort Crook
Camp Mackall 140
Camp Saunders 173
Camp Winfield Scott 94
Campbell, William B. 47
Canada 23
Canadian River 96, 123, 125
Canton, Mississippi 188
Cantonment Burgwin 122, 125
Cantonment Mora 125
Carlisle, Pennsylvania 127
Carlisle Barracks 126–7, 129, 144
Carnton Plantation 5, 196, 199, 200
Carr, Milton 139–41
Carson, Kit 59, 65, 93, 97, 124
Carter, John C. 195, 198, 200
Cascade County, Montana 202
Casement, Colonel 196
Cassville, Georgia 191
Catholic 9, 57–8, 63, 78, 80, 82
Cebolleta, New Mexico 89, 92–4, 97
Celts 155
Central Valley of California 133

Chacon, Chief 122, 124
Champion Hill 186
Chapmen, Lieutenant 145–6
Charleston, South Carolina 147
Charleston, Virginia 59
Chattahoochee River 191
Chavez, General 66
Cherokee Indians 50, 104
Cheyenne Indians 51, 88, 95
Chickamauga, Tennessee or Battle of 178, 188
Chickasaw Bluffs, Mississippi 183
Chilton, Major 116
Chilula Indians 132, 140
Chimarike Indians 132
Chippewa *see* Ojibwa
Chiricahua Indians 51
Cimarron Crossing 117–8
Cimarron Cutoff 55, 95
Cimarron River 118
Cincinnati Daily Commercial 156
Citizenship Act of 1924 137
Cleary, J.W. 145
Cleburne, Patrick 5, 200
Coffman, Edward M. 20
Collins, John C. 202
Colt, Samuel 54, 121
Columbia, Tennessee 200
Columbia Pike 195, 198
Columbus, Christopher 13
Columbus, Kentucky 167–8
Columbus, Mississippi 178–80, 182, 184
Comanche, Indians 51–3, 88, 93, 95, 98–100, 112, 117, 125–6
Comancheria 53
Compromise of 1820 17, 78–9
Compromise of 1850 77–8, 83–4, 86, 135
Confederate States of America 5, 53, 131, 147, 160, 163, 181, 203
Congress of the United States 6, 22, 24, 26, 53–4, 74, 84, 86, 105, 122, 125, 135, 158–9, 184, 202
Connecticut 7, 82
Cooke, Phillip St. George 57–8, 122
Coon Creek 116
Coons Ranch, New Mexico 89
Cooper, Francis Ann 133
Cords, Nicholas 157
Corinth, Mississippi 171–3, 177–8, 182
Coronado, Francisco 52
Corps of Artillerists and Engineers 22
Cortes, Chief 70
Craig, Lieutenant 118
Creek War 48
Crittenden, John 159
Crittenden-Johnson Resolution 159, 184
Crofts, David W. 162

230

Index

Crow River 108
Cucharas River 125
Cunliffe, Marcus 20

Dakota Indians 102, 104–6
Dakota Territory 101, 104
Dakota War 104
Dalton, Georgia 190
Dana, Captain 107
Dana, Congressman 27
Decatur, Alabama 173, 185
Declaration of Independence 10, 50
Democratic Party 43, 48, 53, 79
Demopolis, Alabama 190
Derby, George 36
Detroit, Michigan 103
Dickson, John 202
District of Cairo 171
Dixon, Colonel 172
Dodge, Henry 24
Dodge City 117
Dona Ana, New Mexico 89
Donaldson, Mr. 99
Doniphan, Alexander 60, 68–70, 84
Douglas, Stephen 79
Dumbarton, Scotland 110
Dumfries, Scotland 28
Durango, New Mexico 71–2
Dutton, William 34–6

Easton, Alton R. 71
Edwards, Frank 40
Edwards County, Kansas 116
Eel River 50, 134
Egnal, Marc 175
Egypt 187
Elkmont, Tennessee 177
El Mora, New Mexico 97, 99
El Paso, Texas 69, 71, 92–3
Emancipation Proclamation 6, 174, 184
Embudo, New Mexico 66
Engelman, Adolphus 55
English Civil War 20, 154
Enlightenment 9, 14–5, 22, 27, 50
Escott, Paul D. 150, 175
Evans, General 178
Ewell, Richard 35, 149, 153, 159

Fall River 138
Farrel, Michael 191
Fauntleroy, Thomas T. 116, 119, 122–6, 129
Fayetteville, Alabama 178
Ferguson, Philip Gooch 72
Fifteenth Mississippi Infantry 187
Figuers, H.P. 195, 198
Fillmore, Millard 86, 106
Filmer, John 146

First Cavalry 24
First Kentucky Cavalry 173
First Georgia Rangers 179
First Manassas 171
First Mississippi Battalion 184
First Regiment Dragoons 24, 53, 54, 62, 66, 67, 71, 93, 94, 98, 99, 100, 107, 115, 116, 138, 165
First Regiment Tennessee Volunteers 47
First Regiment Texas Rangers 179
Fisher, Reverend M. 111
Fisher, Richard 96
Fitzpatrick, Mr. 94–5
Five Civilized Nations 49, 50, 103
Flint, F.F. 141–2
Floan, Howard 157
Flying Cloud 165
Foner, Eric 157, 185
Foote, Andrew H. 171
Forrest, Nathan 178–9, 183
Forrest, Mississippi 188
Fort Craig 119, 120, 124, 126
Fort Crook 138 — 47
Fort Donnellson 170–2
Fort Erie 23
Fort Fillmore 122
Fort Garland 124
Fort Henry 170–1
Fort Leavenworth 39, 53–4, 89, 93, 112–3, 115–6, 126
Fort Marcy 91
Fort Massachusetts 123–5
Fort Monroe 129
Fort Mystic 11
Fort Pillow 179
Fort Pitt 21
Fort Ridgeley 107
Fort Ripley 105
Fort Smith 129
Fort Snelling 100–3, 105–9, 111
Fort Sumter 147, 156, 160–4, 167, 183
Fort Union 92, 118–9, 122–3, 125–6
Forty-eighth Colored Infantry 164
Forty-third Mississippi Infantry 188
Foster, John G. 38
Fourteenth Mississippi Infantry 184, 187
Fourth United States Artillery 195
France 154–5
Franklin, Benjamin 15
Franklin, Missouri 45
Franklin, Tennessee or Battle of 1, 5, 174, 182, 187, 192–5, 198, 202
Franklin Female Institute 181
Frémont, John C. 167
French and Indian War 10, 21, 104
Fugitive Slave Act 86, 161

Index

Gains, Edmund P. 23
Galisto, New Mexico 100
Gallagher, Gary W. 150, 157, 159, 175
Gardiner, John W.T. 138
Garland, Brigadier General 122
Genovese, Eugene 151
George II 21
Germany 7, 90, 155
Geronimo 126
Gerster, Patrick 157
Gibson, Thomas 196
Gila Indians 126
Gila River 119
Giles County, Tennessee 29
Gist, States Rights 200
Godey's Lady's Book 115
Gone with the Wind 191
Goose Lake Indians 140
Gordon, Col. George 173–4
Gorman, Willis A. 108
Granbury, Hiram 5, 200
Grand Gulf, Mississippi or Battle of 185
Grand Island Railroad 202
Grant, Mary-Susan 151, 156–7
Grant, Ulysses S. 74, 167–8, 171–3, 181–3, 185–6, 188, 190
Grant Falls, Montana 202
Great Britain 7, 155, 160
Greeley, Horace 158
Green Bay, Wisconsin 105
Grenada, Mississippi 183
Grier, William N. 66, 70, 74, 93, 95–8
Grierson, Benjamin H. 185
Grierson's Raid 186
Guadaloupe Hidalgo, Treaty of 53, 74, 77–78, 87, 204
Guise, Alexander 146
Gulbranson, Ann 90, 195
Gulf of Mexico 46, 55

Hale, Congressman 26–7
Halleck, Henry 171, 173, 177, 182
Hanson, Griffith 111
Hanson, Maria Griffith 111
Hardee, William J. 190
Harmar, Lieutenant Colonel 21–2
Harpers Ferry 174
Harpeth River 196
Harris, Isham G. 161–3
Harrisburg, Pennsylvania 103
Hartford Convention 7
Harwood 65
Hat Creek 139–41, 144, 146
Helm, Benjamin 173
Helm's Cavalry 173
Henley, Thomas J. 135
Henry, Lieutenant 196

Henry, Pat 187, 200, 202
Herrera, David 96
Hewey's Bridge, Battle of 177
Hill, Ambrose P. 30
Ho-Chunk Indians 103, 105, 108
Hole in the Prairie, Colorado 118
Hole in the Rock, Colorado 118
Holly Springs, Mississippi 183
Honey Lake Valley, California 140–1, 145
Hood, John Bell 190–1, 194, 198
Hopi Indians 51
Houghton, Joab 85–6
Houston, Texas 173
Howard, Oliver O. 190
Howe, Major 93
Huero, Chief 124
Humboldt Bay 144–5
Hume, William 28
Huntington, Samuel P. 20
Huntsville, Tennessee? 177
Hupa Indians 140
Hupa Whilidut Indians 132
Hurlbut, Stephen 182

Indian Appropriations Act 135
Indian Territory 129, 160, 162
Indianola 184
Iowa 101
Ireland 28, 42, 90, 111
Isma'il Pasha 187

Jackson, Andrew 7, 26, 29, 35, 43, 47, 60
Jackson, Thomas J. 30, 190
Jackson, Mississippi 179–81, 183–4, 186–8
Jackson Railroad 188
Jackson, Tennessee 182
Jacksonians 23, 26–7, 29, 30, 41, 47, 69
Jamestown, Virginia 9, 154
Jaramillo, Apolinia (Vigil) 59
Jaramillo, Josefa 59
Jaramillo, Maria 59
Jefferson, Thomas 7, 11, 15, 27, 47, 102
Jefferson Barracks, Missouri 107
Jefferson Barracks National Cemetery 202
Jeffersonians 22, 47
Jicarilla Indians 51, 95–6, 118–9, 122–5
Jicarilla Mountains 126
Johnson, Richard W. 19
Johnston, Adam 135
Johnston, Albert Sydney 167–8, 171–3
Johnston, Joseph E. 186, 188, 190–1
Jomini, Antoine-Henri de 25, 35
Jones, Adjutant General 71
Journal of American History 151
Joyner, Charles 152

232

Index

Kansas 39, 53, 79, 105, 112, 115–6, 161
Kansas-Nebraska Act 115, 159
Kayugus Indians 88
Kearney, Stephen Watts 24, 39, 44, 53–4, 57–60, 62–3, 69, 84, 91
Kennesaw Mountain, Battle of 191
Kentucky 19, 108, 153, 159, 167–8, 170–1, 173, 178–9, 182, 184–5
Ker, Captain C. 93, 97
Kibbe, William 141–3, 146
King, Thomas Butler 134
King Philip 11
Kingston, Georgia 191
Kiowa Indians 51, 94–5, 116–7
Klammath Lake 146
Know Nothing Party 80, 90, 175
Ku Klux Klan 174, 179

La Jolla, California 202
Lake Champlain 23
Lake, Mississippi 185–6
Lake Indians 140
Lake Providence Expedition 183
Lamar, Mirabeau 46
Lamb's Ferry 177–8
Lane, Lieutenant-Colonel 71
Lapin Indians 70
La Questa, New Mexico 99, 100
Largo, Sarcilla 69
Las Lunas, New Mexico 100, 122
Las Vegas, New Mexico 57, 70, 81, 89, 92–3, 95, 98–100, 118, 123
Lea, Luke 106
Leal, T.W. 65
Lee, Francis 106–8
Lee, Robert E. 153, 159
Lee, Stephen 65
Lejanza, Mariano Martinez de 81
Leroux, Antoine 96
Lewisburg Road 196
Lincoln, Abraham 6, 78, 80, 104, 131, 147, 150–1, 158, 160, 162–3, 165, 168, 173–5, 182, 184–5, 190
Little Crow 107
Localism 2, 5–8, 16, 22, 155
Loewen, James W. 151, 158, 174
London 50, 155
Looxapalila, Mississippi? 180
Loring, William 186–7, 189–93, 195–6
Los Angeles Mounted Rifles 168
Louis XV 21
Louisiana 10, 21, 167, 171, 180, 183–4
Louisiana Purchase 21, 101
Louisville, Kentucky 80
Love, Captain 72
Lowe, Percival G. 113, 116–7
Lyons, Lord 165

Macomb, Alexander 23
Magazine of History 152
Magoffin, Beriah 167
Maidu Indians 133
Mangas Coloradas 52
Manifest Destiny 2, 6, 8, 9, 11–2, 16, 38, 40, 42–5, 47, 50, 55, 57–8, 76, 102, 135, 204
Mankato, Minnesota 106
Mansfield, Joseph 139
Maplewood Cemetery 201
Markhead 65
Martinez, Antonio Jose 64, 84
Martinez, Mariano 81
Marysville Appeal 130
Mason, Henry 29
Masons 62
Massachusetts 9, 43–4, 154
Mattole Indians 140
Maxey, Samuel Bell 30
Maxwell, Lucien B. 89
Maxwell Ranch 93, 118, 126
May, Charles A. 126–7
Mayflower 10, 55
Maynard, Horace 162–3
McCall, George A. 81–2, 85–8, 91–4
McClellan, Colonel 173
McClellan, George B. 25, 30, 33–4, 38, 48, 158, 170
McClermand, John 182
McDougall, Charles 39, 90, 109, 111, 202
McDougall, Georgiana 109–11, 113, 115, 119, 121, 131, 135, 137, 143, 165, 188, 200, 201–2, 204
McDougall, John, Sr. 11
McDougall, John, Jr. 135
McDougall, Maria Griffith *see* Hanson, Maria Griffith
McDougall, Thomas Mower 131
McDougall Family 110, 165
McElroy, Frank 141–3
McGavock, John 200
McPherson, James 152
McPherson, James B. 182, 190–1
McQuaid 130
McWhinney, Grady 25–6
Mechanicsburg, Mississippi 187
Memphis, Tennessee 1, 107, 129, 164, 168–70, 172, 182, 185, 202
Memphis Legion 172
Mendocino, California 142, 146
Mercer, Lieutenant 146
Meridian, Mississippi 186, 188
Meriwether, David 121
Merrit Lake 116
Mesa Verde 51
Mescalero Indians 51, 122–3
Messervy, Governor 122

233

Index

Metacom 11
Mexican War 16–7, 24–7, 30, 40–4, 47–9, 51, 54, 73–4, 78–9, 89, 92, 94, 108–10, 114–6, 121, 127, 139, 147, 156, 168, 183, 187, 190
Mexico 12, 16, 30, 38–40, 44–5, 50, 51–3, 55, 57, 68, 70, 72–4, 78–9, 83–4, 94, 133
Mill Creek Gap 190
Minnesota 16, 100–5, 107–8, 111, 131, 148, 164, 183, 204
Minnesota Belle 115
Minnesota River 101, 104, 107
Missouri 39, 45, 53, 56, 60–1, 66, 68, 70–1, 78, 111, 171
Missouri Pacific Railroad 202
Mitchell, Benjamin 29
Mitchell, Margaret 203
Mitchell, Mr. 99
Miwok Indians 133
Moache Utes Indians 124–5
modernization 2, 22–3, 103, 203
Modoc Indians 132
Mongollon Indians 126
Monroe, Colonel 91
Monroe, James 107
Montoyo 68
Moqui Indians 87–8
Mora, New Mexico 65, 99, 126
Morotown, New Mexico 81
Mormon War 168
Mormons 44
Morrison, Colonel 179
Morton Station, Mississippi 185
Mosca Pass 124
Motte, Jacob 48
Muchacho Indians 138
Murfreesboro, Tennessee or Battle of 177, 179, 182

Napoleon 11, 25
Nashville, Tennessee 28–9, 107, 172, 194
National Hotel 127–8
National Hotel Disease 127–8
Navajo (Nabajo) Indians 51–3, 62, 69, 87, 92, 94, 104, 122
Nebraska 105
Negley, James 178, 180
Negro, Chief 126
Neighbors, Robert 86
Netherlands 154
New England 7, 11, 15, 26, 43–4, 156–7
New Hampshire 27
New Hope Church, Georgia 191
New Mexico 16, 45–8, 50–1, 53–60, 63–4, 66, 68–9, 71, 74, 76–8, 80–92, 94, 96–7, 101–3, 107, 109, 111–5, 118–23, 125–7, 129, 131, 147–8, 164, 183, 190, 204

New Orleans, Louisiana or Battle of 47, 61, 70
New Spain 12, 55
New York 27, 127, 202
New York City 46, 50, 165–6
Newton, Mississippi 188
Newton Station, Mississippi 185
Nicholson, A.O.P. 158
Nicolet, Jean 105
Nokay River 105
Nongatl Indians 140
North America 40, 46, 105, 153–4, 204
North American Review 23
North Carolina 162, 190, 202
Northern Ireland 28
Northwest Territory 103

O'Bryan, Frances 181, 195, 198
Ocate Creek 123
Ohio 23, 47, 111, 165
Ohio Railroad 188
Ojibwe Indians 103–6, 108
Oklahoma 104
Oregon 44, 89, 138
Oregon Trail 115
Organization of American Historians 152
Ortiz, Thomas 64
O'Sullivan 8, 40–1, 58, 76
Ottawa Indians 104
Oustemah Nisenan Indians 134
Oxford, Mississippi 183

Pacific 10, 46, 53, 89, 104, 168
Paducah, Kentucky 167–8
Paiute Indians 145
Paiute War 145
Pallen, Conde Benoist 202
Panama 165
Paris 10, 155
Parras, New Mexico 70
Partridge 33
Patterson, Gerard A. 152
Peach Tree Creek, Georgia 191
Pearl River, Mississippi? 184, 186
Pecos, New Mexico 57
Pecos River 119, 122
Peel, Sergeant 118
Pemberton, John C. 180, 182–3, 185–6, 188, 190
Pencha Pass 124
Pequot Indians 11
Perryville, Battle of 182
Philadelphia, Pennsylvania 28, 80
Phillipstown, New York 31
Pickering, Timothy 7
Pickett, George 5, 30, 37
Pierce, Franklin 108, 165

234

Index

Pike, Zebulon 45, 101
Pilgrims 11
Pine Mountain, Georgia 191
Pinsker, Mathew 152
Pit River 138–9
Pit River Volunteers 142
Pittsburg Landing 172–3
Point Coupée 185
Polk, James K. 23, 26, 48, 53, 55, 58, 60, 68, 74, 89
Polk, Leonidas 167–8, 171–2, 190–1
Pope, John 33
Prairie Grove, Battle of 173, 177
Presbyterian 28, 199
Price, Sterling 60, 63–8, 70–3, 84, 88, 91
Pritchard's Cross-Roads, Mississippi 187
Proclamation Line of 1763 10, 22
Provisional Army of the Confederate States 168
Pueblo Indians 46, 51–2, 56–7, 65–6, 68, 80, 83, 87–8, 95, 122–4, 126
Pugh, Richard 138, 141
Pulaski, Tennessee 28–9, 39, 107, 174, 176, 178, 194, 201
Pulaski-Elkton Turnpike 178
Purgatoire River 125
Purgetwa, Colorado 118
Puritans 9, 11, 80
Pyramid Lake 146
Pyramid Lake War 145

Quakers 9

Raines, G.J. 145
Ralls, John 71–2
Ramsey, Alexander 102–3, 105–8
Red Bluff, California 138–9, 141
Removal Act 49
The Republican 76
Republican Party 73, 77–8, 80, 151, 157–8, 162
Resaca, Georgia or Battle of 190
Reynolds, A.W. 86
Rhett Lake 146
Rio Conchos, Mexico 72
Rio de la Mora Mountain 94
Rio Grande 46, 53, 55, 57, 61–2, 73–4, 81, 83, 87, 92, 94, 100, 119
Robb, Graham 155
Rochelle Park, New Jersey 202
Rocky Face Ridge, Battle of 190
Rocky Mountains 50, 78, 81, 93, 122, 134, 137
Roff's Ranch 141, 143, 146
Rome, Italy 15, 155
Romero 68
Roop, Isaac 145

Roundheads 155
Rowe, General 130
Russellville, Alabama 173
Rutherford County, Tennessee 179

Sabinal, New Mexico 100
Sacramento, New Mexico 69
Sacramento River 133, 135
Saguache Pass 124
St. Louis, Missouri 105, 107, 202
St. Peter, Michigan 106
St. Vrain, Ceran 59, 67, 123–5
Salt Lake City, Utah 135
Saltillo, New Mexico 70–1
Samson, Mr. 99, 100
Sandy Lake Tragedy 104
San Elizario Presidio 89, 93
San Francisco, California 131, 137–9, 163
San Francisco Bulletin 142, 145
San Geromino, New Mexico 71
Sangre de Cristo Mountains 96, 124
San Joaquin River 135
San Juan, New Mexico 66
San Luis Valley, New Mexico 122–4
San Miguel, New Mexico 57, 70, 99, 100
San Pablo, Mexico 72
Santa Anna, Antonio Lopez de 46–7
Santa Barbara Cañon 126
Santa Cruz, New Mexico (or La Canada) 66
Santa Cruz des Rosales, Mexico 71–2, 74
Santa Fe, New Mexico 45–6, 55–8, 60, 62, 65–7, 85–6, 88–9, 91, 94, 95–7, 118, 126
Santa Fe Trail 45, 50, 55–6, 59, 60, 76, 95, 115
Santa Rita Mountains 52
Sauk Indians 24
Schoepf, Albin Francisco 169
Scientific Revolution 14
Scotland 110
Scott, Dred 156, 175
Scott, Thomas M. 173, 178
Scott, Walter 203
Scott, Winfield 19, 20, 23–4, 44, 74, 165–7, 189
Scribner, Benjamin Franklin 55
Sebesta, Edward H. 151, 158, 174
Second Artillery 91
Second Cavalry 24
Second Dragoons 24, 89, 91–4, 97, 116, 127
Second Missouri 66
Second Tennessee Battalion 174
Seward, William 165, 167
Shasta County, California 139
Shasta Indians 132
Sheridan, Philip 87
Sherman, William Tecumseh 83, 182–3, 189, 190–1, 194

235

Index

Shiloh, Battle of 172–3, 177, 179
Shoshone Indians 52
Sibley, Henry Hasting 102–3, 105–6
Sinkyone Indians 140
Sioux Indians 101–8, 204
Sisserton Indians 106
Sixth Infantry 105, 141, 146
Sixth Military Department 107
Sixth Mississippi Infantry 187
Sixty-fifth Illinois 197
Sixty-sixth Indiana Infantry 195
Skelton, William B. 20, 110, 149, 150, 164, 204
Slack, Captain 67
Smith, Edmund Kirby 149
Smith, Gene 178
Smith, Truman 82
Snake Creek Gap 190
Snelling, Josiah 102
Snyder's Bluff 185
Socorro, New Mexico 89, 91, 95
Socorro County, New Mexico 119
Sola, Vincent de 132–3
Sons of Confederate Veterans 3
South Carolina 7, 25, 159–61, 205
South Dakota 105
Southern Poverty Law Center 151
Spain 45, 93, 132, 154
Spock, Dr. Benjamin 114
Stampp, Kenneth 157–7
States' Rights 5–8, 16, 152–3, 155, 161–2, 164
Steck, Michel 126
Steed's Battalion 186
Steele's Bayou 183
Steen, Major 92
Stewart, Charles S. 38
Stewart, Colonel 197
Stewart, Lucean 123
Stones River 182
Stothart, Isabel 28
Strabane, Ireland 28
Strahl, Ortho 5, 200
Stuart, Jeb 159
The Suland 105–6
Summary of the Art of War 25
Sumner, Colonel 89, 100
Sumner, Edwin 118
Susanville, California 145
Sutter, John 135
Sweden's Cove, Battle of 178

Tafoya, General 66
Taliaferro, Lawrence 102
Taney, Roger B. 165
Taos, Don Fernandez 92
Taos, New Mexico 45, 55–6, 64–7, 81, 89, 92, 94–8, 123–6
Taos Creek 66

Taylor, Zachery 78, 83, 85–6, 105, 127
Tejon, California 135
Tennant, Ann 28
Tennant, Christopher 28
Tennant, Isabelle *see* Stothart, Isabelle
Tennessee 2–3, 5, 8, 23, 28–9, 109, 111, 131, 153, 158, 160–5, 167, 167, 170–1, 178, 182, 191, 194, 200–1, 205
Tennessee River 171, 177
Tenth Louisiana Volunteers of African Descent 164
Terry, B.D. 184
Terry's Texas Rangers 173, 178
Texas 12, 38, 43–4, 46, 53, 57, 73–4, 79, 83–6, 88–9, 92, 94, 127, 168, 179
Thayer, Sylvanus 24, 32–3, 37
Third Infantry 89, 91–3, 97
Thirteenth Amendment 159, 167, 185
Thomas, George 189–91, 194
Three-fifth's Compromise 7
Tilghman, Lloyd 170, 186–7
Tilley, John Shipley 160
Timpas, Kansas 118
Tolowa Indians 132
Tome, New Mexico 62, 89
Tourgée, Albion 157
Trader's Paper 106
Treaty of Mendota 105–6
Treaty of Paris 10
Treaty of Traverse des Sioux 105–6
Trias, Don Angel 71–2
Trimble, Isaac 3, 157
Tsnungwe Indians 140
Tunnel Hill, Georgia 190
Turley 65
Turley's Mill 65
Turner, Frederick Jackson 21
Turner, Nat 174
Tuscaloosa, Alabama 172
Tuscumbia, Alabama 178
Twelfth Louisiana Infantry 173
Twentieth Mississippi Infantry 187
Twenty-Third Mississippi Infantry 187
Tyrone County, Ireland 28

Unification Act 7
United States Arms Training & Doctrine Command 127
United States Army 2, 8, 16–7, 20, 31–2, 38, 46, 52, 87, 97, 108, 110, 114, 121, 123, 134, 140, 144–5, 147–8, 150, 153, 160, 170, 205
United States Army War College 127
United States Navy 111
Utah 86, 145
Utah Indians 88, 92
Ute Creek 123
Ute Indians 119, 121–4

Index

Valdez, Captain 96
Valley of Chamas 81
Van Dorn, Earl 173, 183
Varnell's Station 190
Venable, Aaron 29
Vera Cruz, Mexico 53
Vicksburg, Mississippi or Battle of 181–6, 188
Victoria, Queen 7
Vigil, Donaciano 81
Virginia 11, 110, 116, 153–4, 162, 167, 174, 183, 190, 202

Wahpeton Indians 106
Walker, Robert 71–2
War Department 24, 54, 134
War of 1812 7, 15, 19–21, 23–4, 37, 54, 74, 116, 166
Washington, George 15, 24, 102, 127, 189
Washington, John Macre 84, 89
Washington, D.C. 70, 83–6, 106, 127–9, 147–8, 165, 182, 202
Water Holes, Colorado 118
Waters, Mr. 99
Webster, Daniele 43–4
Weightman, Richard H. 85–6
Weller, Governor 141
West Point 6, 8, 10, 15–7, 19, 21–7, 29, 31, 36, 40–1, 44, 47–9, 59, 68–9, 73, 101, 109, 127, 147, 149, 152–3, 159, 167, 183, 187, 190, 203–4
Wharton, John A. 178–9
Wheaton, Dr. 34
Wheeler, Joseph 190
Whig Party 43, 46, 48, 53, 55, 73, 77, 79, 80

Whilkut Indians 140
Whiskey Rebellion 127
White, Ann 95–6
White, James M. 95
White, Virginia 95
White Massacre 95
Whittlesey, Joseph 75, 95
Wilcox, Cadmus 30
Wilkinson, James 45
Williams, Roger 9
Williams, Thomas 48
Williams Station 145
Wilmot, David 79
Wilmot Proviso 77, 79, 80
Wilson, John 134–5
Winchester, Alabama 178
Winnebago *see* Ho-Chunk Indians
Winnemucca, Chief 145
Winona, Minnesota 106
Wintun Indians 133
Wirtz, Horace R. 76
Wisconsin 101, 104, 106, 111
Wiyot Indians 132, 140
Woodard, Colin 153–8, 163
Woods, Michael B. 151
Woodward, C. Vann 151
Woodward, Thomas G. 173
Wootton, Dick 96
Wurtemburg Academy 29

Yazoo Pass, Mississippi 183
Yokuts 133
Yuba County, California 130
Yurok 132

www.ingramcontent.com/pod-product-compliance
Ingram Content Group UK Ltd.
Pitfield, Milton Keynes, MK11 3LW, UK
UKHW041942140426
5217IPUK00014B/610